# Journalism in a Culture of Grief

# Journalism in a Culture of Grief

Carolyn Kitch and Janice Hume

Routledge
Taylor & Francis Group
New York   London

Routledge
Taylor & Francis Group
270 Madison Avenue
New York, NY 10016

Routledge
Taylor & Francis Group
2 Park Square
Milton Park, Abingdon
Oxon OX14 4RN

© 2008 by Taylor & Francis Group, LLC
Routledge is an imprint of Taylor & Francis Group, an Informa business

Printed in the United States of America on acid-free paper
10 9 8 7 6 5 4 3 2 1

International Standard Book Number-13: 978-0-415-98010-4 (Softcover) 978-0-415-98009-8 (Hardcover)

| Library of Congress Cataloging-in-Publication Data |
| --- |

Kitch, Carolyn L.
   Journalism in a culture of grief / Carolyn Kitch, Janice Hume.
     p. cm.
   Includes bibliographical references and index.
   ISBN 0-415-98009-7 (hardback : alk. paper) -- ISBN 0-415-98010-0 (pbk. : alk. paper)
     1. Journalism--Social aspects--United States. 2. Grief--Social aspects--United States. 3. Mass media and culture--United States. 4. Death in popular culture--United States. 5. Death in mass media. I. Hume, Janice. II. Title.

PN4877.K578 2007
302.230973--dc22

2007004041

**Visit the Taylor & Francis Web site at**
**http://www.taylorandfrancis.com**

**and the Routledge Web site at**
**http://www.routledge.com**

*This book is dedicated to the memory of our parents:*

*Albert Bertram Kitch and Aimee Lou (James) Kitch*

*Marcus Foster Hume and Norma Jean (Pickens) Hume*

# CONTENTS

## PART III: THE JOURNALISM OF RITUAL AND TRIBUTE

# ACKNOWLEDGMENTS

We would like to thank our colleagues for the institutional and motivational support that made this project possible, including: at Temple University, Dean Concetta Stewart and Department of Journalism Chairs Patricia Bradley, Bonnie Brennen, Thomas Eveslage, and Andrew Mendelson; and at the University of Georgia, Dean E. Culpepper "Cully" Clark, Interim Dean Leonard Reid, Associate Dean for Research and Graduate Studies Jeff Springston, and Journalism Department Head Kent Middleton. Several graduate students provided research assistance, and we are grateful to them as well: at Temple, Guillermo Avila-Saavedra, Eliza Jacobs, Melissa Lenos and Susan Robinson; and at the University of Georgia, Gary Guffey, Melanie Jarrett and Brian Lee. Janice Hume's mom, Norma Pickens Hume, spent a long day at the Guntersville, AL public library helping to gather the obituaries examined in Chapter 4.

This book is a collection of studies that now form a whole but began as individual projects, and many colleagues from across the country (and nearby) provided moral support and valuable help with our research. They include: Carolina Acosta-Alzuru, Tanya Barrientos, Joseph Bernt, Fred Blevens, Bonnie Bressers, Simon Bronner, Caryl Cooper, Dane Claussen, Fabienne Darling-Wolf, John Ferre, Bob Franklin, Denise Graveline, Joseph Harry, Sam Harvey, Barry Hollander, Ann Hollifield, Carol Holstead, Mark Johnson, Peggy Kreshel, Hugh Martin, Sharon Mazzarella, Patricia McNeely, David Mindich, Janice Peck, Earnest Perry, Bill Reader, Bryan Reber, Barbara Reed, Karen Miller Russell, Chad Stebbins, Linda Steiner, Edward Trayes, Betty Houchin Winfield, and Barbie Zelizer.

We are grateful for the insights of the anonymous reviewers of this manuscript and for the editorial guidance and creativity of Matthew Byrnie, Stan Spring, Susan Horwitz, Suzanne Lassandro, and Elise Weinger at Routledge/Taylor & Francis.

Earlier versions of some of these studies have been presented at the annual conferences of the Association for Education in Journalism and Mass Communication and the International Communication Association, and have been published in scholarly journals. We acknowledge and appreciate that the following publications have allowed us to reuse these articles as part of the content of this book:

Hume, J. (2005, Winter). Life and death in a small town: Cultural values and memory in community newspaper obituaries. *Grassroots Editor, 46*(4): 1-8. [Chapter 4]

Kitch, C. (2007). "It takes a sinner to appreciate the blinding glare of grace": Rebellion and redemption in the life story of the "dark" celebrity. *Popular Communication, 5*(1): 37-56. Reprinted by permission of Lawrence Erlbaum Associates. [Chapter 5]

Kitch, C. (2007). Mourning men joined in peril and purpose": Working-class heroism in news repair of the Sago miners' story. *Critical Studies in Media Communication, 24*(2). Reprinted by permission of Taylor & Francis Ltd. [Chapter 7]

Hume, J. (2003, Spring). "Portraits of grief," reflectors of values: The *New York Times* remembers victims of September 11. *Journalism & Mass Communication Quarterly, 80*(1): 166-182. [Chapter 8]

Kitch, C. (2003, May). "Mourning in America": Ritual, redemption, and recovery in news narrative after September 11. *Journalism Studies, 4*(2): 213-224. Reprinted by permission of Taylor & Francis Ltd. [Chapter 8]

# INTRODUCTION

The American way of death, which historically has shuttled between the extremes of denial and desire, seems tending toward desire these days. The instantaneous monuments that are tossed together with flowers, stuffed animals and personal messages, such as those that followed the deaths of Princess Diana and John F. Kennedy Jr. and the TWA Flight 800 disaster, suggest that the country is ready, even eager to connect with ideas of death and the past, no matter how superficial that connection may sometimes be.

—*Time* **magazine (Rosenblatt, 2000, p. 28)**

Today, the only surprise of this newsmagazine passage is that the examples, all from the 1990s, somehow seem to have happened a long time ago. We have seen so much public grief since then. Nationally and locally, death has become a visible aspect of twenty-first century public culture, on roadsides where crosses mark car-crash sites and in more formal memorials, all across the United States, dedicated to those who died not just in wars, but also in tornadoes and industrial accidents and shootings. Prime-time television dramas teem with the grisly details of corpses, mysteries solved by coroners, and characters who speak to dead people. Murder, fatal accidents, natural disasters, and war always have made news, but now journalism does something more, covering grief rituals and saluting "heroes" as a routine part of reporting deaths.

As Tony Walter (1991, 1994, 1999a) has noted, this widespread media interest in death refutes the historian Philippe Ariès's (1974) well-known claim that by the twentieth century, death had become a taboo subject for public discussion. While Ariès may remain correct that the deaths of individuals, removed from the home to the hospital, are "hidden away," the attention paid to deaths that are seen as socially symbolic has never been more public. Indeed, as it is conducted in and through mass media, public mourning has returned to an almost Victorian level of ritual—what Ariès called "the romantic, rhetorical treatment of death" (1974, p. 56).

The extraordinary events of September 11, 2001, to which a chapter of this book is devoted, certainly placed the subjects of death and grief in the American cultural spotlight, creating what was perhaps the most public national discussion of loss and memorial that was not connected with an ongoing war. Yet the shift had begun to happen before the turn of the twentieth century, as *Time* essayist Roger Rosenblatt contended. The "desire" he identified in that 2000 "Memorial Day Special" cover story had been building for at least two decades. It had grown out of several separate phenomena that were precedents for the more recent events discussed in this book: the emotional public response to the opening of the Vietnam Veterans Memorial in Washington; the devastation caused by the disease of AIDS, and the creation and migration of the AIDS quilt; spectacular accidents such as the explosion of the space shuttle *Challenger*; the news that two teenage boys had shot and killed a dozen of their classmates at Columbine High School in Colorado; the unexpected deaths of iconic celebrities including Princess Diana, John F. Kennedy, Jr., and Kurt Cobain; and the bombing of the Alfred P. Murrah Federal Building in Oklahoma City.

During the same period, the more routine processes of battling disease and facing death were becoming a common topic of best-selling books, television talk shows, and journalism. The *New York Times* attributed this trend to the aging and mindset of the Baby Boom generation. In an editorial about Joan Didion's 2005 book *The Year of Magical Thinking*, a memoir about her husband's death and her daughter's illness, the newspaper proclaimed:

> Assuming that Ms. Didion has struck a generational chord—think of that huge one on the piano at the end of "A Day in the Life"—it seems fair to expect a melancholy river of death-themed books, plays and movies until the last of the baby boomers follow their predecessors into the grave. This could be a very good thing. It has been more than 40 years since Jessica Mitford wrote *The American Way of Death*, and society still has not overcome its squeamish denial of death's existence. (Downes, 2006, Sec. 4, p. 11)

In direct contradiction of this last phrase, this venerable newspaper was already well invested in the broader media trend. Throughout 2006, *Times* front-page stories included features about personal coaches for the terminally ill and their families; about memorial Web sites, an extension of obituaries for individuals; and about roadside memorials, an article that was illustrated with photographs picturing the mothers of the dead next to the markers (Gross, 2006; St. John, 2006; Urbina, 2006b). The *Times* began that year with a themed Sunday magazine section titled "The Lives They Lived," profiling well-known and lesser-known but inspirational people who had died in 2005. This special issue closed with a short photo essay about Private Christopher Taffoya, who had received the Purple Heart for wounds he suffered in Iraq in 2003 and who had gone on to serve in the equestrian unit that conducts military funerals in Arlington National Cemetery. In captions, he was quoted as saying "I never lose sight that this is an honor" and "This is a job greater than ourselves … the last thing families remember" (Councill, 2006, p. 62). At year's end, the same setting provided the backdrop for the newspaper's front-page photograph of a horse-drawn carriage bearing a flag-draped coffin processing through Arlington, saluted by volunteers who were there to lay Christmas wreaths throughout the cemetery (A day for laying wreaths, 2006, p. A1).

In popular journalism today, the passing of even a minor celebrity merits "commemorative" newspaper features and entire magazine issues. The summary journalism of *People* magazine's 2005 year-end issue was threaded with death, including not only the usual "tributes" to stars who had passed away that year, but also "A salute to America's fallen heroes in Iraq and Afghanistan" and three articles of witness testimony about Hurricane Katrina, the Asian tsunami, and the London Tube bombings (*People*, 2005, December 26). The commemoration of dead celebrities has accelerated to the extent that when George Harrison died in 2001, he was featured on three times as many magazine covers as John Lennon had been in 1980; in 2003, Johnny Cash received five times more coverage in entertainment and newsmagazines than Elvis Presley had received 26 years earlier (Kitch, 2005, p. 69).

A number of scholars have begun to address the phenomenon of public grief and the preoccupation with death as a social factor in modern life. The geographer Kenneth Foote (1997) toured the country to document its many memorials to Americans whose violent deaths have become part of regional as well as national memory, from witches executed in eighteenth-century Salem to the nineteenth-century Haymarket rioters in Chicago, from victims of the 1889 Johnstown flood to civil rights workers slain in twentieth-century Mississippi. Charlton

McIlwain (2004) has traced the theme of death in recent fictional television shows such as *Six Feet Under* and *Crossing Over*. Marita Sturken (2007) has analyzed the marketing of tragic events, through consumer products and tourism, with regard to the Oklahoma City bombing and the events of September 11.

Few researchers, however, have studied how the theme of death plays out in news media, which in fact have become the primary forum for the conveyance and construction of public grief today. In newspapers and newsmagazines and on television, themes of death and memorial are woven together in hard news and features. These news stories create a broader cultural narrative in which the distant past and the "breaking" present, the most prominent public figures and the most ordinary citizens, merge into a single, ongoing story about meaning of loss, mourning, and sacrifice in America.

This function is not unique to journalism, of course; it is, instead, one of many examples that journalism itself is a cultural process, embedded within a much broader (and older) web of cultural practices. Narratives about death always have had powerful cultural implications. Joseph Amato argues that death "causes people to tell stories" that can be "shaped by moral judgment, fashioned for the sake of argument, made buoyant by metaphor, or given meaning by the rituals of culture and the promise of religion" (1993, p. 259). Moreover, as many scholars have noted, death stories are less about the dead than about the living. Public accounts explore what the anthropologists Richard Huntington and Peter Metcalf call the "dialectical relationship between the meanings of life and death," a system in which "death can be understood as an indicator of life" (1979, p. 2). Death stories told publicly also resonate with audiences because of their strong connection with cultural and religious ritual.

Journalistic media help to enact what sociologists call "civil religion," a phenomenon first described by Émile Durkheim nearly a century ago. Durkheim claimed that "[t]here can be no society which does not feel the need of upholding and reaffirming at regular intervals the collective sentiments and the collective ideas which make its unity and its personality," and that there is little difference between "the processes employed to attain these results" and "regular religious ceremonies" (1973/1915, p. 201). Like "regular" ceremonies, civil religion relies on rituals, especially in times of social crisis. The religion scholar Frederick Bird explains that rituals

> provide spoken and embodied vocabularies for communicating and reconfirming intense feelings of respect, awe, sorrow, loyalty,

tenderness and attraction. ... Without these ritual forms, persons often find it difficult to communicate these sentiments. ... Ironically, ritual codes because of their stylized form seem to facilitate greater articulateness. (1980, p. 24)

The audience is involved (or at the very least, implicated) in this process along with journalists. As Barbara Meyerhoff notes, rituals "must be convincing. People must recognize what rituals are saying, and find their claims authentic, their styles familiar and aesthetically satisfying" (1977, p. 200). If this verification takes place through journalism, then journalism is not merely a body of texts; rather, it is a dialogic process akin to oral storytelling, in which the role of the audience "is to respond to the storyteller, helping her or him shape future versions of the tale" (Bird, 2003, p. 30) and in which the selection of cultural symbols seems to come from "the people" as much as from leaders such as politicians or journalists.

Accordingly, this study embraces the theoretical understanding of news as a form of ritual culture, a model deriving from the early communication theories of Durkheim (1973/1915) and George Herbert Mead (1934). In this view of production (and reception), journalism unifies readers into communities and nations, articulating and affirming group values and identity (see, for example, Carey, 1989; Edy, 1999; Fiske & Hartley, 1978). As this body of literature contends, journalists accomplish these goals by telling stories and creating characters who stand for something larger than themselves, something that is cultural and historical rather than personal and momentary.

In some of the death coverage discussed in this book, journalism embraces national mythology and archetypal characters. In other examples, news coverage serves as a public forum in which—through the telling of a tale with villains and heroes—shared values are defined and lasting lessons are learned. In all cases, this journalism conveys cultural stories employing familiar elements arranged in recognizable order, stories that recur across media and over time to create a broader understanding of the meaning of death.

Method in this study therefore flows from theory, combining narrative analysis (a study of the structure of the text) and discourse analysis (a study of the relationship between the text and its cultural and political context). While it devotes closer attention to story elements and structure, narrative analysis is methodologically similar to framing analysis, a study of "principles of selection, emphasis and presentation composed of little tacit theories about what exists, what happens and what matters" (Gitlin, 1980, p. 6), and of "keywords, stock phrases, stereotyped images, sources of information and sentences that provide thematically reinforcing clusters of facts or judgment" (Entman, 1993, p. 52; also see Goffman, 1974). Therefore, while it analyzes news coverage through the lens of "story" rather than "frame," this study draws and builds on both areas of communication research.

Narrative analysis—a search for the common thematic and structural choices reporters and editors make—has become a common tool for understanding journalism (see, for instance, Barkin, 1984; Bird & Dardenne, 1997; Dahlgren, 1999; Darnton, 1975; Eason, 1981; W. Fisher, 1985; Lule, 2001; Rock, 1973; R. Smith, 1997; Zelizer, 1990). This method takes note of the events and anecdotes in stories (*what* is in them and what is left out) as well as overall plot development (*how*, in what order and with what language, the story is told, how it opens, how its conflict is established and resolved, and how it ends) and characterization (*who*, within the story structure, emerge as the most salient players and how they interact). When studying related material, the researcher considers not just each story's individual content and structure, but also recurring characters and subplots across all evidence. The researcher attempts to understand the connotative as well as denotative meanings of media language and imagery: what is suggested generally about culture, as well as what is literally depicted with regard to the reported event or profiled news subject (Barthes, 1977).

It is at this second level of communication that a news narrative acquires symbolic meaning within its particular time and place and enters into public discourse, a dialectical and fluid set of ideas about cultural ideals and political power. Discourse analysis considers "the ideational function of language," notes Norman Fairclough, "viewing language as a social practice" (1995, pp. 18, 54). "Critical discourse analysis," he explains, "explores the tension between these two sides of language use, the socially shaped and socially constitutive" (p. 55). Through representative, even mythic, characters, writes Jack Lule (2001), news narratives can "provide examples of good and evil, right and wrong, bravery and cowardice," offering "models *of* social life and models *for* social life" (p. 150) and "enact[ing] social dramas that sustain social order" (p. 36). John Shelton Lawrence and Bernard Timberg call this quality "mythic adequacy," which they list as "one important criterion of newsworthiness," explaining:

> News stories that are "mythically adequate" not only tell us something about the world of events. They also provide confirmation for the faith that we can be finally victorious over the forces that besiege us. Certain kinds of news stories thus take on the character of a ritually structured affirmation of hope. (1979, p. 328)

Such journalism constructs as well as reflects social values. As Sally Moore and Barbara Meyerhoff write, "Ritual may do much more than mirror existing social arrangements and existing modes of thought. It can act to reorganize them or even help to create them. This is particularly striking in the secular ceremonies of our own day" (1977, p. 5). Moreover, they contend, ritual is a willful declaration of unity: ritual "provides an explanation, implies meaning and comprehensibility … rituals of promises about continuity" (p. 17).

A number of academic and industry studies have examined news coverage (especially television news coverage) of terror, crime, and disaster, focusing primarily on the role of reporting during crisis as it is under way (see, for instance, Altheide, 2002; Deppa et al., 1993; Graber, 1980; Nimmo & Combs, 1985; Paletz & Schmid, 1992; Shearer, 1991). Other writers have examined the cultural functions of obituaries (Hume, 2000; M. Johnson, 2006; M. Siegel, 1997). Far less scholarship has considered the extent to which death has become a common and ongoing theme in general news. Yet news reports about death carry a special authority. Because they are based on fact—on real people who died in real circumstances and real people who mourn them—they seem to have an authenticity and transparency, an evident "truth," even as they perform ritual processes of tribute and commemoration. They also create a sense of intimacy and inclusion, allowing a broader audience to mourn along with the central characters, even to feel that they are somehow a part of private ceremony.

Indeed, the mediated sharing of the stories of strangers' deaths may be the most common death experience in modern culture. Cheryl Jorgensen-Earp and Lori Lanzilotti note in their study of memory and grief in the construction of public shrines: "As a sense of local community dissolves, as our own relatives (and ourselves) are removed beyond personal control to die in hospitals, we are provided with mediated substitute families whose violent deaths are replayed in our living rooms" (1998, p. 156). Even when the general public do not know the dead and may live far removed from the situation that is the focus of attention, their connection is culturally real, an example of Ernest Borman's notion of "symbolic convergence" in communication and his model of the role of fantasy in rhetoric (1982a, p. 301). The studies in this book illustrate what he calls "the archetypical shared fantasy theme that participants in a rhetorical vision use to fit new events into the explanatory system of their vision" of a coherent social world (p. 296).

Audiences have an imagined but meaningful role as witnesses to these deaths, as Robert Jay Lifton explains in his discussion of news coverage of atrocities in Bosnia: "When television bring us to scenes of killing and dying, it can make us survivors by proxy," a role that prompts audiences "to bring our own minds to the experience of victims, to imagine what they are feeling," and to remember the importance of the deaths (1992, Sec. 2, p. 26).

In his study of memorial ritual after the Oklahoma City bombing, the historian Edward Linenthal notes that

> a nationwide bereaved community ... is one of the only ways Americans can imagine themselves as one; being "together" with millions of others through expressions of mourning bypasses or transcends the many ways in which people are divided—by religion, by ideology, by class, by region, by race, by gender. (2001, p. 111)

When a disaster occurs, such communion is achieved through news media, which can create, if only temporarily, a feeling of consensus. Death stories provide an opportunity to discuss shared ideals and values, presumably held by the great and the common alike. Death is the ultimate equalizer, and it is made meaningful in journalism (and other cultural forms) as an ideal itself, which the historian Ralph Houlbrooke calls "the ideal of the final trial of fortitude" (1989, p. 24).

Some scholars claim that the increasingly common journalistic discussions about this "final trial" offer a new way for reporters to cover religion (for instance, Hoover, 1998). Yet news always has addressed issues of mortality and morality. The historian David Paul Nord argues that "the characteristics of American news—its subject matter and its method of reporting—are deeply rooted in the religious culture of seventeenth-century New England" (2001, p. 31). He notes the scandal that ensued after a stillborn, deformed child was born in 1637 to Mary Dyer, a supporter of the religious radical Anne Hutchinson (and later herself a Quaker martyr); when the Massachusetts governor ordered the body exhumed, reported a British news sheet, "a crowd of more than 100 gathered to gape at the grotesque little corpse. Mary Dyer's 'monstrous birth' was news" (2001, p. 31). Death stories filled the very first Colonial newspaper, *Publick Occurrences: Both Forreign and Domestick*, whose topics included fever, smallpox, fire, and war; one article told of "a very tragical accident ... an Old man ... The Devil took advantage of the Melancholy. ... found him hanging by a Rope" (1690, p. 1).

James Franklin, editor of the *Pennsylvania Gazette*, asked his readers to send reports of "every remarkable Accident, Occurrence, &c. fit for publick Notice." "Apparently they did," Nord writes: the newspaper reported drownings, hangings, a murder trial, and the death of a 100-year-old woman (2001, p. 53). David Copeland also lists "melancholy accidents and deplorable news" as staples of this era's journalism, including coverage of crimes, disasters, accidents, sex scandals, monstrosities, and executions. Of the latter, he writes: "Not only could a story provide precise descriptions of the carrying out of a sentence, but the readers could also feel that a valid moral decree had been upheld" (1997, p. 82). Yet confirmations of morality were less compelling than the sheer entertainment value of reports of violent death: "What made these short stories interesting reading was the sensationalism, the unexpected and explicit grotesqueness. The brains and bowels were necessary to capture the interest of the readers" (Copeland, 1997, p. 85).

Though newspapers of the new republic engaged in partisan boosterism, not all of their content was political, notes Gerald Baldasty, who found "vivid stories about death from rabies, accounts of executions, [and] tales of love gone wrong" (1992, pp. 6–7). "Penny press" newspapers retained interest in remarkable death and melancholy news, although, as Andie Tucher notes, "society grew increasingly secular" and "the sensationalism began to outstrip the moralism" (1994, p. 11). As Americans settled new territories, newspapers and dime novels told spectacular tales of gunfire and other deadly dangers of "violent death in the Old West … exaggerat[ing] it out of all reasonable proportion," and creating romantic myths that a century later would be retold in film and on television (Dykstra, 2000, p. 279).

A different kind of fatalistic romance played out in the deathbed scenes of mid-nineteenth-century Victorian fiction, as well as in the surrounding popular culture of elaborate funerals and funerary art. In newspaper obituaries, the deceased were "removed by the omnipotent author," "scathed by the wing of the destroying angel," "paled by the mighty Death King," and "torn from our midst by the fell destroyer" (Hume, 2000). Periodicals contained poetry such as "On the Death of an Infant," from the July 1850 issue of *Harper's New Monthly*, beginning with this stanza:

> His languid eyes are closing,
> On the pale, placid cheek.
> The lashes dark reposing,
> So wearily, so weak
> He gasps with failing breath
> A faint and feeble strife with death;
> Fainter and fainter still—'tis past
> That one soft sigh—the last. (p. 183)

But the Civil War brought a change to public sentimentalization of death. Gary Laderman (1996) argues that during the war, a detached response to the remains of the dead was a reasonable and patriotic sensibility. After the war's end, journalistic treatment of death shifted from sentimental to scientific. In *Putnam's*, for instance, an article written by a doctor posed the question "Is death painful?" No, he replied: "There is reason to believe the opposite is true—that dying usually is as painless and physically as pleasant as sinking into a sleep" (Buffet, 1870, p. 312).

James Farrell (1980) similarly traces the abandonment of sentiment to the late nineteenth century, partly "as the major American religious denominations increasingly stressed a loving, beneficent God, [and] eased some anxieties which had earlier emanated from religious teachings" (p. 7), partly because of the increasing cultural importance of science and technology, and partly because of a growing funeral industry. It also was during this era, the century's opening two decades, that journalism itself, including the craft of obituary writing, was professionalized and standardized (Hume, 2000). Many scholars, including Philippe Ariès (1974), have dated a profound shift in public attitudes, a "looking away" from death, to the moral as well as mortal devastation of World War I. This characterization of the modern era remained unchallenged through the 1970s, when Ernest Becker published his Pulitzer Prize-winning book *The Denial of Death*, claiming that "the idea of death, the fear of it, haunts the human animal like nothing else; it is a mainspring of human activity ... to overcome it by denying in some way that it is the final destiny for man" (1973, p. ix).

Nevertheless, as an established part of twentieth-century news content, obituaries and other death stories have long had human-interest appeal. One 1935 reporting guide claimed: "News of the death of a well-known person is always certain to interest thousands of readers. ... The bigger the renown of the dead person, the bigger the appeal of the story. ... The more sudden and unexpected the death, the better the story" (Porter & Luxon, 1935, pp. 190–191). As celebrity news content increased throughout the century, the "dead celebrity" became a way for journalists to engage in collective nostalgia while according such figures iconic popular-culture status.

Certainly the appeal of the dead celebrity has not diminished. At the same time, as Herbert Gans (1979) noted in his study of "news values" at national news media during the 1960s and 1970s, the symbol of the common man also has become powerful in news. John Hartley explains that ordinary people who appear as news subjects "serve as potential points of identification for the audience" and are presumed to share the audience's experience and opinions (1982, p. 90). Characterized in death news stories as either victim or mourner, the figure of the common American makes it possible for strangers to feel involved in a tragedy, symbolically uniting the dead and the living and transforming private emotions into public ones.

Today, otherwise uninvolved people respond empathetically to news of the deaths of young soldiers, who might have been "anyone's" son or daughter, growing up in any "typical" American town (see Cloud, 1998). In cases of more routine death, the trends toward personalized newspaper obituaries and online obituary sites open to public view what once would have been private knowledge (see Ferré, 2005). And in coverage of murder or disaster, television news programs and newspapers transmit images of mourning rituals that seem to be a form of direct communication from the grieving subjects to the news audience. "Because these violent incidents transcend the private grief of immediate family and community," write Jorgensen-Earp and Lanzilotti, "they blur any concept of a boundary between what has historically been called the public and private spheres" (1998, p. 151).

News also can be instructive, providing, according to the sociologists Tony Walter, Jane Littlewood, and Michael Pickering, "not just pictures in words and text of appropriately grieving people, but outright advice on the proper way to grieve" (1995, p. 589). The result is behavioral modeling that can transcend the specific circumstances of grief. The nighttime candlelight vigils held in New York City parks after September 11 may have seemed unique to that event, yet mourners had made the same gesture, in the same public space and in front of news cameras, more than two decades earlier when John Lennon was murdered.

News coverage of more recent tragedies—from drunk-driving casualties and airplane crashes to terrorism and natural disasters—has continued this educational process. Citizens are ready with ritual when a local child is murdered or an office building collapses: by the broadcast of the evening news, they will have assembled candles, teddy bears, flags, photographs, hand-lettered signs, and ribbons. When hundreds of thousands of "ordinary people" traveled to Washington, DC, in June 2004 to wait in line to view the body of former U.S. President Ronald Reagan, they knew not only that they would be covered by news media, but also that they would become "the story" itself. Just as journalists already know the script for coverage of such a story, writes Ernest Borman,

> Audience members, too, have learned how to interpret and appreciate such performances. ... The end result of the television coverage is an interpretative (*sic*) dramatization that provides the possibility of audience participation. ... When we are drawn

into the scripts we share the social reality they portray with their
implied values, motives, and explanations. (1982a, p. 135)

There are certain kinds of public figures in whom cultural ideals are
inscribed, and the occasions of their deaths and funerals are opportunities for public reassessment of those ideals, a reckoning with what
has been lost and what has been preserved in national life. Sometimes
the symbolic figure was, or was connected to, a national leader, such as
Reagan or such as John F. Kennedy, Jr., whose 1999 death prompted a
similar level of news coverage of public grief that really was more about
his father than about him. Sometimes the mourned figure or figures
are symbolic in coverage of major national events through which the
American character is assessed, such as those who died on September
11, soldiers who since have died in Iraq, or casualties of earlier wars
now seen as particularly valorous. Sometimes grief coverage focuses on
ordinary people who strike some symbolic nerve—whose lives are seen
as especially admirable, whose deaths are seen as instructive, or whose
circumstances are understood as the sort of challenge that brings out
"the best in us."

The definition of "us" in this kind coverage, as it appears in U.S.
media, is expressed as American. Journalists identify and explain death
stories (and many other kinds of stories) in terms of their meaning to
the nation—even if the concept of the nation is symbolized by the small
town or the common man. Therefore, the events discussed in this book
are American: not only did they happen in the United States, but their
lasting significance has been assessed according to American ideals.

The 10 studies that comprise this book provide a portrait of the
role of journalism in public ideas about death—and the role of death
in the public functions of journalism—in American society today. The
chapters analyze separate incidents, and they represent very different
types of death. Yet familiar characters and plots, morals and lessons,
reemerge from one study to the next, confirming not only the narrative
qualities of such news but also the nature of public ideals about life and
death today in America.

These studies are organized into three sections that explore major
threads in the coverage of death in news media. The first section considers kinds of death news that are unusually traumatic, involving disaster, murder, or scandal. It opens with a study of coverage of six recent
natural disasters in the Midwest and West, considering how reporters
used war metaphors and religious references in order to make sense of
the arbitrariness of such events (chapter 1). This survey is followed by a
close look at specific cases that not only involved shocking death stories

but also prompted national outrage. One explores what happened to "the story" of death when bodies were not handled with the usual care—when there was no ritual leading to closure—during a scandal at a Georgia crematory and during the chaos of Hurricane Katrina in Louisiana and Mississippi (chapter 2). The other analyzes the press's own self-criticism in coverage of the shooting of 10 Amish girls in a one-room schoolhouse in southeastern Pennsylvania (chapter 3).

Reporters' first duty in such cases is to function, on behalf of the community, as witnesses to a terrible situation. But then they must do something more. Paradoxically, these least explicable situations are the ones that most demand explanation. News coverage of such events therefore seeks villains to whom blame is assigned, and, if possible, heroes among survivors or rescuers. This kind of journalism also seeks some kind of thematic closure, a positive message that is understood to have arisen out of horrible events.

The book's second section further explores these "lessons learned" from deaths that gain public attention. Its subjects range from the common to the famous; what unites them is that, in coverage of their various deaths, all of them are understood as examples of ideals larger than themselves. The obituary pages of small-town newspapers, such as the *Guntersville* (Alabama) *Advertiser-Gleam* (chapter 4), make room for the simple details of life stories, reporting hobbies and idiosyncrasies alongside more official accomplishments and causes of death. They paint a collective portrait of community identity and values. Yet so do the life stories of major celebrities, who, according to retrospective journalistic tributes, almost always are revealed to be "just like us." This is true even of stars who led lives of sinful excess, who become candidates for public forgiveness and inspire popular discussion about religion and redemption (chapter 5).

This section also considers how victims of accidents become sacrificial symbols, reminders of social rules and values that somehow seem to have been lost in the fast pace of modern life. The accidental deaths of teenagers (often in car crashes and/or related to alcohol or drugs) are unfortunately not unusual events, and yet they are written about in journalism as though they were; they serve as moral fables, as warning and instruction, as one more chance for the living (chapter 6). A far different set of circumstances—the deaths of coal miners in an industrial accident—nevertheless was similarly instructive, reminding a national news audience of the "traditional" values and lifestyles of simple, rural folk (chapter 7). Both these kinds of stories drew on the metaphor of family, as an ideal communal model for coping with tragedy (closure) and as a promise that life goes on (continuity).

Closure and continuity are the main themes underlying the third section of this book, which considers the healing function of journalism and the uses of patriotism and national mythology in news. These studies confirm Michael Kearl and Anoel Rinaldi's claim that "social rituals involving the dead contribute to the collective integrity and solidarity of the political groups employing them" (1983, p. 695). All of these chapters examine journalism that not just reported on but *enacted* public ceremonies, paying ritual tribute to Americans whose deaths were seen as nationally momentous. Both newspaper and magazine journalism took on such ceremonial duties very soon after the events of September 11: *The New York Times* eulogized the victims of those attacks by celebrating their typicality in "Portraits of Grief," while newsmagazines wrote in the first person plural, speaking on behalf of the nation, and provided a month-long storyline that paralleled the stages of a funeral ceremony (chapter 8).

The final chapters discuss two highly patriotic events that were widely covered by news media. The death of former President Ronald Reagan was followed by a 10-day pageant of ceremonies that had been planned for a decade, and yet, according to news stories, this public tribute seemed to have emerged spontaneously and surprisingly from "ordinary" people (chapter 9). The nostalgic backdrop for memory of the generation Reagan represented had prevailed in Washington only a week earlier, when the National World War II Memorial was dedicated and reporters showed up for one last chance to record veterans' stories of the war (chapter 10). Yet in this case the subjects refused to cooperate, dodging questions about their own exploits and instead talking about their friends who had not lived to see the memorial built.

Their response confirms Jay Winter's declaration that "war memorials [are] sites of symbolic exchange, where the living admit a degree of indebtedness to the fallen which can never be fully discharged" (1995, p. 94). Ultimately, though, he notes, "[t]he living can go about their lives in freedom because of the selflessness and dedication of the men who fell" (p. 95). Winter's statement illuminates not just the social function of war memorials, but also the social function of public discussions about death in general, and his comment surely applies to the subjects of every chapter of this book. All of these death stories, as told in news media, are ultimately an acknowledgment of what the living owe the dead—of how we must honor them, of which stories we should tell about their lives, and of what we have learned from them.

# I

## Disaster, Trauma, and Respect for the Dead

# 1

## AT WAR WITH NATURE
### Coverage of Natural Disaster Fatalities

All deaths are sudden, even if long expected. In one moment is life; the next, death. Yet the random and violent loss of life during natural disasters seems particularly newsworthy, those sudden deaths especially tragic. When an earthquake in San Francisco or tornadoes in Kansas wreak multiple fatalities, communities small and large share the stories and, to varying degrees, experience the grief. The element of surprise, the bitter and surprisingly egalitarian role of chance in determining death and survival, and the turmoil of recovery are all part of the story. And though nature's violence often takes victims by surprise, covering it becomes almost routine for reporters who train and plan for disasters. Indeed, the Dart Center for Journalism and Trauma notes that "the majority of journalists witness traumatic events in their line of work," including natural disasters (Smith & Newman, 2005). It follows that journalists would tell similar stories at disaster sites, often invoking the same kinds of metaphor and cultural-historical context. News coverage of disasters, according to Katherine Fry, who wrote about television reporting of the Midwest floods of 1993 and 1995, "is a socioculturally sanctioned form of telling and, through a unique format, constructs its own reality" (2003, p. 138). This chapter examines some of the shared stories of deadly natural disasters, to seek to understand their function in the social construction of death.

The role of journalism during a disaster is complex, and coverage can inspire both criticism and praise. The *Christian Science Monitor*, following the Asian tsunami of 2004, wrote about "How to tell the story of the dead without offending the living." It noted "a wave of criticism" of the press from those who called coverage of the tsunami a "corpse show" or "disaster porn." The article explained that the audience's proximity to a disaster can determine how graphic the coverage of deaths will be "and warned 'that the line between'" exploitation and depiction of reality can be a hair's breadth of opinion (Leach, 2005, p. 11). William C. Adams criticized the Western media's ethnocentrism. He wrote: "Overall, the globe is prioritized so that the death of one Western European equaled three Eastern Europeans equaled 9 Latin Americans equaled 11 Middle Easterners equaled 12 Asians" (1986, p. 122). Aaron Parrett noted the U.S. media's neglect and sparse coverage of the effects of a deadly 1964 flood on the Blackfeet Indian Reservation in Montana. It reflected, he argued, "the dominant culture's tendency to minimize or overlook such events when the worst of the damage is experienced by a minority population" (2004, p. 23). Such neglect, even if subconscious, can suppress the history of minority groups: "Mainstream media accounts of events become the semi-official narratives that eventually emerge as 'standard' history, a process that overwhelms minority voices as the event is articulated and retold" (p. 31).

Yet the psychiatrist Beverley Raphael acknowledges the positive role of media coverage of tragedy in natural disasters. One way victims gain "mastery" over feelings of fear, shock, and helplessness, she says, is "giving testimony," including through interviews with news media (1986, p. 94). Talking to press and sharing "communal rituals, ceremonies, celebrations, and public statements may also be vehicles for individual and group release of feeling," which aids in recovery (p. 95). In fact, the simple act of recognizing that victims have suffered provides, at the most basic level, "psychosocial care for disaster-affected people and communities," she writes (p. 245). The media's human-interest stories "are likely to underscore the suffering and need of the affected community. This media attention again indicates to victims that their plight is being taken seriously" (p. 246).

The news media, particularly television meteorologists, work to warn audiences of impending disaster, and much of the scholarly attention paid to press coverage of disasters has been on its ability "to influence people's preparedness and response." But according to Marla Perez-Lugo, media serve important functions through all phases of disaster, perhaps most of all during the actual event (2004). Her study of hurricane coverage found that the press provided emotional support and companionship, created a sense of community, and connected isolated individuals with the outside world. "During the impact of the hurricane, the media–audience relationship was motivated more by the people's need for emotional support, companionship, and community ties, than for their need for official information" (p. 219).

Beyond the immediate informational and social function, press coverage of disasters teaches cultural lessons. Fry notes: "News functions to capture and canonize certain historic events and moments. … Journalists and news organizations become cultural authorities, authorized to shape, interpret, and present certain events and phenomena." She argues that both the form and content of news shape "our collective understanding and memory of how these natural phenomena ought to be regarded, and how nature should behave." Television coverage of the Midwest floods "visually presented them as battles with Mother Nature in the mythic heartland" (2003, p. 137). She writes: "Nature was pitted as the enemy against human (particularly Midwestern) victims who were constructed as a collective protagonist fighting in solidarity against the waters' onslaught" (p. 138).

Ted Steinberg argues that this tendency to regard natural disasters as "morally inert phenomena—chance events that lie beyond the control of human beings" enables political inaction and helps to preserve a particular set of social relations (2000, p. xxiii). Irene Ledesma, in her historical study of community survival following natural disasters, charges that U.S. historians "have long ignored the social and political implications of natural disasters" and suggests that disasters be considered a social as well as a natural force (1994, p. 73). "We will go further in understanding the past when we stop treating natural disasters as capricious acts of God and view them instead as the politically consequential affairs they really are" (p. 82).

All death stories are potent and provocative, and examining them tells us something about American culture and values. In particular, scholars have pointed to "sudden deaths" that elicit a set of cultural responses, including the establishment of bereavement communities, heightened feelings of guilt and the need to assign blame for a crisis (Fast, 2003, p. 285). Thus far, the literature on "sudden deaths" has focused more on human-caused tragedies, such as the 1999 murders at Columbine High School, and not on disasters of nature.

The question becomes: How does the press tell the story of natural disasters, particularly those that cause large numbers of fatalities? This chapter examines local, regional, and national coverage of natural disasters that occurred in 1989, 1991, 1994, 1995, 1997 and 1999, in California, Oklahoma, Texas, Kansas, North Dakota and South Dakota. Included were 154 newspaper articles and 31 abstracts of network broadcasts reporting selected earthquakes, tornadoes, and blizzards that killed at least 20 people. This coverage appeared in *The Washington Post, USA Today, The St. Louis Post-Dispatch, The St. Petersburg Times, The Topeka Capital-Journal, The Chicago Sun-Times, The Houston*

*Chronicle, The New York Times, The Boston Herald, The San Francisco Chronicle, The Los Angeles Times, The Oklahoman, The Forum* (Fargo, ND), *The Wichita Eagle, The Argus Leader* (Sioux Falls, SD), and *The Dallas Morning News,* and on ABC, CBS, NBC, and CNN. Coverage was accessed via LexisNexis, the Vanderbilt Television Archives, online archives at individual newspapers, and microfilm of those newspapers not available electronically (scrolled by dates of the disasters).

## COUNTING THE DEAD

Accurately reporting the number of fatalities caused by a disaster is one of the first and most difficult tasks for journalists. The chaotic situation at the scene and problems with power outages and damaged phone lines or cell towers make it difficult for rescue workers and the press to determine and then communicate who might be dead, or simply missing. For example, the day after a devastating earthquake struck Northern California in 1989, *The Washington Post* told readers "the total number of dead and injured could not be established early today in the widespread confusion that followed the sudden shock of the quake. At sites of collapses throughout the area, rescue personnel worked by flashlight in the darkness to search for victims or extricate them from the rubble" (Weil, 1989, p. A1). In Oklahoma in May 1999, following "an evening of terror" as "tornado after tornado battered the state," *The Oklahoman* reported "the vastness of the destruction and seemingly endless barrage of tornadoes left officials unable to determine the exact number of dead or injured" (Ellis, 1999, p. A1).

Yet as this sample of disaster coverage indicates, establishing a concrete toll becomes increasingly important, and following most significant events, government officials and the press soon begin to speculate on the number of dead, often overestimating. Two days after that 1989 earthquake, *The San Francisco Chronicle* reported a grim prediction: "State officials put the death tally at more than 200, but yesterday they called that count 'only an estimate.' They said about 30 bodies have been recovered but conceded the count would probably climb dramatically" (Shilts & Sward, 1989b, p. A1). Estimates reached as high as 250 for potential fatalities on a particular stretch of the Nimitz Freeway that collapsed during that earthquake—*CBS Evening News,* among others, reported that more than 200 people were killed—yet when the dust settled, the number of dead was 41 (Bowen & Rather, 1989). *The San Francisco Chronicle* noted: "In a series of interviews, officials are blaming unadulterated chaos for the huge miscalculations published around the world" (Carlsen, 1989, p. A17). As one official noted: "We were shooting from the hip. ... A microphone was pushed in our faces every 10 minutes, and we responded the best we could" (p. A17). The newspaper, as well as CBS, speculated that the number of cars on the road was probably fewer than had been predicted because commuters had hurried home early to watch baseball's World Series on television (Blackstone, Bowen & Rather, 1989).

Ten years later, in the aftermath of a deadly tornado in Oklahoma, *USA Today* reported that officials "still were struggling ... to assess its toll—particularly in human lives" and noted the scene was too chaotic to know whether everyone had been found (Weiberg, 1999a, Amid chaos, p. A4). The paper reported 100 people missing, but noted "officials still were trying to determine who among them might have died and who might just be away" (Wieberg, 1999a, Residents, p. A4). *NBC Nightly News* also voiced concerns that the death toll would rise (Avila, Brokaw, Cummins & Williams, 1999). But eventually in the arc of disaster coverage, estimated death tolls begin to come down in number, as well as the official reports. For example, in Andover, Kansas, following a tornado in 1991 that destroyed a mobile home park, the official death tally dropped "as authorities identified bodies and discovered that some fatalities had been counted more than once," according to *The St. Louis Post-Dispatch* (Twister death toll, 1991, p. A10). Fatality estimates following a tornado in Wichita, Kansas, began "falling ... as residents who had fled to shelters succeeded in locating each other" (Manning, 1999).

As journalists attempted, despite significant difficulties, to attach a death toll to these tragedies, at least in some instances they tried to provide a kind of context or comparison. They reported that a Los Angeles earthquake in 1994 was not as deadly as the San Francisco quake of 1989, which, according to multiple reports, was not as devastating as the historic earthquake that destroyed the latter city in 1906. CBS noted that Californians were still waiting for "the big one" (Bowen, Chung, Hughes, Rather, Threlkeld & Whitaker, 1994). *USA Today*, following deadly 1999 storms in Oklahoma and Kansas, provided statistics on the number of tornado deaths by year and the highest tornado death tolls historically, including storms in 1925 that killed 689 people in Missouri, Illinois, and Indiana, and tornadoes that killed 317 in Natchez, Mississippi, in 1840 (Sharp, 1999, p. A19).

## MORE THAN NUMBERS

Statistics, of course, were only a small part of these disaster stories. Journalists struggled to describe the deaths, to give "causes" beyond just the earthquake, or tornado, or blizzard. Sometimes these descriptions were not specific to an individual person. Following the 1989 earthquake, *The San Francisco Chronicle* told readers of fatalities in the city's warehouse district: "The causes of death ranged from decapitation to severe blood loss. Most of the victims were in their cars, leaving work, when caught in the avalanche of falling bricks and mortar from the building" (Shilts & Sward, 1989a, p. A1). Another article began with a generalization ("There are as many ways to die in an earthquake as there are frailties in our flesh. Bricks crush, metal cuts. Sheer terror can stop the human heart"), then continued with information about specific victims killed in collapsed buildings or on the freeway (Robertson, 1989, p. A4). *The Forum*, in Fargo, North Dakota, told readers of deaths and injuries from frostbite, exposure, and carbon monoxide poisoning during the harsh winter of 1997. It then assigned specific causes to names of the deceased, including a 40-year-old woman whose car went into a ditch, a 26-year-old man who fell through a roof while shoveling snow, and a 41-year-old who walked away from his stranded pick-up truck and died from exposure (Crawford, 1997, p. A1). Similarly, *The Dallas Morning News*, following a deadly storm, listed victims by name and causes: a 68-year-old woman drowned, a 26 year old crushed, a teenager hit by lightning (1995, p. A31). Network television coverage typically listed just numbers of deaths, though sometimes victims' relatives or friends described singular deaths in more detail (see, as an example, Lewis & Schneider, 1994).

The violent nature of many natural disaster fatalities made describing them problematic. The events were newsworthy, and the journalists attempted to describe accurately the horrific conditions, yet they seemed uncomfortable with graphic descriptions of victims. In these cases, property damage became a metaphor, a tool for describing deaths of people. Network television coverage, of course, did not broadcast images of bodies but showed scenes of damaged buildings and flattened highways while discussing fatalities. Newspapers, with their verbal pictures, did the same thing. The *San Francisco Chronicle*, reporting the rescue and recovery operations on the collapsed highway, noted that "some cars, flattened by thousands of pounds of concrete, were just 12 inches high" and quoted workers who said that the victims under the rubble were "unable to escape injury" (Sandalow & Congbalay, 1989, p. A5). The same newspaper quoted a police officer:

He saw cars that were turned into tombstone-like wedges of steel 18-inches thick. "I knew...that there were (dead) people inside. I wondered who they were, what they had looked like, where they were going. It was numbing. (Bizjak & Sandalow, 1989, p. A1)

Numerous articles following tornadoes in Kansas, Texas, and Oklahoma reported deaths by describing property damage. For example, a 50-year-old woman "died of injuries she sustained when a tornado destroyed her home" (Cramer, 1999b, p. 11). A husband and wife died in 1995 "when a tornado picked up their home and dropped it across the street" (Tornadoes hit state, 1995, p. 12). *The Wichita Eagle* described a man "found face down in water and debris from the storm. Nearby stood the remains of a twisted trailer's hull and a tree snapped in two" (Wenzl & Elliott, 1999, p. A1).

In some instances, newspaper coverage of these disasters did describe in greater detail the bodies of victims and the anguish of family members. *The Houston Chronicle*, in an article titled "Terror on the Plains," related a man's description of his father's death: "A minivan lifted by the tornado crashed through the wall and roof, crushing his father's head and chest" (Sallee, 1999, p. A25). *The Topeka Capital-Journal* described an infant, "not yet a month old, who looked like a doll lying on top of wood nails, tree branches, and other debris" (Man dies, 1999). An 80-year-old Oklahoma woman died "after a week of treatment for a head injury and crushing-type injuries" (Plumberg, 1999, p. A1). Relating the aftermath of a Los Angeles earthquake, one article quoted an emergency technician:

He said the worst thing he saw was a woman "still alive, lying face down on her king-size bed. A beam had fallen across her," he said. Unable to move it ... he ran for help, returning a few minutes later only to find her dead. "These people had 4 seconds to get out. They had no time. They were just grinded in there." (Apartment complex, 1994, p. A6)

*The Wichita Eagle* related the anguish of discovering the dead, quoting a witness who said she "will never forget the scream. ... The cry began suddenly, then filled the air over Andover like a sorrowful testimony to the surrounding destruction. It was the reaction of a woman uncovering her dead husband" (Perez, 1991, p. A11). Other articles reported the identification of victims by family at a temporary morgue ("That's my father and my brother. Oh, my God, oh, my God, what am I supposed to do?") or the moment when a family member, still hoping for her child's rescue, was told the bad news ("Ma'am, listen to me. Your son, how old is your son? ... This son is dead, ma'am. He is dead.") (Fitzgerald, 1991, p. A15; O'Neill & Chu, 1994, p. A1).

Sometimes coverage described the moments of death, as related by witnesses, including a "3-week-old ... who was sucked from his mother's arms when the storm raged," a man electrocuted by a power line while attempting to rescue a child trapped by earthquake debris ("as soon as he touched the line, his body went stiff as a board"), and a Los Angeles police officer who "plummeted from a freeway overpass when his motorcycle skidded out of control on a buckled swath of the Antelope Valley Freeway. 'His lights were still flashing and he just came tumbling down'" (Kaplan & Krikorian, 1994, p. A1; Lives crushed, 1994, p. A4; Weiberg, 1999a, p. A4).

Numerous articles described not only the deaths of people but the deaths of named pets and other animals as well (see, as examples, Cramer, 1999c; Johnson, 1999; Owen, 1999; Tornadoes kill 3 in 1995; Trammell, 1991). For example, one Oklahoma couple had taken shelter in a bathroom with their pet dachshund, Sammy, and when the storm was over, husband and dog were dead: "It just took [them] away" (Cramer, 1999a, p. A1).

## MONSTERS AND WAR ZONES

While damage to inanimate objects became the metaphor for the deaths of people, coverage of natural disasters examined for this chapter personified the storms, blizzards, and earthquakes, which seemed to destroy purposefully, creating war zones. These living entities were often credited with supernatural power. Storms "marauded," "skipped," and were "furious" enough to crush cars and houses "like soda cans," shear trees "as if someone had taken a giant chain saw to them," and stack mobile homes up "like dominoes." *The San Francisco Chronicle* called the 1989 earthquake "unbelievable," telling readers "it brought death, and fire, and darkness and fear in the very deepest pit of the stomach. If you were here, that memory will never leave" (Nolte, 1989, p. B3). *The Los Angeles Times* quoted a quake survivor in 1994: "It felt like Godzilla had picked the building up, shook it, couldn't find a toy and threw it back down on the ground" (O'Neill & Chu, 1994, p. A1). *The Oklahoman* called a 1999 tornado "a huge, brown, raw monster. Incredible" (Hutchinson & Jackson, 1999, p. 15). And amateur videos of the storms, broadcast on network television, showed what those monsters looked like. Writing for a national audience, *USA Today* described a storm: "To those who ran from its dark tentacles or cowered under its howling fury, it was a monster, loud as Hell, black as Death." The monster, the paper told readers, "flattened subdivisions and most of a downtown. It tossed one mobile home into a pond—a baby with a bath toy—and stripped the skin off another like a banana" (Hampson, 1999, p. A1). Ten years earlier, *USA Today* had told readers the Bay Area earthquake "shook you like God was coming down" (Howlett & Nichols, 1989, p. A1).

By far, war was the reference most often used to describe the devastation resulting from these disasters. Over and over again, a disaster site was described as a war zone, a tornado as an atomic bomb's mushroom cloud, earthquake damage as if a bomb had exploded. NBC quoted the Oklahoma governor: "It certainly looked like a huge battle has taken place" (Talley, 1999). One witness described quake-ravaged Los Angeles: "Devastation. It's like a war zone. Walls knocked over. The stores are boarded up. The National Guard is all over the place. People camped out. Petit Park is like a tent city" (Crittenden & Hutchinson, 1994). In an Oklahoma neighborhood damaged by a tornado:

> The once comfortable street resembles a scene from World War I: Trenches of rubble offset by an occasional leafless tree against the stark horizon. For [one woman], who was tossed 50 feet through what had been the front of her house, the moments after the tornado hit could have been the aftermath of an atomic bomb. "When I got to my feet, there was no noise. No birds. No cars. It was just like a thick, heavy film of death hovering over a pile of debris." (Willing & Levin, 1999, p. A17)

Another 73-year-old woman "thought about being in Germany in World War II" and "had a creepy feeling" (Hampson, 1999, p. A1). The epicenter of the Los Angeles earthquake of 1994 was likened to Beirut, the scene "nearly apocalyptic" (Kaplan & Krikorian, 1994, p. A10).

Many Oklahoma tornado stories looked back to the 1995 bombing of the Alfred P. Murrah Federal Building. For example, in May 1999, *The Topeka Capital-Journal* told its readers about damage in their neighbor to the south: "The damage looks like the Murrah Building, but instead of nine stories tall it's spread out over a large area" (Talley, 1999). *The Oklahoman* quoted a resident of a damaged apartment building: "It looked like a war zone. … It was the Oklahoma City bombing all over again" (Ellis, 1999, p. A2). Disaster sites were also described as "hell" and "a madhouse," an earthquake as a "Disney ride" or "waves on an ocean," and tornado sounds as trains. One roof during a tornado "rippled in and out 'like it was breathing.'"

Yet as often as the devastation was vividly described, so too were the recovery efforts. *CBS News* assured viewers that people in Oklahoma were "survivors" and that they were receiving help (Bowers, Pitts & Rather, 1999). According to reports of both storms and earthquakes, rescue workers used specially trained dogs, infrared technology, and listening devices to find survivors and bodies. Firefighters, police, and everyday citizens worked methodically and tirelessly to restore order. As one shaken worker told the *San Francisco Chronicle*: "It's like hell up there—people have lost their families up there. … There's always hope of life. If I was (trapped on the freeway), I know others would do this for me" (Sandalow & Congbalay, 1989, p. A5).

## CELEBRATING VALOR, REMEMBERING THE LOST

Reports of death and destruction in the disaster coverage examined for this chapter were punctuated with stories of heroism and remembrances of lives lost. Such memorials reflected particular cultural values and strengthened communities, aiding in recovery from the tragedies. Readers of the *San Francisco Chronicle* likely found it comforting that when the 1989 earthquake hit Candlestick Park during a World Series, "the California people knew themselves, instinctively, what to do. They decided to keep their heads. A panic would have killed thousands of people, not hundreds, but there was no panic" (Nolte, 1989, p. B3). Readers learned: "Wherever lives were threatened throughout the region, stories of valor and compassion abounded" (Shilts & Sward, 1989b, p. A1). *The Dallas Morning News* reported, following a violent 1995 tornado, "spontaneous acts of heroism saved several lives" (Loftis & Lopez, 1995, p. A29). "Throughout Los Angeles," following the earthquake of 1994, "there were tales of courage—of strangers helping strangers because, as one man said, 'it seemed like the right thing to do.' By day's end, many people owed their lives to that spirit. And many more had been touched by it, as they watched the progress of several daring rescue missions on television" (Kaplan & Krikorian, 1994, p. A10). As recovery from these disasters progressed, articles noted community support. *USA Today* told readers that in Oklahoma tornado victims had been "buoyed by the massive outpouring of donations and offers of help, a tradition among people whose ancestors were raised in tougher times on the Plains" (Levin & Bowles, 1999, p. A4).

Soon after each disaster, journalists began focusing on individual stories of sacrifice and heroism, particularly about those who died. One mother in Oklahoma gave her life for her son, telling him "I love you" as a tornado sucked her from under a bridge (Hutchinson & Jackson, 1999, p. 15). A Dallas man died trying to pull a carload of people out of a ditch during a storm (Minutaglio & Garcia, 1995, p. A30). A Kansas woman was surely "checking on other people to make sure they were all right when she was killed," according to *The Wichita Eagle* (Flynn, 1991, p. A5). A husband died shielding his wife from "waves of debris" (Cramer, 1999a, p. A1). A 23-year-old father died from injuries received when trying to rescue his family from their burning apartment (Owen, 1999, p. 4). Finally, *The Wichita Eagle* told the frightening story of a

27-year-old "hero" who died on his birthday saving his sister and her family. He held them together as they were sucked out by the storm, twisted round and round, and dumped six lots away. They survived, but he did not (Ranney, 1999, p. A1).

As breaking news turned into "follow-up" kinds of stories in the wake of these disasters, the press began concerted efforts to remember, individually, more of the victims. *The Wichita Eagle* counted "The lives lost" and "Those who died," publishing photographs and short memorials of 1999 tornado victims. *The San Francisco Chronicle* noted "Quake Victims—The People Behind the Statistics" (1989, p. A10). In each installment of a 1999 series called "Portraits of Life," *The Oklahoman* reminded readers: "They were like us. They worked, played, had families and looked forward to 2000. Then, Monday night, tornadoes claimed their lives, but not their memories, not their smiles, not their hugs, not their effect on others." In a series that preceded its own "Portraits of Grief" (part of the Pulitzer Prize-winning coverage of the terrorist attacks of September 11, 2001), *The New York Times*, thousands of miles from the epicenter of the Bay Area earthquake of 1989, published "The freeway dead: Portraits from Oakland—a special report." It noted:

> The coroner's list was like a census report on the polyglot Bay Area: Victims were Asian, black, white, Hispanic. There was a Palestinian, a refugee from Vietnam, Midwesterners, Easterners. Most were not native to the Bay Area: They had come for economic opportunity, for personal or political freedom, for the climate, the beauty. (Reinhold, Navaro & Rabinovitz, 1989, p. A1)

All of these stories were structured much like typical newspaper obituaries, remembering work achievements, memberships, hobbies and families, and focusing, if only briefly, on the personalities of the deceased. What distinguished them from obituaries was that they were published together, as part of the disaster coverage rather than on traditional obituary pages.

Some victims were singled out, remembered in more than one report or in lengthier articles, for a variety of reasons. In addition to those noted for sacrificing their lives for others, coverage focused on stories that seemed particularly tragic, such as a Texas family that lost five members in a single storm (Jacobson, 1995, p. A31), or the earthquake death of a formerly homeless man who had been adopted by his neighbors and became "a surrogate brother to many neighborhood children" (Kaplan, 1994, p. B1). Some were remembered for public service during their lives, such as a motorcycle police officer killed in the 1994 Los

Angeles earthquake who was featured by both *NBC Evening News* and the *Los Angeles Times* ("He rode the freeways, the boulevards, the side streets and the alleys, proudly sitting astride his thundering Kawasaki Police 1000, spiffily uniformed in a shiny white helmet, shiny black boots, and, of course, shiny inscrutable sunglasses"), an elementary school teacher ("She was just a treasure. … She was one of those teachers that comes along once in a blue moon"), and a Baptist minister (He "lived a long life that was an inspiration") (Ayres, 1994, p. A16; Alanis, 1995, p. A21; Sallee, 1999, p. A25). The *Argus Leader* remembered "a local hero" who froze to death in his car; the 63-year-old, while attending high school, had been the first freshman ever to make the all-state team in basketball (Tucker, 1997, p. A1). Finally, some deaths were given extra attention in newspaper reports because of television coverage, including a 23-year-old Berkeley woman who died on the Bay Bridge in the 1989 earthquake. As the *San Francisco Chronicle* noted, "Her death will also be remembered by millions of television viewers who saw the shocking film footage of the car plunging over the edge of the bridge's broken section. A video, shot by tourists following a few cars behind, was shown on network newscasts" (Viets, 1989, p. A21). Another man, rescued four days after the same earthquake, "had received thousands of cards and letters from schoolchildren worldwide … along with at least 50 movie and TV offers from producers." After he died, he was remembered for embodying "the Bay Area's hope and stubborn determination after the quake" (Congbalay, 1989, p. B6).

Local and national coverage provided information about memorials, and some funerals were covered as news stories (see, as an example, Dow & Rather, 1989). Services for the motorcycle officer and elementary teacher each drew more than a thousand people—*CBS Evening News* showed scenes of the police officer's funeral—and in Dallas, two thousand mourners remembered the family that lost five members (Chung, Hughes & Rather, 1994). "The 3 1/2-hour service was punctuated by tears, but there also was a conscious effort by surviving family members and friends not to allow the gathering to become gloomy" (Jacobson, 1995, p. A31). In Oklahoma, "American flags popped up by the dozens … tied to headless stop signs, car antennas, anything left standing. Those that flew from flagpoles were at half staff for the 38 Oklahomans who died" (Levin & Bowles, 1999, p. A4). Other, more intimate kinds of memorials were noted, too, such as the elementary students who put a note on their lost classmate's chair and decided no one would sit there for the rest of the school year, or the child who sent a helium balloon to his deceased father with a note saying "I love you, I miss you and I finally made it to first grade" (Jacobson, 1995, p. A35; Owen, 1999, p. A4).

Some of the articles about individual deaths hinted at responsibility, though none ever blamed the victims outright. *The Argus Leader* noted that "alcohol was involved" when two men froze to death during a 1997 blizzard (Tucker, 1997, p. A1). Articles listing the dead in California noted their casual attitude about earthquakes, that worrying about earthquakes was low on the list of priorities, or that most who died gave little thought to earthquakes (Reinhold, Navarro & Rabinovitz, 1989, p. A1). *The Wichita Eagle* pointed out, in one man's obituary, that he "didn't like to go to the storm shelter" (Those who died, 1991, p. A4). Numerous tornado articles noted that victims waited too late to seek shelter or died trying to take cover. Writing about a death in Kansas, *The Washington Post* quoted a man who lost his father-in-law: "He wanted to lock his damn house. ... He never made it" (Walsh, 1991, p. A3). *The Wichita Eagle*, in an article titled "Rubble tells a bitter truth," considered the high death toll following a 1991 tornado: "With 6 minutes warning, why were so many killed here? 'Because they lived in a mobile home park,' said Andover Mayor Jack Finlason during a news conference. ... 'They didn't have basements'" (Rubble, 1991, p. A1).

## THE SPIRITUAL AND SUPERNATURAL

A major theme in coverage of these natural disaster fatalities was the influence of God, chance, and fate in the tragedies. Just as it coupled horror and heroism, news coverage juxtaposed stories of death and survival, of darkness and light, of wreckage and renewal. These images were scattered throughout the coverage, but on occasion a news article addressed the spiritual aspects of disaster outright. *USA Today* covered a "bittersweet Mother's Day" church service in a tent erected in the wreckage of an Oklahoma tornado. It quoted a Baptist minister: "Hope will outlast the darkness. ... God has never been nearer to you than he is right now. There's nothing so radiant as when the sun breaks through the clouds after a storm. We will never, ever be the same again, but we will rise from the rubble" (Hoversten, 1999, p. A3). *The Oklahoman*, covering a 1991 storm, quoted a Methodist minister who disagreed with the phrase "act of God" often used to describe the cause of a natural disaster:

> We're just letting them know that this is not an act of God as is termed through government agencies. ...We've told them that it's one of those things of nature that happens and God has good things for them. The people I know [who] have been affected have great faith and have put it in proper value. Life goes on. (Tornado victims, p. A1)

In the Bay Area following the 1989 earthquake, the *San Francisco Chronicle* asked an Episcopal priest what he might say "to a widow struggling to find the hand of God in that hellish jumble of death and destruction." The priest replied:

> But that was only one moment in time. There are also moments of resurrection. This life and its injustice is not the last word. The people who died were not unjust. This world does not give us that kind of justice. ... There will be an awful lot of folks in church on Sunday. ... One reason they will be there is to say "Thank you for life," and to touch base with something even deeper than the fault lines we live on. Thank God there are ritual and liturgies in the church to help people get back to sanity. (Lattin, 1989, p. C9)

Time and again, the people quoted in these disaster stories repeated the same notion—that God was not responsible for the destruction, but had a hand in the survival and any good that might come from the trials of storms and earthquakes.

For example, one man, who survived being stranded in a car during a blizzard, said he asked God to pull him out safe and received help from a mysterious man who later could not be found or identified. "But I feel lucky. I really do. God was good to me and maybe that was my guardian angel sitting there. I feel bad thinking about the families of the other guys, though" (Kranz, 1997, p. A1). CBS told viewers about a "miracle baby" rescued in the mud in Oklahoma (Mitchell & Pitts, 1999). Another Oklahoma family survived in the only room left standing in their house after a tornado. "We could hear the whole house and furniture projecting against the walls. It totally lifted the roof off our house. If we had been in any other room we would be dead right now. ... It's only by the grace of God that we were saved" (Tornadoes kill 3 in, 1995, p. A1). Still another woman, her husband, and two sons "huddled in their hallway linen closet for protection." She told *The Oklahoman*: "We said a prayer that God would watch over us," and "when they emerged from the closet they discovered it was the only thing left standing in their home" (Ellis, 1999, p. A1). An earthquake survivor told the *San Francisco Chronicle*, "I thank my God ... that I am alive" (Nolte, 1999, p. B3). A woman told the Associated Press: "We heard it coming and—whoa, whoa Jesus—we called on his name and I felt his arms come around us and saved us from that tornado. And I thank God for that" (Tornadoes kill at least 30, 1999, p. A3).

Survivors told journalists they believed God's role in the disasters was even more complex than simple protection from danger. Said the 8-year-old niece of the Kansas man called a hero because he died saving his family: "God must have used Uncle Chris to save us because if he hadn't been there to take care of us, I would have died. Daddy would have died, too" (Ranney, 1999, p. A9). A woman who lost both her husband and her home said: "I think God took our home away to make it easier on me, because I think if I had to go back and see all our memories, I couldn't handle it" (Owen, 1999, p. 4). A few articles told readers of unanswered prayers. A Los Angeles woman "learned her prayers were not answered" when news came that her son had died (Hutchinson, 1994, p. A1). An Oklahoma woman, after finding the body of missing neighbor, said: "We prayed for God to lead us to her before we went out . ... We hoped to find her alive" (Doucette & Sutter, 1999, p. A1). A witness to the collapse of a Bay Area freeway said he "watched in horror" as it crumbled. "Then I started thinking of all those people on the freeway and I said, 'Please God, let that freeway hold.' But I knew it wouldn't hold'" (Dietz, 1989, p. A4). But in the same article, another man spoke of being thankful to survive: "At first it was just total silence. ... People couldn't believe it. I sat there in shock and thanked the Lord a few times."

Several articles noted the belief among survivors that the dead had passed on to a better place. A 4-year-old Oklahoma girl, according to her mother, was "in heaven with her great grandmother" (Cramer, 1999c, p. A6). In Kansas, the report of the death of a 79 year old woman quoted her son: "She was not afraid of death. She was right with the Lord; she knew her salvation was true, and she studied and longed for the day that Jesus would take her home. ... I think she's happier than she's ever been because, she's at home now" (Koetting, 1991, p. A4). The "Profile of Life" featuring the Oklahoma woman who died protecting her son noted: "She was a very spiritual lady; she had a lot of faith. This boy is not having any trouble with it for the simple fact that he has all the faith she taught him. He knows she went to be with the Lord. That's what he'll tell you. She went to a better place than here. She taught him the reality of life and death" (Bentley, 1999, p. 20).

If God was responsible for survival, but not for death, then what was? According to some press coverage it was the fickle hand of fate, "nature's cold caprice" (Torres & Johnson, 1994, p. A4). The *San Francisco Chronicle* explained to readers: "But in a disaster as sudden and selectively devastating as Tuesday's earthquake, one cause of death emerges as the lowest common denominator: coincidence. It was the simple accident of being in the wrong pace at the wrong time. People died because of where they were when the world broke apart" (Robertson, 1989, p. A4). *ABC Evening News* noted the "illogic" of earthquakes (Claiborne, Jennings, Muller, & Rose, 1994). Storms in Texas "randomly took neighbors, co-workers and friends—and threatened but somehow spared many others" (Minutaglio & Garcia, 1995, p. A30). Articles conveyed surprise that victims came from "all walks of life, neighborhoods" (Minutaglio & Garcia, p. A1). Yet, time and again, articles noted that it could have been worse, that more could have died, had it not been for the World Series (and lighter traffic on the freeways), for the spontaneous acts of heroism of family and neighbors, for the calm reaction of people who kept their heads, and for the televised warnings of the impending storms. *USA Today* reported that three television meteorologists were front-row guests at an Oklahoma church service: "The broadcasters got a more rousing welcome—two standing ovations—than ... any ... of the other officials who attended" (Hoversten, 1999, p. A3).

In the end, most coverage focused at least in part on how thankful survivors were simply to be alive. An Oklahoma man asked, "How can you feel anything but lucky?" (Willing & Levin, 1999, p. A17). *USA Today* quoted the Oklahoma City police chief: "A lot of people have lost everything, except what they can dig out of the rubble. Most are in good spirits, though there's not a whole lot to be happy about except to be alive" (Wieberg, 1999b, p. A4). In Kansas the governor told the Associated Press "we feel blessed" that the fatality count was lower than it could have been. A San Francisco man "poured champagne into paper cups for his friends and said, 'This is an earthquake celebration, because we're still alive'" (Shilts & Sward, 1989a, p. A1).

## DISCUSSION

Like death itself, natural disasters are sudden, even if long predicted. Journalists expect to cover them, they train for them, and they even have a national organization (the Dart Center) dedicated to easing the trauma of them. But when an earthquake or deadly storm hits, the event is jarring not only for victims but for the press, too. Journalists must react quickly to tell the story, to get critical information to readers and viewers. The most important stories to tell are about the people who died.

When news of a disaster breaks, the first reaction is to describe the chaos and to get a handle on the numbers of lives lost, as well as the amount of property damage done. That need to quantify is so strong that the press often overestimates the number of fatalities, and then later backtracks to explain reasons for the miscalculation. Beyond reporting death tolls, the disaster coverage seeks to give more specific information about the causes and moments of death. Twisted metal, snapped trees, and crushed buildings become metaphors for the bodies of human victims because those images abound and are easy to invoke. Occasionally, however, the press reports more detail about the actual bodies. Words describe what still photography and television will not show—corpses of family, friends and neighbors.

As this coverage suggests, journalists have a hard time finding analogies strong enough to describe the disaster scenes and the events that caused them. Neighborhoods destroyed become war zones, the damage like an atomic bomb's wake. A storm or earthquake takes on supernatural qualities. It becomes a monster wreaking havoc, a random killer of innocents. Even more shocking is the realization that death crosses geographic and cultural barriers, claiming victims from "all walks of life."

Yet these horrible scenes are juxtaposed with more uplifting stories. Time and again, these articles point to spontaneous acts of heroism, to crowds that opted for calm over panic, to neighbors who provided help, to rescue workers who toiled until the last victim was rescued or found. Only one article in the sample of 185 examined told a different story. *The Wichita Eagle*, following a brutal 1991 storm, quoted a survivor: "It looks like a war. ... Worse than a war. Last night there was nothing but people stumbling around here in shock. A lot of people were so much in shock, they couldn't help. You know that's a lot of shock when you can't help save someone's life" (Mann, 1991, p. A1). This is a different image, an anomaly that would offer little comfort to readers and viewers who surely want to believe they and their neighbors would behave admirably, would help resolve a crisis rather than add to it. The vast majority of articles and network news abstracts examined for this chapter reassured readers they would, indeed, do the right thing.

Coverage of these disasters also commemorated the dead in a variety of ways. Newspapers and television covered funerals and memorial services, and shared more intimate remembrances, like that of a first-grader who sent his dead father a message attached to a helium balloon. Some victims received extended coverage—if they lost their lives heroically, or if they represented some tragedy even greater than the norm, or if they had become well known through other media coverage, particularly television. Obituary-style reports gathered the victims into one place and offered tiny synopses of what had been valued in their lives. Those stories, shared with a larger audience, became instructive as well as reflective of community values.

Finally, press accounts of these fatal disasters focused on the notion of God in interesting ways. Time and again, victims gave God credit for the miracle of their survival, but did not blame God for their losses. They prayed for themselves and others, and they expressed the belief that the dead had gone on to a better place. And they reported feeling happy and grateful in the aftermath of the destruction.

Such a reaction might not come as a surprise to scholars who have looked at the role of faith and religion in American culture historically. Steinberg (2000) notes that Americans at the turn of the twentieth century stopped referring to natural disasters as God's judgment on evil people, and instead attributed them to the randomness of nature. James A. Morone has written about the public outrage expressed when some ministers opined that God had allowed the September 11 terrorist attacks as punishment for an amoral culture. Quite the opposite image became part of public consciousness. He notes:

> When the planes struck … people rushed to help one another. Ordinary men and women refused to abandon strangers as they made the long flight to safety. … The many stories all testify to a deep, shared community, to powerful bonds. … The images from that terrible day construct a formidable sense of us. (2003, p. 496)

Likewise, press coverage of these disasters revealed "a formidable sense of us" by sharing stories of a faithful people who help neighbors and strangers alike, who deal with tragedy with courage and optimism rather than fatalism.

The disaster coverage examined for this chapter indicates that the press serves a greater role than simply providing information about preparedness and response, though that role is important, too. The press strengthens community ties by commemorating the lost lives, and by celebrating the heroic attributes of both the dead and the living. Such coverage, as Fry (2003) notes, shapes and interprets the collective understanding of these events. The press allows victims to "give testimony," which, Raphael (1986) argues, would help them gain mastery over their fear and grief. Coverage recognizes their suffering and shares their stories locally, regionally, and nationally. These victims know with certainty that their plight has been taken seriously.

# 2

## DEATH RITES INTERRUPTED

*Responsibility and Remembrance in Coverage of the Tri-State Crematory Scandal and Hurricane Katrina*

What responsibilities do the living have for the dead—for the corpse and for the memory of the deceased? In a communication age, when both individual and mass deaths are shared publicly, what role does journalism play in articulating such responsibilities? John McGowan writes that "some people, though by no means all ... believe that they owe something to the dead and express that belief through a variety of words and deeds" (2002, p. 301). Those obligations, he notes, involve remembrance, acknowledgment of significance, rituals of burial and mourning, justice, forgiveness, continuity, and piety. Though McGowan argues "the dead gain nothing from our piety toward them even as the neglected living cry out for our attention," he does acknowledge that "piety is ... inescapable" (pp. 344–345).

Whether obligations to the dead are real or perceived, whether they are moral, psychological, or political, the rites surrounding death are among the most sacred in any culture. Douglas J. Davis considers such rituals "to be symbolic of human nature, expressing the way people transform the given facts of biological life into values and goals of humanity" (1997, p. vii). He writes: "The fact that practically all human societies possess some formalized death rites, alongside the otherwise practical task of disposing of a body, suggests that funerary ritual possesses some very positive function in human life" (p. 5). For religious cultures with a belief in an afterlife, the funerary rituals serve as transition between this life and the one to come, and people who are not religious in a traditional sense also place great emphasis on such rituals. Davis says, "Even in secular contexts, rites are performed to locate the dead firmly in the past and in memory" (p. 2).

Rites of death become so important, culturally, that they seem almost mandatory. McGowan argues that "mourning—the public enactment of grief—is expected, even demanded" (2002, p. 307). Funerary rituals, according to Giblin and Hug (2006), bring home the reality of death in a culture that tends to deny death, and help the living deal with grief. Yet sometimes the socially prescribed customs and ceremonies are hindered or rendered impossible. Bodies are not tended; the deceased are not recalled in ways that celebrate their significance or that foster cultural continuity. This chapter considers what happens when there is a public disruption in established death rituals by examining press coverage of two highly publicized instances of such disruption: the Tri-State Crematory scandal and the aftermath of Hurricane Katrina.

## THE EVENTS AND THE JOURNALISM STUDIED

In January 2005, Ray Brent Marsh was sentenced to 12 years in prison for discarding more than 300 corpses he had been paid to cremate. The decision followed a 10-hour hearing the presiding judge called "the longest victim impact session I've ever been through in all my years on the bench." Two dozen relatives of people whose bodies had been "stacked and strewn" on the property of the Tri-State Crematory in the community of Noble, Georgia, vented their wrath and confusion about the bizarre crimes that had sparked international attention. As *The Atlanta Journal-Constitution* reported: "Most ... spoke of having nightmares, being unable to sleep, experiencing depression, seeking counseling, taking anti-depressants and being unable to control their behavior." The newspaper quoted a woman who "called the Tri-State scene a 'horror movie, macabre, horrifying, sick to the point of vomiting. All I had left of my brother were black bones'" (Arey, 2005b, p. B1). At the end of the emotional hearing, Marsh apologized to the families and asked for forgiveness, not for his crimes but for his "sins" (Weber, 2005).

Press coverage of the Georgia crematory scandal began in February 2002 when federal authorities received an anonymous tip and discovered hundreds of bodies scattered on the crematory grounds, hidden in the underbrush and stuffed into vaults. The difficult and intense search for decaying corpses preceded civil suits and criminal charges in a case that spanned three years. As family members brought in for testing the ashes they had believed to be deceased relatives, many learned they had been given cement dust instead. Marsh was eventually charged with

787 felony counts, including 439 counts of theft, 122 counts of burial service fraud, 179 counts of abuse of a corpse, and 47 counts of making false statements, according to the *Journal-Constitution*, which pointed out that punishment for the offenses could have added up to more than 8,000 years in prison (Arey, 2005b, p. B1).

The case did not go to trial; Marsh pleaded guilty to theft and fraud. In the end, many of the 24 victims who attended the sentencing hearing (and many of the more than 240 who sent victim impact statements) felt confused, angry, and frustrated. As Thane Rosenbaum noted in an essay published in the *National Law Journal*: "For many of these relatives, the plea agreement failed to achieve any sense of relief, closure or moral justice ... but perhaps even more painfully, the truth and story behind his crime—what he did specifically, and why he did it—will never be known" (Rosenbaum, 2005, p. 26).

More than once in press coverage the mystery and the story were likened to a horror novel. Yet Stephen Prothero had a different observation. In an essay published shortly after the discovery of corpses in Georgia, he wrote:

> I find myself returning not to Stephen King but to the Catholic writer Flannery O'Connor. O'Connor hailed from rural Georgia, and this story might have sprung from her imagination. ... Like all of O'Connor's work, the Tri-State case is inflected with the issue of race. Ray Brent Marsh is black, and Walker County is lily-white. ... When the Tri-State Crematory story first broke, a colleague of mine asked, "Is there no limit to sin?" The answer, in Noble, Georgia, as in O'Connor's fiction, seems to be no. (2002, p. 6)

For Prothero, the story was about race, sin and grace. The work of those who combed the grounds looking for corpses was "holy" (p. 7).

The first section of this chapter analyzes regional and national press coverage of the Georgia crematory scandal, paying particular attention to its focus on death rituals, its portrayal of the living victims, and its religious imagery.

On August 29, 2005, Hurricane Katrina pounded the American Gulf Coast, flattening communities and killing more than 1,800 people, though an accurate and final death toll is difficult to pinpoint. Press coverage of the massive storm and its aftermath was extensive, including the human suffering, the economic loss, and the government's astonishing inability to deal with relief efforts. One particularly interesting thread in the press coverage of Katrina focused on the bodies of victims. From the hours and days immediately after the storm, when retrieval of bodies took a back seat to rescue work, to eight months later when corpses were still being recovered and identified, local, regional, and national press accounts highlighted the treatment of the dead and in doing so considered the obligations of the living to the dead.

Such coverage became a legal issue when a government official announced plans to bar the press from covering the collection of corpses, and several news organizations were denied access to recovery efforts (Marquez, 2005). When CNN filed suit against the Federal Emergency Management Agency, and a judge issued a temporary restraining order in an initial hearing, the government changed its policy.

The second portion of this chapter will discuss press coverage of the victims of Hurricane Katrina and the efforts to return them to their families.

This study examines coverage of the Georgia crematory scandal and the issue of body recovery following Katrina in the local, regional and national press. Local coverage includes *The Atlanta Journal-Constitution* for the crematory scandal and *The New Orleans Times-Picayune* for hurricane recovery. National coverage includes articles located using LexisNexis Academic and Academic Search Premier in national and regional newspapers and in magazines, including *The New York Times, USA Today,* the New York *Daily News, The Philadelphia Inquirer, The Washington Post, The Houston Chronicle, People, Rolling Stone, Jet, Cross Currents, Human Events, Society, Black Enterprise, Maclean's, Time, The Economist,* and *The American Prospect.* For Katrina coverage, broadcasts of National Public Radio, as well as reports from the Knight-Ridder wire service, also were considered. Of course, these databases likely did not produce every story written about the crematory case or the hurricane recovery, but they provide a manageable sample to analyze the coverage, including a variety of publication types. In all, 195 articles were examined.

## COVERAGE OF THE CREMATORY SCANDAL

Descriptions of the corpses were common in articles reporting the Tri-State Crematory scandal. Over and over again, words like "ghoulish," "macabre," "appalling," "horror," "gruesome," "grotesque," "atrocity," and "horrendous mess" were used to describe the scene on the crematory grounds (Arey, 2003c, p. B1; Copeland, 2002b, p. A10; Ripley, Berestein, Berryman, DeQuine, Land, & van Dyke, 2002, pp. 41–42; White, 2002, p. B1; Deneen, 2002, p. 48; Crematory declared, 2002, p. 12). As *People* magazine noted, it was "like something out of a Stephen King novel" (Fields-Meyer, Helling, & Sider, 2002, p. 141). The bodies were "stacked like cordwood," "dumped like garbage," rotting, scattered, piled, stuffed, discarded, stashed, jammed and crammed in various locations on the crematory grounds (Stacked like, 2002, p. 38; Ensure crematory, 2002, p. 23; Ripley et al., 2002, pp. 41–42; Arey, 2002a, p. B1; Copeland, 2002c, p. A3; Fields-Meyer, Helling & Sider, 2002; 111 unidentified corpses, 2003, p. 12; Stanford, 2002, p. C1; Crematory operator, 2002, p. D8). *The Atlanta Journal-Constitution* quoted the Georgia chief medical examiner at length about the search for corpses in the woods and underbrush:

> If you separated the brush you could see skeletal remains or degenerating body bags, things like this. In some of the piles of trash you could see bodies. … I remember against a tree there was a vault that was upside down. Later on, we found the vault with human remains. (Arey, 2003, June 20, p. B1)

The article portrayed this examiner as being bewildered by what he found, and quoted him as saying, "It is still very difficult to find words to describe it. … I'd say it was beyond the life experience of even fairly seasoned professionals like myself." County worker Stan White, among the more than 450 county, state, and federal emergency workers called to the scene, assured the *Journal-Constitution* that the workers handled "every body and casket with care, with great care," but he reported having nightmares as a result of the clean-up. He told the newspaper: "I dreamed they [the bodies] would be coming out of the body bags at me … grabbing at me and everything" (Arey, 2002g, p. C6).

Articles also regularly repeated that concrete dust or powder, earth, wood chips, and potting soil had been passed off as the ashes of the deceased (Arey, 2002b, p. B1; Copeland, 2002b, p. A10; Hart, 2004a, p. A15; Stacked like, 2002, p. 38). One family had scattered a portion of what they thought were remains near the eleventh hole of the deceased's favorite golf course. His niece told *People* magazine, "When they scattered his ashes . . . they could see light shining through the ashes, and they sparkled" (Fields-Meyer et al., 2002, p. 141). The family, according to the magazine, had been "plunged into an emotional maelstrom" when they realized the shimmering dust was powdered cement.

The problem became, for officials in Georgia, Tennessee, and Alabama, how to deal with such an inconceivable crime. Or was it a crime? *The New York Times* quoted a Georgia district attorney who explained the dilemma: "There are laws against desecration of graves, desecration of bodies that have been interred, but this is just something you really don't contemplate happening" (Firestone, 2002, p. A16). Officials first charged Marsh with two counts of theft by deception for each identified body. One count was for taking money for a cremation that did not occur, and the other was for not returning the correct remains (Firestone,

2002, p. A16). Yet the *Journal-Constitution* reported court deliberations on the question: "Is a human corpse the property of another so that it might be the subject of theft by taking?" (Arey, 2004d, p. B5) And "theft," even if correctly applied, did not seem appropriate for the magnitude of Marsh's crime. As coverage of the lawsuits began, one attorney described "a family culture of disrespect" for the dead, another called the scandal "perhaps the greatest deception ever," and another accused Marsh of "depravity" (Arey, 2004c, p. C2; Federal civil, 2004, p. E2). Politicians called it a "betrayal of trust" and an "incredible transgression of the universal respect for the dead that we have" (Arey, 2002c, p. A1; Tri-State opinion, 2002, p. C5; Arey, 2002d, p. D3). As Georgia's medical examiner said: "The horror of it is that this was a man, who ... was entrusted with the care of loved ones. ... We take care of our trash much better, frankly." Yet there were no laws that fit. As Marsh's lawyer told the *Journal-Constitution*, "We have heard officials cite our cultural mores against disrespect of the dead, but until last summer, it was simply not a felony in Georgia in the ways alleged in this case. The state cannot simply make up criminal charges and apply them after the fact to a situation our leaders find either politically popular or politically sensitive" (Arey, 2003b, p. E1).

Marsh's lawyer, quoted in *The New York Times* after the guilty plea was made public, said the idea that his client could have gotten thousands of years in prison was "a bit of overkill," particularly for a case "where none of the allegations had anything to do with a living being . ... There was nothing done inappropriate to the bodies other than not cremating them" (Hart, 2004b, p. A16). Rumors had circulated that bodies had been mutilated or sexually assaulted, and that some had been at the site for 15 years, but those allegations were reported to be false (Arey, 2002b, p. B1; Arey, 2002e, p. C1).

A few articles did attempt to grapple with the implications to death rituals of the unfolding events in Georgia. *Time* magazine noted:

> There is a time to weep, a season to mourn. But there is not supposed to be a second time to do it again from the beginning. Last Tuesday about 100 alumni of grief filed into the Oakwood Baptist Church in Walker County, Ga. Clutching candles and tissues, they were forced to revisit the rituals of death. This time they prayed not for the souls of the dead but for the bodies. (Ripley et al., 2002, p. 41)

The article provided information about other scandals in the funeral industry, yet said proposed regulations rarely got anywhere. "Most people don't want to deal with death until it happens, and not even then." An article in *The American Prospect* said:

We tell ourselves that the rituals by which we preserve or destroy corpses reflect moral seriousness, the strength to acknowledge death and integrate it into our lives, and respect for the deceased. We presume that the failure to value a dead body implies a failure to value the person who once enlivened it. (Kaminer, 2002, p. 9)

But writer Wendy Kaminer disagreed with that sentiment. She spoke about and to a woman upset by the treatment of her mother by Tri-State:

"I can only think of my mom, of her lying out in the wind and cold, tossed into the ditch like an old shoe," one woman poignantly lamented. "I feel somehow I have let her down. I loved my mom. She was an old lady and I wanted her death to be dignified."

"That's not your mom in the ditch," I want to remind her. "She's well beyond indignity. The manner in which her body is treated after death has nothing to do with the manner in which she died." (2002, p. 9)

The *Journal-Constitution* published a lengthy article in its "Religion Faith & Values" section, titled "Last sacred rite." It noted the "tender care many people believe is due the dead," and quoted religion scholars: "Despite religious beliefs that the spirit has left the body, disposal of human remains is considered by many people to be a sacred duty, carried out as a way of honoring the memory of people who are loved." The attachment to remains of loved ones is "the source, probably, of all funeral ritual" (White, 2002, p. B1).

Indeed, according to an article published in *Society*, "From ancient times the desecration of a corpse was considered to be a deep affront against the gods themselves" (Deneen, 2002, p. 48). And in twenty-first-century Georgia, coverage of the crematory scandal included numerous references to religion. In his sentencing hearing, Marsh himself referred to his crimes as "sins" and asked for "forgiveness" rather than leniency (Weber, 2005). A Chattanooga, Tennessee man whose wife's body was found at the crematory site spoke not of forgiveness, but of punishment: "God's going to punish him, but he's got to be punished on this end, too" (Arey, 2004e, p. A1). *The American Prospect* debated whether Marsh's actions constituted sin. "The betrayal of trust and the disrespect of grief are despicable—in that betrayal lies sin—but the lack of sentiment about dead bodies doesn't reflect a moral lapse so much as a sentimental one" (Kaminer, 2002, p. 9). The argument was that for those who do believe in life after death, the impulse to sanctify corpses might be misguided. "If you believe in immortality, as most people apparently do, why worry about an empty vessel that the soul or spirit leaves behind?"

Families of the deceased grappled with this notion, according to the *Journal-Constitution,* which wrote about a prayer service held to "address such questions on a community-wide scale." One Tennessee woman told the newspaper she believed her uncle's soul had left the body at the crematory site and gone to heaven, "But that doesn't make it any easier." Another man said he believed the "essence" of his mother is "far removed from all the commotion around Noble." The Baptist pastor officiating at the service told those attending: "From a Christian perspective, the Bible teaches that to be absent from the body is to be present with the Lord." Yet a Methodist minister whose parishioner had been among those sent to Tri-State for cremation understood the families' anguish. The body, he told the newspaper, is "God's temple ... there's a certain accepted and appropriate manner for dealing with the physical remains. To deviate from that norm, such as in the case here, brings an outcry of a horrible injustice not just against the body, but against the spirit." And a religion specialist interviewed for the article spoke of the Taoist view that "a person has two souls, one that leaves after death and one that lingers near the body. If the corpse is not properly handled, the soul that is its guardian becomes angry. ... It becomes a 'hungry ghost.'" The point, he said, was that there is an obligation to the dead (White, 2002, p. B1).

Surprisingly, many of the religious references were to Marsh, the accused. *People* magazine noted that before his arrest, Marsh was "two months away from becoming a deacon at his church" (Violation, 2002, p. 122). *USA Today* reported that he was a treasurer of his church, and a former member of his county's Board of Family and Children Services, and *Time* quoted a bewildered neighbor who noted he came from "churchgoing people" (Copeland, 2002, February 19, p. A3; Ripley et al., 2002, pp. 41–42). Articles told readers that a jailed Marsh was "relying heavily on a Bible provided by his sister" and that he continued reading the Bible at home under house arrest (Arey, 2002a, p. B1; Violation, 2002, p. 122). The *Journal-Constitution* reported when a judge loosened restrictions confining Marsh, which enabled him to attend church services, and it noted that the Marsh family "prayed the Lord" would send the right attorney (Arey, 2002l, p. C1; Arey, 2003a, p. C3). Marsh himself, responding to death threats against him from an angry community, said, "If the Lord's ready for me to go, then I'll go. The Lord is my protector" (Arey, 2002h, p. D1). At his sentencing hearing, he asked forgiveness for his "sin" but offered no reasons why he discarded rather than cremated the bodies sent to Tri-State.

According to press reports, Marsh had reason to worry about his safety. Newspapers and magazines analyzed for this study focused on victim anger and confusion, from the time the first bodies were discovered all the way through the sentencing hearing. As one victim told *People*, "We were upset, then sad. Now we're angry. ... How could someone do this to us?" (Fields-Meyer et al., 2002, p. 141) The *Journal-Constitution* quoted furious family members who vented their feelings about Marsh ("You scum, you deserve to die." "I hope you rot in hell." "You will get what you deserve." "They ought to blow off his kneecaps and send him to prison in a wheelchair" [Arey, 2002k, p. B1]). And the newspaper reported on threats made to the defendant, including one caller who said on tape, "I wish you would hurry up and get [Marsh] out so we can kill him. ... We've spent enough [money] on him. What he needs is hanging. I'd like to help hang him. We need to build a big fire under him" (Arey, 2002j, p. D1). Marsh's attorney reported numerous death threats, shots fired on his property, and trespassers (Arey, 2003e, p. B1; Mungin, 2002, p. H3).

Rather than the theft or fraud, many victims focused on deceased loved ones, and some wore T-shirts with their pictures (Arey, 2002f, p. E3). One woman stood outside the courtroom holding a placard with her mother's photograph. "I don't want you to forget her. ... I'll never forget her, never forget what Brent Marsh did to her" (Arey, 2004f, p. A1). As a lawyer for the families told the Associated Press, "This ruined the memory about the passing of their loved ones" (Associated Press, 2004, August 23). The grave of one woman's mother-in-law had been exhumed and found empty. She told *The New York Times*, "We don't even know where she is" (Families raise, 2002, p. A19). A man lamented that "there will be no closure until my mother is found" (Arey, 2003b, p. E1). Another woman, quoted in *USA Today*, said, "It's disgusting to think our son was tossed to the side without any regard" (Copeland, 2002a, p. A3). One man had not told his 87-year-old mother that his brother's body was among those missing. "I've never told her what happened. It would kill her," he told the *Journal-Constitution*. "No person deserves to be treated like that. It's turned my life around" (Arey, 2005a, p. E3).

Other family members expressed feelings of guilt. A Georgia woman told *USA Today*, "You try to go on, but now it's all coming back again. You think he [her father] was done properly, the way he wanted. Then you find out he's been in some shed or out in some field decaying" (Copeland, 2002a, p. A3). The Georgia attorney general, quoted in the *Journal-Constitution*, said: "This case has touched a nerve, and exposed the raw emotions of countless citizens who thought they had achieved some measure of closure with respect to the death of their loved ones" (Arey, 2002d, p. D3).

Family members expressed an overwhelming need for information, to know not only what happened, but why. *The New York Times* noted that much of the families' passion sprang from their desire for answers they would never receive (Hart, 2004a, p. A15). Some were upset that a plea deal substituted for a trial. "We're not going to learn what happened if we don't have the trial. I want to see all the pictures of my mother, and I want everything they have concerning my mother" (Arey, 2004e, A1). A woman from Florence, Alabama begged Marsh at his sentencing hearing: "Please speak to me, Brent. If not today, any day, ever. … Please help me, only you can set me free" (Arey, 2005b, p. B1). Marsh told those at the hearing they would not get the answers they desired, he said, "not for lack of a desire to give those answers, but the lack of the answer." As he spoke, *The New York Times* reported, "the courtroom erupted in sobs and sighs" (Hart, 2004a, p. A15).

Just as the religion scholar Stephen Prothero had predicted in his essay "Bodies in Limbo," race became a part of the Tri-State Crematory story, which he likened to a Flannery O'Connor novel. As the story broke, a number of African American funeral directors "quickly sought assurances that a persistent rumor that black bodies were cremated while white ones were not was untrue" (Arey, 2003c, p. B1). As one official said, "The rumor and innuendo that existed was incredible." The *Journal-Constitution* reassured readers: "Many unidentified remains were African-Americans." Officials told the newspaper that fewer African Americans had brought DNA samples of missing family members in for identification. The Georgia medical examiner said, "I have no explanation for why that is" (Arey, 2003c, p. B1). And articles about a possible change of venue for the trial talked about the necessity of finding a new county that matched demographically with Walker County, Georgia, and its four percent African American population (Arey, 2003d, p. C1).

As the investigation progressed, victims and the community expressed outrage, encouraging a "lynch mob atmosphere," according to a coalition of ministers and civil rights leaders who protested a decision by the state not to provide Marsh extra protection (Law and order, 2002, p. H3). The *Journal-Constitution* reported a "racial epithet" had been uttered during a bond hearing. In an editorial that urged officials to ensure Marsh's safety, the newspaper noted: "Aggrieved family members, in published articles and on the Internet, have made no secret of their wishes to see him dead" (Arey, 2002i, p. B1). A witness in one of the court hearings noted that the Ku Klux Klan in northern Georgia had been monitoring Marsh (Arey, 2003f, p. B1).

Marsh attributed at least some of the anger to his public face. He said: "This is the South and I'm a black man and I'm involved in the community in a leadership role. ... A lot of people don't like that. They might run me off the road or shoot at me" (Arey, 2002h, p. D1).

Finally, most of the coverage of the crematory debacle dealt in some way or other with the restoration of social order—the massive efforts at clean-up and identification, the civil and criminal court proceedings and efforts at reform. They told readers about a proposed bill in the Georgia legislature "that would require inspections of all crematories and penalize abuse of human bodies and body parts," and another that would make abandonment of a dead body a felony (Fields-Meyer et al., 2002, p. 141; Arey, 2002c, p. A1). The governor of Georgia promised to extend the inspections beyond the crematories, to funeral homes as well (Stacked like, 2002, p. 38). One article speculated that such statutes would likely appear in many state and federal penal codes (Deneen, 2002, p. 48). Others gave information about proper cremation procedures, and assured readers that this "tragic abuse" was not widespread nor would it be repeated (Copeland, 2002b, p. A10; Wilson, 2002, p. 3). They noted that cremation had been rising in popularity, and estimated that by 2025 nearly half of all Americans would choose cremation over traditional burial (Copeland, 2002a, p. A3). *Black Enterprise* included a consumer-oriented article on burial rights and how to choose a crematorium (Evan, 2002, p. 281). Articles reported on the millions of dollars in restitution that had been paid to some of the families (Arey, 2004a, p. D1).

The press noted, too, that the site of the debacle would be "preserved as a private 'sanctuary' ... a dignified and respectful use of the properties where the bodies were found." About an acre of the crematory property would be "left undisturbed forever" (Arey, 2004b, p. D3).

## DEATH AND HURRICANE KATRINA

Just as with the crematory coverage, descriptions of corpses were commonplace in the sample of articles about death and Hurricane Katrina. Early coverage focused on bodies "floating in the streets" that were "being ignored" by rescue workers still intent on searching for living victims of the storm. *The New Orleans Times-Picayune* quoted an anonymous official: "We had to push bodies out of the way to get our boat through the streets ... to pick up survivors" (Anderson, 2005a, p. A4). The same article told readers of unconfirmed reports of bodies stacked near the city's convention center. Often, bodies were described as bloated, rotting, and disfigured.

One particular corpse, that of Alcede Jackson, remained on a front porch for two weeks, as the *Times-Picayune* described, "wrapped in a plastic bag and covered in a blanket beneath a sign quoting the evangelist John and commending Jackson to 'the loving arms of Jesus'" (Krupa, 2005, p. A1). Two days later, another *Times-Picayune* article, by a different reporter, noted the same man, saying "his horrible, long wait is a scar on our neighborhood, and our city" (Grace, 2005, p. A1). *The New York Times* wrote about a corpse waiting for recovery near an automated teller machine on Union Street. "Its feet jut from a damp blue tarp," the story described, "its knees rise in rigor mortis. Six National Guardsmen walked up to it on Tuesday afternoon, and two blessed themselves with the sign of the cross" (Barry, 2005, p. A1). Knight-Ridder reporters described a woman's corpse "hung up on a cyclone fence, her arms outstretched as if she had been caught running from something" (Tsai & Fitzgerald, 2005). On September 28, nearly a month after the storm, the *Times-Picayune* reported the identification of three bodies found in St. Tammany Parish, including that of a 42-year-old man whose "body ended up near a heap of debris days after he struggled to survive in his flooded home, where he wrote a goodbye letter to his wife." The article noted: "Though the bodies represent only a fraction of the dead pulled from Hurricane Katrina, the three identifications made public ... this week put some of the first faces on southeast Louisiana's death toll" (Gordon, 2005, p. A1).

Identification of bodies was slow and tedious, and news coverage often reported the numbers of anonymous bodies that had been recovered and speculated about how many might still be waiting for discovery. The longer the wait, the more difficult the identification because of "prolonged exposure to the elements" (Anderson, 2005b, p. A1). Knight-Ridder Washington Bureau reporters Pawlaczyk and Garcia told the story of a woman who had to identify the bodies of her parents: "She told the attendant to unzip the bag holding her father, but he hesitated. 'He just unzipped it a little bit, just past my father's ear,' she said. 'That was enough. I knew that was my father's ear. They wouldn't unzip my mother's bag. They said they found them together. I guess that will have to be enough'" (2005). An article about a makeshift morgue said workers were "surrounded by nearly 900 corpses one month after Katrina" and called it a "hellish reality" and incomprehensible (Jensen, 2005, p. B1). As weeks passed, the descriptions became more graphic. As the *Times-Picayune* reported on October 17:

> Many of the dead were "floaters" who lay in water or mud for days, swelling the bodies and rendering their appearances undistinguishable by race or gender. The number of wallets or other identification found on the bodies was "minimal." ... Clothing

was ragged, "animal activity" had removed flesh and many finger-
prints were unreadable. Many died away from their homes. Bodies were found washed up on house porches that were not their
own. (R. T. Scott, 2005, p. A1)

As months passed, stories reported the difficulties of even knowing when a body was found. The National Public Radio program *All
Things Considered* told the story of a student volunteer relief worker
who thought he saw something, and alerted officials. Remains of three
people were discovered buried in rubble (Block, 2006). As late as March
2006, seven months after the storm, bodies were still being discovered in
New Orleans, as *The New York Times* noted: "Skeletonized or half-eaten
by animals, with leathery, hardened skin or missing limbs, the bodies
are lodged in piles of rubble, dangling from rafters or lying face down,
arms outstretched on parlor floors" (Dewan, 2006, p. 1A). Numerous
publications wrote about the problem of family members returning to
damaged and destroyed properties, finding loved ones themselves. *USA
Today* quoted a sheriff: "For people to come home to that damage and
then to make that gruesome discovery—that doesn't seem fair to me"
(K. Johnson & Willing, 2005, p. 1A).

For public and press, the idea of so many untended corpses was
bewildering and shocking. *The New York Times* told its readers: "What
is remarkable is that on a downtown street in a major American city,
a corpse can decompose for days, like carrion, and that is acceptable"
(Barry, 2005, p. A1). And just as happened following the discovery of
untended bodies at the Georgia crematory, rumors began to circulate.
Rumors were repeated by public officials, published in the press, then
debunked. In an article about how such rumors were spawned, *The
Philadelphia Inquirer* listed several: that hundreds of bodies floated
in shark-infested waters or were consumed by alligators, that 1,200
people had drowned in a school, that 30 to 40 bodies were stacked
in a freezer at the New Orleans Convention Center, that hundreds of
bodies languished at the Superdome. "It never happened," the paper
noted (Gillin, 2005). A New Orleans area fire chief, during an interview
with Knight-Ridder, called "hurricane urban myth" the rumor that 22
bodies had been found bound together with a single rope (Pawlaczyk,
2005). Rumors were so strong regarding bodies in the Superdome that,
according to the *Times-Picayune*, federal officials finally arrived there
with a refrigerated 18-wheeler and three doctors—to find only six bodies (Thevenot & Russell, 2005, p. A1). The New Orleans coroner, interviewed on National Public Radio, explained it this way: "Times like
this, people hallucinate. I mean, you know, people are not themselves

and they think they saw things. I mean, they're not lying, you know, but they think they saw things that never happened" (Montagne, 2005).

That the bodies were deserving of respect was another common theme in the sample of Hurricane Katrina coverage examined for this chapter. Shortly after the storm, federal officials used such an argument when explaining why accurate death toll numbers were not available. "You have to deal with these bodies with respect and get them properly secured" (Anderson, 2005a, p. A1). Reporters told of makeshift memorials, not at burial sites but literally with bodies. The *Times-Picayune* wrote: "They practically scream out their message: that this is a person, not a body" (Grace, 2005, p. A1). Time and again, the press reassured readers that the dead were being treated with dignity (Jensen, 2005, p. B1; Norris, 2006; Pope, 2005a, p. A9). Workers who struggled to identify victims called them "individuals" rather than bodies or corpses (Scott, 2005, p. A1). *The Houston Chronicle*, quoting a Texas relief worker, assured readers that the bodies were more than numbers: "Each one ... represents a person who had a family and a life" (Hedges, 2005).

Recovery workers' jobs were described as "solemn" and "sacred" (Perlstein, 2005, p. A1). National Public Radio's *All Things Considered* included a report from a Family Assistance Center where a genetics team worked to identify bodies. It noted: "Across one wall is a quotation from William Gladstone, 'Show me the manner in which a nation cares for its dead and I will measure with mathematical exactness the tender mercies of its people'" (R. Siegel, 2006). Yet the issue of respect for the dead became ammunition in the well-publicized political squabbling in the wake of the hurricane. The governor of Louisiana and the mayor of New Orleans criticized the federal government for what the former called a "lack of urgency and lack of respect. ... In death, as in life, our people deserve more respect than they have received" (Tsai & Fitzgerald, 2005).

Naturally, because recovery and identification of bodies was so difficult, and because many Gulf Coast residents were unable to return to their homes, traditional funerary ritual was interrupted or, in some cases, rendered impossible. As *The New York Times* explained: "The uncertainty has produced anguish in a community known for attaching special importance to final goodbyes, with elaborate rites and elegant cemeteries" (Dewan, 2005a, p. A18). As "routine processes for handling the dead [were] re-established," the *Times-Picayune* reported, even victims who had been identified would have to wait weeks, even months, for burial (Gordon, 2005). The newspaper told readers that authorities were withholding release of some that had been identified "because of a concern that families will rush to plan funerals and then be disappointed by the delay in receiving the remains" (Scott, 2005, p. A1).

The funeral for one identified man, whose family was lucky enough to bury him a month and a day after the storm, was missing some traditional elements, including the line of cars driven to the burial site since the cemetery was unable to accept new caskets. Many of the deceased's friends, too, could not get back into town for the event. For his daughter, the problems "heaped more despair onto the month's unending trauma" (Gordon, 2005, p. A1). One funeral director suggested that families hold memorial services before they had bodies, or as another story called them, "empty casket funerals" (Dewan, 2005a, p. A28; Ott, 2005). The *Times-Picayune* reported a "big increase in cremations and in temporary burials" (Pope, 2005b, p. A6). According to the newspaper, "These are not bodies that look like they are going to a funeral home" (Jensen, 2005, p. B1).

Still more problematic were the bodies that could not be identified, or whose families could not be contacted or were unable to make provisions for burial. In February 2006, five months after the storm, *The Washington Post* reported "200 unidentified or unclaimed victims" were "inside a fleet of refrigerated trucks." According to the article, the state of Louisiana had initially decided to bury the bodies at a cemetery site in Carville, Louisiana, and construct a memorial.

But that did not sit well with many in New Orleans who argued that a proper burial includes the sense, spiritual and geographical, of "going home." Most of the dead come from the city. "I told them we cannot be burying New Orleanians outside of New Orleans," Mayor C. Ray Nagin said of his protests to state officials. (Whoriskey, 2006, p. A4)

One concern about the proposal was that there were no regular bus routes to the site, but mainly citizen and city protests were that most victims "would prefer to have been buried in their homeland, so they can be with their families" (Norris, 2006).

Coverage of deaths in Hurricane Katrina, similar to that of the crematory scandal in Georgia, focused on the frustration and wrath of family members dealing with the disaster. The massive scale of the evacuation and rescue efforts for the living, and the enormity of the scale of property damage, created havoc for families as they tried to make provisions to find and bury loved ones. Fear and grief gave way to anger (Latson, 2005; Ott, 2005). One woman was furious when authorities lost for three weeks her parents' bodies that had been recovered immediately after the storm (Pawlaczyk & Garcia, 2005). Another woman, whose mother died at the New Orleans Convention Center, told National Public Radio of her frustration. The family had attached a note to her body with the names and phone numbers of her children, yet locating the body later was "agonizing." She said:

> We called. I would call. My sisters would call. We contacted the White House, we contacted our congressman, we contacted the mayor's office. ... Couldn't sleep because we felt like, "She's out there somewhere and we have to find her." ... I know she's at peace now. I know she can rest in peace. We know where she is now. There's still some answers we want. We never found out: When was she picked up? Who picked her up? Where was she kept? How was—there's so many unanswered questions. I still don't know how the system could be so messed up. (Siegel, 2005)

Families who knew where their relatives were became impatient as logistical problems delayed the release of bodies. As one article noted, "Anger of relatives seems to waft with the faint odors of death through the post-Katrina morgue at a former grade school." In that article, a man said of his great-aunt, and of government officials, "She's a little old lady who drowned in her attic. ... I think they're so incompetent. I'm afraid now they're going to lose her" (Simerman, 2005). One family staged a formal protest. The two sisters stood outside a facility that held their mother's body, one with a sign: "Free the Souls held hostage at St. Gabriel morgue" (Scott, 2005, p. A1). In April 2006, more than seven months after the storm, a woman whose family never found the body of her 6-year-old nephew told *The New York Times*, "In my opinion, they forgot about us." Angry at ongoing efforts to rebuild the city, she said: "They did not build nothing on 9/11 until they were sure that the damn dust was not human dust; so how you go on and build things in our city?" (Dewan, 2006, p. A1) The woman believed victims of the terrorist attacks of September 11 had been treated with more dignity.

Finally, coverage of death and Hurricane Katrina focused on process and the return of social order, just as did that of the Tri-State Crematory saga. At first, police and National Guard were prohibited from touching corpses, "except to tag them and report their location" (Krupa, 2005, p. A1). Then articles described the tedious search for the dead, first by recovery workers who broke through doors and slogged "though hip-deep, foul-smelling muck," later aided by cadaver dogs (M. Brown, 2005, p. A2; Latson, 2005). Articles told of processes of "collecting corpses and zipping them into body bags;" of creating maps showing retrievals; of transporting them in refrigerated trucks; of using DNA and other methods of identification; of assessment and autopsy (El-Ghobashy, 2005; Hedges, 2005; Pawlaczyk, 2005; Siegel, 2005, 2006; Simerman, 2005). Much of this work for Louisiana victims was done at a newly established morgue in St. Gabriel, "a vast necropolis, a city of death capable of processing 144 bodies a day" (Ott, 2005). As discussed earlier, articles assured readers the bodies were treated with respect and dignity.

## DISCUSSION

Local, regional and national press coverage of the Tri-State Crematory scandal and the aftermath of Hurricane Katrina did offer clues as to what happens in a culture when there is a rift in its death rituals. And it sheds light on how the press might contribute to the anguish and conflict—and to the healing.

In coverage of both, articles reflected a social inability to understand or even to cope with the situations at hand. Journalists seemed obsessed with the state of the bodies, and repeated descriptors that implied shock and surprise. Their selection of emphasis offered hints into the nature and degree of the cultural reaction to such anomalies. Public officials as well as the victims affected could not comprehend what was happening, or that such things could occur in the United States. In the wake of the confusion, wild rumors circulated in Georgia and along the Gulf Coast. And while the press eventually debunked the rumors, journalists also aided in their transmission.

In both cases, too, families of the deceased moved from a state of confusion and grief to one of anger, and the press reported that progression. The rage seemed strongest when facts were scarcest. Families literally begged for answers, and were often disappointed. Too, when families were impeded from fulfilling their obligations to the dead (those of respect for the corpse, rituals of burial, and remembrance), they lashed out—at public officials following Katrina, and at the accused and beleaguered Tri-State Crematory owner. Resuming the culturally established rites of death was important and necessary before calm and order could be restored. Significant for the press were the importance of ritual and the strong need for information.

The desire for public memorial and remembrance was also evident in both sets of coverage. Families of the deceased, neighbors, and even strangers showed their determination to remember. Makeshift memorials were placed literally on the corpses waiting for recovery after Katrina, and family members of those whose bodies were never cremated spoke up about the memory of their loved ones—they attended court hearings wearing T-shirts and carrying placards with photographs.

Place became important, too. Families demanded to recover the bodies stashed at the Tri-State Crematory. They needed to know where the remains were and to determine where those remains would finally rest. People in New Orleans, and eventually government officials, believed the unidentified victims of Katrina in New Orleans should be laid to rest in New Orleans, not elsewhere. They needed to be in their homeland.

Religion and race were often discussed in coverage of the crematory scandal, but less so in the sample of Katrina articles examined. It is important to note that issues of race played a significant role in overall Katrina coverage, particularly in articles describing the political battles that followed the storm on the national, state, and local levels. However, race and religion played less significantly in this sample of coverage that dealt just with deaths. Not so in Georgia, where Ray Brent Marsh, the villain in the crematory scandal, was portrayed as a fallen sinner who displayed no respect for the dead. In a culture and era when families turn over the difficult task of dealing with the dead to expert strangers, this represented a terrible breach of trust. Karla FC Holloway, in her book about African American mourning, talked about the trust placed in African American funeral workers in the mid-twentieth century. "The biased social codes of the day were very much in play. So, when black men embraced the burial business, they were responding not only to a business opportunity but also to a sense of cultural responsibility and community necessity" (Holloway, 2002, p. 16). Thus, Marsh's crime was much more than a sales transaction gone wrong. Marsh's "sin" was incomprehensible, treated as worse almost than murder, even while officials had a hard time defining it beyond the crimes of theft and fraud.

In both cases, the bodies themselves became characters in the dramas, first simply to illustrate a momentous crime and disaster, but later as a way for people to grapple with the nature of death.

Douglas Davis has noted that funeral rites (including disposal of bodies) serve as a transition between this life and the one to come, and they serve secular roles of placing the dead firmly in the past and memory. Families involved were forced to revisit the rituals of death and to think about their deceased loved ones. Where were they? Had they been grossly mistreated, or were the untended corpses simply empty vessels? Had their memories been tainted? Press coverage in New Orleans relayed the idea that it was worse for a family member to discover the body of a loved one killed in Katrina than for public officials to do so. The corpse was not to be seen by family until cared for by experts.

Finally, much of the coverage of both events focused on healing and the restoration of social order. Georgia courts dealt clumsily with the needs of victims, offering financial remuneration but no answers to wrenching questions. Following Katrina, government relief efforts were overwhelmed by the magnitude of the disaster. Yet in the end, in both cases, articles portrayed a multitude of community and public officials working to repair damage and to ensure a return to normalcy. That normalcy included public spaces for burial and remembrance, a fulfillment of the obligations of the living to the dead.

# 3

## WHO SPEAKS FOR THE DEAD?

*Authority and Authenticity in News Coverage
of the Amish School Shootings*

On the morning of Monday, October 2, 2006, a milk truck driver named Charles Roberts entered a one-room Amish schoolhouse in Nickel Mines, Pennsylvania, heavily armed and prepared for a siege. He released all but 10 girls, ages 6 through 13, before boarding up the doors and windows. Though later evidence would indicate that he had planned to sexually molest the girls, when state police arrived he shot the girls and then killed himself. By the next morning, five girls were dead, and this small town in rural Lancaster County was inundated with journalists representing local, national, and international media.

During the week following the tragedy, journalists attempted to explain this event in terms of broader news themes, including other recent school shootings and the escalation of gun violence in the United States. News media covered the girls' funerals, which, though private, entailed a long cortege of buggies traveling down a public highway, a scene widely photographed and published or aired in media. Based on clues in Roberts's suicide note and final phone call to his wife, reporters speculated about his motives, ultimately inconclusively. Given the absence of a logical explanation for what had happened—and given their lack of access to the grieving families within a community that even in normal times goes out of its way to avoid media attention—reporters then turned to the timeless theme of innocence lost. The story became one of "when worlds collide" (a phrase used by three newspapers), a cultural feature about what happens when the evils of the "outside" world make their way into a small rural community.

Farming communities long have represented both core national values and an exception to modern life. They function culturally as imaginary spaces, yet because they are real places, they are an especially effective symbol in journalism. The people who live in these communities similarly function as wishful symbols who are nevertheless very real. Katherine Fry explains that, in news coverage, rural people "are strong, accept challenges, and work through their difficulties by drawing on the strength and cooperation of their neighbors. They value hard work, family, God, the land, and their country," and they live amid "safety, security, and continuity" (2003, p. 36).

In this case, nearly all news media ignored the details that made such a simple portrait problematic for Lancaster County, where farmland increasingly is interrupted by sprawling housing developments and outlet malls. Area residents hardly could have been shocked by murder occurring in their midst, after two other spectacular murder cases there during the previous eleven months: in November 2005, 18-year-old David Ludwig of Lititz killed his 14-year-old girlfriend's parents before running off with her, and in April 2006, 21-year-old Jesse Dee Wise murdered six members of his family, including his grandmother and a 5-year-old, in his grandparents' Leola house. Only the Lancaster *Sunday News* revisited these cases, asking in a headline "What's Wrong Here?" and answering, "Lancaster County's three deadly rampages in less than a year are linked to isolationism and a sense of entitlement." This suggestion was a direct challenge to the notion that rural people are inherently caring and neighborly; moreover, it referenced modern societal problems that have led to a culture of violence of which Lancaster County is only a part.

Yet such a perspective was rare in coverage of the Amish school shootings. Instead, newspapers contained illustrative photographs of pastures and of buggies driving into the sunset. Several reminded readers of the popular 1985 film *Witness*, about an urban police detective who is sheltered by an Amish family so that he can protect a child who witnessed a murder while traveling through Philadelphia (a story in which Lancaster is a sanctuary, a place where boy and man are hidden away from "the world"). This was the backdrop for the great majority of news coverage of the Amish school shootings: a land of agrarian purity violated by the outside world.

The killer himself was not an outsider; Carl Roberts was a local resident known to many Amish families in the area. He was, however, "English," the Amish term for anyone who is not Amish, and, because he used guns and had a great deal of ammunition with him, Roberts came to stand for the violence of modern life, now visited on "Paradise" (the name of a nearby town where several of the murdered girls lived). What's more, hundreds of outsiders literally did invade Paradise in the days after the shootings. Some of them were tourists, described in media alternately as "mourners" and "gawkers." Many more of them were reporters and news crews.

Indeed, during the week after the killings—with Roberts dead and his motives still very unclear—the media themselves became villains in this story, and news organizations took up this theme while jockeying for a favorable position within it. The journalistic *content* that later would be most scrutinized was produced by print photojournalists. Nevertheless, the greatest criticism of "the media" in this story fell on television journalists, who were resented less for what they reported than simply for being there with their trucks and their electric cables and their lights. Also resented were representatives of "big-city" media in general. These debates thus centered not only on media responsibility versus insensitivity, but also on which kinds of media have the most journalistic authority and capacity for empathy—the authenticity of "insider" status—in a culturally and geographically specific tragedy. Nearly all of this discussion took place in print rather than broadcast media.[1]

With regard to routine news coverage, journalistic authority tends to be assessed in terms of institutional reputation, resources, facticity, impartiality, credibility, and the ability to create consensus (see, for instance: Allan, 1999; Gans, 1979; Hartley, 1982; Tuchman, 1978, among many others). Yet when a crisis event shines the media spotlight on a vulnerable subculture, journalistic authority also becomes a matter of cultural expertise, sensitivity, and identity—factors that involve not merely the conventions of the production process but the perceptions of the news audience as well. Such a situation elevates the need for news organizations to create and maintain "a relationship with their audience based on their values, on their judgment, authority, courage, professionalism, and commitment to community" (Kovach & Rosenstiel, 2001, p. 61). Creating and validating this relationship was one evident goal of news coverage of the Nickel Mines shooting.

This chapter provides an analysis of such reflexive criticism as well as the major themes of coverage in 20 American newspapers representing local and non-local perspectives. The study attempts to answer the following questions: How did journalists use the Amish killings as an occasion to discuss their own standards and behavior in covering a sensational murder? Were there differences between local and non-local newspapers in terms of the narrative themes they emphasized? At all levels of coverage, how did reporters define "the community" affected by the murders (what kinds of people were accorded the status of "insiders" in this story)? How were these shocking murders ultimately explained to people outside the community?

The evidence for this study includes coverage from three categories of daily newspapers: those within 50 miles of Nickel Mines (local); those within 100 miles of Nickel Mines (regional)[2]; and the top-10-circulation newspapers in the U.S. (non-local, or national).[3] One of the newspapers in the last category, *The Philadelphia Inquirer*, is also in the second, qualifying as a regional paper, while five others are within 150 miles of Nickel Mines.[4] Of newspapers not included in any of the categories above, only one, the *Pittsburgh Post-Gazette*, devoted ongoing, staff-written coverage to this event, and so it too has been included in this study.[5] Hundreds of newspapers across the country and the world[6] covered this event, giving it considerable play and using it as a springboard for editorials about school safety and gun control, but most used wire-service photography and text that either was from the wire services or was reprinted from one of the northeastern papers in the above groups. Since most of the newspapers studied here used wire-service material in addition to their own reporting, wire-service coverage was included in the analysis as well.[7] The journalism discussed in this chapter was published during the month following the event, from Tuesday, October 3, 2006, the day after the shooting, to Tuesday, October 31, 2006, by which time daily, continuing coverage of this event had stopped, even in the Lancaster papers. This body of evidence includes 512 articles (not counting letters to the editor or photo captions).

## "AGONY IN AMISH COUNTRY": MAIN THEMES OF THE INITIAL COVERAGE

The first reports of this story were documentary, showing the school and a photograph of the gunman, as well as pictures of Amish people talking with authorities or gathered in groups in fields near the school. With these initial reports, several newspapers established "logo" phrases that would be used in the rest of their coverage: "Death of Innocents" (Lancaster *Intelligencer Journal*); "Rampage in Paradise" (*Philadelphia Daily News*); "Tragedy in Amish Country" (Harrisburg *Patriot-News*); and "Agony in Amish Country" (*Philadelphia Inquirer*). News text recounted what reporters had been told in press briefings by Col. Jeffrey Miller, the Pennsylvania State Police Commissioner: that Roberts was a local resident and father of three who drove a truck that collected milk from area farms; that once inside the school he had let the boys and several women go before barricading himself inside with 10 girls; that in a phone call with his wife he had said he was seeking revenge for something that had happened two decades earlier; that he shot the girls and then himself within minutes of the arrival of state police; and that (at that point) three girls were dead and the rest had been taken to hospitals.

Two and three days after the shootings, reporting become more psychological, expressing shock and asking: Why? With the death toll by then at five girls (plus Roberts), newspapers emphasized the innocence of the victims, with article heads such as "Rural Peace Shattered" (which ran with the subhead "Monday's schoolhouse killings happened at the unlikeliest of places") (Scolforo, 2006a, p. 1A). This coverage was dominated by two explanatory subthemes. One was the question of the possible motives of the killer (Gammage, 2006, p. A1; also see E. Barry, 2006, and Hambright, 2006a). The second was an explanation of the Amish way of life. Some articles in the latter category described Amish customs and values, which according to *USA Today* include faith, forgiveness, stoicism, and interdependence (Goodstein, 2006; also see Hampson, 2006, p. 3A; Kraybill, 2006; Weaver-Zercher, 2006; Wright, 2006). Others provided pastoral descriptions of Lancaster and the Amish community, portraits that, while essentially true, were greatly romanticized.

The Allentown *Morning Call* quoted a non-Amish local resident's characterization of the community: "If you lived here and your house burned down, you wouldn't have to be Amish to be helped. I like to think of this as like America used to be" (Gostomski & Micek, 2006, p. A1). Over its front-page aerial photograph of one of the graveyard ceremonies, *The Washington Post* used the title "A season of loss in a small town" (2006, p. A1), and in text, the same newspaper used poetic language to describe the scene:

> All day they trudged across the dusty farm fields here—white-bearded Amish patriarchs, women in black dresses and white bonnets, strapping young men with cropped hair and tanned arms. They came, too, in their metal wheeled black buggies, drawn by lathered horses that built clouds of gray dust on the gravel byways, somber but dutiful people on timeless missions of grief. (McCaffrey & Ruane, 2006, p. A3)

As this quotation suggested, the idealization of the community was laced with exceptionalism and fatalism. "If any community must endure the execution of five little girls and the wounding of five others, the Amish come better prepared than most," wrote the *Philadelphia Inquirer*. "This community is the definition of close-knit" (Vitez, 2006, p. A14).

During the first few days of coverage, journalists also tried to explain the crime by connecting it to broader news themes. These included school shootings and general school safety (for instance, Lash & Cleary, 2006; Schools, 2006; Securing, 2006); gun violence and the need for gun control (for instance, Common tragedy, 2006; Gottlieb & Workman, 2006; Kinney, 2006); and the calm leadership of the police commissioner and the heroism of police and medical rescue personnel in the face of "terrorism" (for instance, Raffaele, 2006; Reilly, 2006; Thompson, 2006).

Although it also was present in early coverage, the theme of journalistic intrusion received more attention when the newspapers began to do summary and analytical pieces the Sunday after the shooting, and this focus intensified over the following week. Such criticism focused partly on professional practice: the mere presence of so many journalists (especially those in news trucks) in a rural area, and their act of questioning and photographing the Amish. It also focused on product: newspapers' publication of images captured by telephoto lenses, resulting in close-up views of the faces of Amish people, especially young children and mourners riding inside buggies during funeral processions. Of the 13 newspapers in this study that were viewed in print format, only the Lancaster newspapers (largely) refrained from using these kinds of photographs—which violated not only the grieving families' privacy but also the general wish of the Amish not to be photographed at all. Such images appeared in elite publications such as *The New York Times* and *The Washington Post*, and they were used extensively in three newspapers: the Harrisburg *Patriot-News*, the *Philadelphia Inquirer*, and the New York *Daily News* (interestingly, a group that includes a local paper, a regional paper, and a non-local/national paper). Discussion on the other newspapers' Web sites, including reader posts, indicates that the Wilmington and Allentown newspapers used these images as well.

The sections below detail the newspapers' own discussions of press coverage of this event. Through these seemingly reflexive debates, reporters, editors, and columnists assessed the role of journalism during a perceived "crisis" event, while also arguing over the question of who had suffered the crisis—of who was an insider and who was an outsider, and of who is allowed to speak for the dead and the grieving in particular circumstances. Within these debates, journalists provided another layer of explanation about the special meaning of these murders.

## "SHOW SOME RESPECT": THE LOCAL COVERAGE

Reporters for the newspapers closest to the crime described the scene as though they, too, were area residents appalled by the media spectacle.

The *Lancaster New Era* described the media village that had sprung up within hours of the event, quoting a traffic policeman: "'You get these people from New York that are information hungry and it is kinda (*sic*) 'annoying,' Anderson said, although he quickly added that the media had been very polite" (Umble, 2006, p. A8). Two days later, the same paper was much more critical:

> … the horde of television and newspaper reporters … gathered along the roads … snapping pictures of every Amish person or buggy that passed in front of the media gauntlet. … [There were] about 40 satellite trucks and television crews from New York, Philadelphia, Baltimore and Harrisburg, plus 75 cars belonging to reporters. …
>
> One member of the media apparently tried to sneak into the private funerals, state police said, by dressing as an Amish woman. … Another man said he chased a cameraman out of his driveway when he heard the man say, "Is this where we're going to set up?"
>
> "I understand it, but it ain't right," he said. "They're infringing. The media's so ignorant they asked one woman if they could get on her roof and film the funerals." (Kelley & Stauffer, 2006, p. A1)

The other Lancaster newspaper, the *Intelligencer Journal*, contained a similar vignette:

> While the media waited to capture photos of the funeral procession, an elderly Amish man leaning on his cane walked slowly past the cameras. A television reporter leapt into his path, begging him to speak on camera for "just a second." He shook his head no, and after a few moments of pleading, she finally let him pass. An Amish man inside his buggy who was not part of the funeral procession called out, "Show some respect." (Itkowitz, 2006, p. A7)

Both the Lancaster *Sunday News* (produced jointly by the *Intelligencer Journal* and *New Era* staffs) and the *York Sunday News* published photographs of news trucks, reporters, photographers, and television cameramen. In a rare local-newspaper use of such imagery, the Lancaster *Sunday News* published a photograph that showed the faces of young Amish boys but that emphasized the fact that the buggy carrying the boys was forced to pass by a long line of news trucks bearing satellite dishes (Smart, 2006, p. A1). The York newspaper used the headline "Fatal Attraction" and the subhead "Media Horde Descends upon Amish Country." In this Sunday commentary column, a reporter for the York newspaper provided an eyewitness account that portrayed big-city reporters as not only preying, but also inept:

> I watched as the man was interviewed by a TV crew from, I believe, Philadelphia. Another TV crew waited by the road and yet another was lurking not far away. ... Little did he know, but the man was about to become the victim of a serial gang-interview. ... After his third or fourth interview, I didn't have the heart to bother him. ...
>
> The media descended upon this village like a turkey vulture on a fresh roadkill. Up and down the main highway, traffic was clogged with TV news vans and the tell-tale signs of lost reporters, trying to drive while looking at a map, usually upside down, while their cars swerve onto the shoulder. (Argento, 2006, p. B1, B6)

The Wilmington (Delaware) *News Journal* (which, though it is in a different state, is only 40 miles away from Nickel Mines), went so far as to advise its readers: "Don't read this story, stop tuning into the news coverage and let the media-shunning Amish heal in peace. Lost in the media blitz is the necessity for communities to be left alone to heal" (R. Brown 2006, n.p.). (The *News Journal* nevertheless published 55 articles of its own.)

In all of these newspapers, reporters wrote as observers rather than perpetrators of "the media blitz." So did the Harrisburg *Patriot-News*, which contained this self-referential anecdote about Amishman John Fisher, who "was fielding questions from *The Baltimore Sun* and New York *Daily News* when his cell phone appeared to ring. ... Later, he told *The Patriot-News* he would sometimes pretend to get a call to get away from the bothersome questions of reporters" (Victor, 2006, p. A6). The *Patriot-News* offered an interesting twist when Barry Fox, its television critic, interviewed reporters and producers for the three local television stations, whose "responsibility as local broadcasters" worked against "the competitive nature of their business" as "news crews from around the world descended on the scene." The article quoted Dan O'Donnell, the news director of WGAL, the NBC affiliate based in Lancaster and Harrisburg: "There were a few tears in our newsroom ... you can't help but be affected by it as a human being" (B. Fox, 2006, p. A4). (This would turn out to be the rare exception to newspapers' consistent demonization of the role of television news in this story; here, though, the television station most closely associated with Lancaster also was validated as a sensitive member of the community, not an intruder from the outside world.)

Published 50 miles away from Nickel Mines, *The Patriot-News* was the geographically closest newspaper to contain critical commentary about its own reporting, offering a mix of the justifications offered by local and regional newspapers. In an essay titled "About Our Coverage," executive editor David Newhouse wrote: "While some in the national media may bully their way into Lancaster County and cover the Amish as if they are a circus sideshow, these are our midstate neighbors." At the same time, he defended the paper's inclusion of photographs showing the faces of Amish people in its coverage of "a terrible news story": "The Amish, tragically, have found themselves thrust in the middle of it. … We have tried very hard to balance our job of telling the story with our tremendous regard for these people of faith and peace" (Newhouse, 2006, p. A3). This defense of inherent newsworthiness—with the explanation that the Amish, unfortunately, just happened to find themselves inside a major news story—characterized the discussions in newspapers published farther away.

## "SERVING A HIGHER PURPOSE": THE REGIONAL AND NON-LOCAL/NATIONAL COVERAGE

One of those papers was the Allentown *Morning Call*, published 74 miles away. Challenged in print by one of her newspaper's own columnists, editor Ardith Hilliard replied: "Breaking news is something you cover as soon as it unfolds. … How do you tell a story like that without showing the people directly affected?" (Carpenter, 2006, p. B1).

A more adamant defense was mounted by Amanda Bennett, editor of *The Philadelphia Inquirer*. In a Sunday commentary piece titled "Reporting a Tragedy, with Compassion," she described in detail the precautions taken by the paper's staffers, especially its photographers, in covering the crime that had taken place 59 miles from the city. Photographer Barbara Johnston, Bennett explained, had attended the state police briefing at which rules were set for reporters, and then she had asked permission to stand in a resident's driveway in order to shoot the funeral cortege of buggies. Bennett quoted Johnston's justification of this "most important photo" and included the broader view of photographer Scott Hamrick, who said: "I believe that when I have to intrude into a tragedy, I am serving higher purpose. If we forget our history we will not learn and thus are doomed to repeating the sorrow and sadness" (Bennett, 2006, p. C7). Elsewhere in the newspaper, the *Inquirer* tattled on other news media, especially television: "Television news trucks lined the rural lane, their generators belching smoke, cables crossing the pavement, satellite dishes poking into the sky. Reporters in high heels dabbed on makeup, preparing for their live stand-ups" (Grogan, 2006, p. A15).

Both the *Inquirer* and *The Baltimore Sun* used the phrase "When Worlds Collide" as a title (Pompilio, 2006; Woestendiek, 2006). In the *Sun*'s view, what the Amish community collided with was not just modern violence, but also "modern technology." A major feature in the *Sun* was illustrated by two photographs: one of a horse and buggy driving through a gauntlet of television reporters illuminated by bright lights, and the other of an Amish man being interviewed, surrounded by television news cameramen and photographers (as in the local papers, this was a sleight-of-hand image in which the *Sun* photographer himself was invisible). Published 76 miles away from Nickel Mines, the Baltimore newspaper echoed the contempt for television reporters expressed by the Lancaster and York newspapers: "TV reporters primped before their on-air appearances, taking out curlers and putting on makeup." On an inside page, a caption beneath a large photograph contained this self-conscious explanation: "Amish farmer Amos Esh drives his horse-drawn combine ... while harvesting corn in his field in Strasburg, Pa. Esh agreed to talk to a reporter as long as it didn't interfere with work, and he politely tolerated a photographer's presence" (Woestendiek, 2006, pp. 1A, 6A).

*The Washington Post* (112 miles away) used similar wording and the phrase "a collision of cultures," to conflate the media with "the world" of outsiders, and included similar anecdotes (T. Jones, 2006b, p. C5). One article told of an Amish farmer who "felt a surge of gratitude" when his neighbors "angrily chase[d] a television crew away ... . The TV trucks with their loud generators and the photographers with their clicking cameras ... [could] spook the horses" (T. Jones, 2006b, pp. C1, C5). Like the *Inquirer* and the Allentown *Morning Call*, the *Post* ran a Sunday commentary defending its own use of photographs of the Amish by claiming that "this was a story of historical magnitude that does warrant coverage." This essay also justified close-up shots of the Amish by noting that "many were taken through telephoto lenses from as far as 100 yards 'with respect and dignity'" and that the aerial shot of a graveyard procession that appeared on the *Post*'s front page had been taken from a helicopter that "did not hover" (Howell, 2006, p. B6).

*USA Today*, also published in Washington, DC (112 miles away), used a close-up photograph of a woman holding an infant inside a buggy within a funeral procession, directly above part of an article that noted: "The Amish, who have shunned publicity in the wake of the killings, issued a statement Wednesday asking the media to refrain from 'close-up gawking and picture taking'" (Levin, 2006, p. 4A). Though it, too, published one close-up shot of an Amish child's face, *The New York*

*Times*'s photographic coverage of the people of Nickel Mines was more distant, as was its tone, evident in this removed yet strangely honest passage:

> ... the strain of having hundreds of reporters, photographers and their high-tech equipment descend on an area that often seems as if it is from an earlier century was apparent.
>
> "I'd just as soon not give you any information about our culture to send out to the world," said Ammon Fisher Jr., who helped his father carve tombstones for the girls. "What good does that do?"
>
> Driving on Mine Road in Georgetown, an Amish man in his 20's swerved his large mule-drawn hay cutter toward a crowd of reporters. "We all wish you would just pack up and leave," he told one. (Urbina, 2006c, p. A14)

## "THERE IS NO OTHER WAY FOR US TO REACH OUT": COVERAGE OF THE AMISH RESPONSE TO MEDIA

One unusual dimension of all the concern about this media coverage was the fact that, unlike most grieving families of murder victims, the Amish themselves are not in the media audience. While some may subscribe to a local paper, those around Lancaster are served by their own German-language newspapers, and, by forgoing electricity, they have no regular access to television or the Internet.

One of the few news media to acknowledge this disconnect was *The Pittsburgh Post-Gazette*, which, while it is published 253 miles away from Nickel Mines, represents an area of western Pennsylvania also with an Amish community. The Pittsburgh paper published several profiles of Amish life in its own area, while also reporting from Nickel Mines. Interestingly, one of its articles contained a Nickel Mines resident's criticism of *local* coverage of the event:

> "I'm glad our children aren't subjected to television. They won't see the coverage," said Sam Fisher, an Amish man who manages the auction house that has served as a parking lot for the TV trucks whose crews are roaming the countryside. ... Mr. Fisher, a patient and courteous host to a vast international press corps, became so angry yesterday that he said he wanted to throw out the media on his own. "I saw some of the photographers taking pictures of an Amish man and woman in a buggy, so I stepped in to stop it," he said. "When I found out one photographer was local, it made me all the madder." (Simonich, 2006, p. A4)

The relationship between the Amish and the media took a few unexpected turns two weeks after the shootings. First, the family of the murderer and families of the dead schoolgirls used the local newspapers to extend their thanks to the community for its kindness and help. Both Lancaster papers printed a statement issued by Marie Roberts, the killer's widow (see Hambright, 2006b; Stauffer & Kelly, 2006). The *Intelligencer Journal* also printed a letter of thanks from the parents of Naomi Rose Ebersol, one of the murdered girls, whose father gave an interview to the paper in which he said, among other things, that he was not angry at the media (Hambright, 2006c; Letter from the Ebersok, 2006).

Second, the Lancaster *Sunday News* printed a statement by the Nickel Mines Accountability Committee (the group managing monetary donations), which thanked contributors, the local fire and police officers and medical personnel who responded to the emergency, various charitable organizations—and the media (or, at any rate, *some* media):

> We thank people from the news media who sensitively reported our tragedy to the world and in many cases wrote thoughtful commentary that helped the world grapple with values that are dear to us—forgiveness, nonviolence, mutual caring, simplicity and life in a community of faith. Above all, thank you for the acts of kindness you showed us even while you were doing your reporting work. (A message, 2006, p. A7)

Perhaps most striking was a gesture made by *Die Botschaft*, a German-language Amish newspaper published in Millersburg, Pennsylvania. Two weeks after the shootings, it addressed the non-Amish community for the first time in its 30-year history with a front-page essay, in English, titled "Thank You." In order to make the non-Amish aware of this, the newspaper's editor, Elam Lapp, contacted local reporters, and his message appeared in *The Lancaster New Era* and the Harrisburg *Patriot-News* (Brubaker, 2006b; Courogen, 2006; Scolforo, 2006b). "There really is no other way for us to reach out," Lapp explained. "We could have printed the message the way we did, but if [the media] didn't pick it up, who is going to see it?" (Courogen, 2006).

All of this content bolstered the status and authority of the local press. Lapp's comment provided powerful evidence that news media *do* perform a community-building function—a claim that was a central theme in local press references to the victims as "our neighbors"—and conferred insider status on the local press, if only in these specific circumstances. The Nickel Mines Accountability Committee's statement confirmed media characterizations of the "local values" of Lancaster

County (forgiveness, mutual caring, simplicity), privileged newspapers in its use of the word "wrote" to describe the act of journalism, and implied that its appreciation was primarily for the *local* newspapers that had "sensitively reported our tragedy *to the world*."

## "SPEAKING THE SAME LANGUAGE": AUTHENTICITY AND AUTHORITATIVE LESSONS

Such praise legitimized the extensive media criticism appearing within the local press, even though almost none of that commentary was *self-critical*. Instead, the "the media hordes" that had "descended" upon the Lancaster area were made up of journalists from other news institutions. Especially demonized were "bully" reporters from urban areas, which were repeatedly named in press criticism: New York, Philadelphia, Baltimore, even Harrisburg. The implication was that, by virtue of their residence, these journalists were incapable of being sensitive to a rural community, let alone the Amish. Local-press accounts portrayed big-city reporters as out of their element in Lancaster county: physically clumsy, logistically disoriented, stupidly careless of safety, and inappropriately vain. They were defined as not just inept but inauthentic, lacking the authority to cover this story. These descriptions turned a common news stereotype on its head: in this case, it was not the country folk but the city folk who were rubes and buffoons.

In some of this coverage, the local journalists themselves were invisible in the scenes they painted. In other articles, they were present as sympathetic local characters who were hesitant to make a bad situation worse ("I didn't have the heart to bother him") and who had the confidence of their subjects (as with the Amishman who confided in the Harrisburg reporter that he "pretend[ed] to get call to get away from … reporters"). The local press conflated itself with the "first responders" and with the residents of Lancaster County. They celebrated the generosity of "neighbors" who held quilt auctions and chicken barbecues to raise money for the families of the injured girls (see, for instance, Kelley & Umble, 2006). In one front-page feature in the Lancaster *Sunday News*, an area resident claimed:

> Except for dress, you'd have hardly thought there were any different cultures around here. … Surprising perhaps, for people outside the area, we were all speaking the same language … and not just English, but a language of caring, a language of community, a language of service. And, yes, a language of forgiveness. (H. Adams, 2006, p. A1)

In its article deck, the newspaper asked: "After that tragic day, a deeper respect among English, Amish?" (p. A1). In this feature, the local newspaper was incorporated into "the English" who were learning to "speak the same language" and presumably had gained the respect of the subjects of this event—which now was understood as crime that had happened to the area, not just to particular girls in particular families.

Unable to claim empathy, reporters and editors for the newspapers representing the three closest big cities—Philadelphia, Baltimore, and Washington—nevertheless claimed to have felt sympathy, insisting that they had taken every professional precaution to ensure sensitive coverage (see, again, Bennett, 2006; Howell, 2006; Woestendiek, 2006). The regional and national papers were more likely to provide overviews of journalistic ethics, discussing the use of specific kinds of photographs, privacy considerations, and standards for practice that governed journalists' on-site work in this case. Similarly, the larger and farther-away papers were more likely to discuss the purpose of journalism—the day-to-day decision-making process about what is newsworthy, as well as journalism's broader societal mission of explaining the events of modern life. In these discussions, journalists described the event as "breaking news" and as an "unfolding" story that "warrant[ed] coverage." They also claimed that "this was a story of historical magnitude" and that, therefore, detailed coverage of it "serv[ed] a higher purpose," ensuring that "we" would not "forget our history." Overall, these journalists defended their coverage in terms of their obligation to report and explain news to people beyond the Amish community—a stance from which they had the authority to identify the story's lasting lessons.

Chief among those lasting lessons were the Amish's stoic acceptance of their fate and their choice to forgive the killer and help his family. *The Washington Post* justified its declaration that this was a story "of historical magnitude" by explaining that "the world has learned so much from the Amish this past week, about faith, humility and immediate forgiveness, all done by example" (Howell, 2006, p. B6). Two of the newspapers whose use of close-up photographs of Amish children's faces seemed most exploitative, the New York *Daily News* and *The Philadelphia Daily News*, ostensibly justified these images in headlines that emphasized this theme: "Amazing Grace" (H. Kennedy, 2006, pp. 24–25) and "A Day of Mourning and Forgiveness" (Geringer, 2006, pp. 4–5). The poetic pastoralism of coverage further contextualized this lesson, suggesting that "grace" was the way of people connected not only to each other, but also to the land and the cycles of nature. The Lancaster *New Era* wrote: "Autumn will pass and winter come, and in the spring the Amish farmers in adjacent fields will plow and plant again" (Brubaker,

2006a, p. A1). As these examples confirm, the same concluding themes were conveyed by local as well as non-local press.

In prose and in photographs, the Amish ceased to be a group of distinct people and instead became signs, standing for innocence lost in "our" modern world. As Herbert Gans (1979) notes, the broader "news value" offered by a tragedy in a small town is a symbolic, inspiring one, conveyed through a story in which the resilience of "good" people facing grief stands for the resilience of the American character itself. *The Philadelphia Inquirer* declared that the "victims' families showed the best part of humanity" (Gimbel, 2006, p. A21). Major newspapers, even elite ones, contained nostalgic portrayals of simple but heroic people—in the prose of *The Washington Post* and *The New York Times*, the "patriarchs" and "strapping young men" who inhabited an "area that seems as if it is from an earlier century" (McCaffrey & Ruane, 2006, p. A3; Urbina, 2006c, p. A14). Through this stereotyping, the Amish were idealized, an elevation that was part of the most common professional rationale (after the newsworthiness of the shooting itself) for reporters' close attention to their lives: that "the world" might learn from the example of these noble people.

The forgiveness theme seemed to provide closure to the story. The New York *Daily News* concluded: "Their remarkable lack of bitterness, their refusal to rage or to demand vengeance, seems to offer an important lesson: though a quiet grief hangs over the pastoral country here, peace is returning too" (H. Kennedy, 2006, p. 25). At the same time, though, this theme confirmed how inexplicable "the story" really was. The Amish unwillingness to grieve publicly (the "stoic acceptance" of their fate) created a strange and unusual absence in news coverage of murder, which more commonly features an openly weeping family, and made it difficult for news organizations to report the phenomenon of community grief (though they did so nonetheless). The complexities of the Amish response were acknowledged in some journalistic commentary. Writing an op-ed piece for *The Pittsburgh Post-Gazette*, a religion professor took issue with both the nostalgic nature of coverage and the implications that the Amish stood for the broader American population:

> The horror of Monday's events would have grieved us had they occurred down the road at a public school. That the killings occurred in a one-room Amish schoolhouse exacerbated the anguish, for the Amish and their little school are, in many of our minds, somehow "ours," a reservoir of our supposedly more innocent past.
>
> I am glad that Americans are grieving Monday's horrific events. … Still, I would hope that those of us outside the Amish

community would work hard to resist the notion that the Amish are "ours." They are not. (Weaver-Zercher, 2006, p. H1)

Further, he stressed that the Amish commitment to nonviolence and refusal to seek revenge are distinctly *atypical* of American values: these people, he wrote, are "anything but quaint" given that, "in the United States, forgiveness is radically countercultural" (p. H1).

His point echoed the message of Ammon Fisher to *The New York Times*: that the Amish intentionally live apart from others, and they do not intend for others to identify with them. Fisher's comment ("I'd just as soon not give you any information about our culture to send out to the world. … What good does that do?") contradicted the pervasive media defense that the intense coverage of the Amish during this tragedy promoted understanding and tolerance that inspired the nation. Instead—in a reversal of the common news explanation that the Amish are unprepared to cope with the violence of the modern world—Fisher suggested that the outside world is not equipped to understand Amish culture, nor is it meant to.

It is in fact very hard to understand the Amish within the boundaries of common news narratives (or news frames). As cultural symbols, the Amish characters in this news story potentially could have raised provocative questions about social responses to violence and disaffection. In many ways this story presented an opportunity for nuanced discussions about American beliefs and behavior, as well as the mission and nature of journalism and the way journalists tell stories. Clearly speaking as an insider in this story, the Lancaster *Intelligencer Journal* began to address these possibilities in its own summary of the final meaning of the story:

> Violence befell the Amish community, but violence is not the Amish way. Nor is vengeance. The Amish offer witness to another way of responding to a wrong. They believe in committing to the hard work of healing. They reject an agenda of creating more pain and misery. If only the world would listen, then something good could rise from the horror. (Hawkes, 2006, p. B1)

Overwhelmingly, however, news media did not embrace the story's narrative and symbolic complexities, instead choosing to focus on the happier note in the last sentence above. Throughout the coverage, reporters repeatedly claimed to sensitively represent the Amish to others—and yet, in fact, readers learned little about the Amish. Instead, in this news story, the Amish functioned symbolically as an ideal vision *of people other than themselves*—as "us," or at any rate as transferable, admirable qualities that we must regain and remember.

In the end, this story was less about a fatal tragedy than it was about a self-congratulatory notion of community, an idealized concept of collective identity in which journalists' authority derives from their authenticity as members of the (imagined) social group. In this role, reporters were indeed able to speak for the people whose innocence had been shattered by the unexpected violence in Nickel Mines, even if they could not speak for the dead or their immediate families—because, in reflexive journalism, the crime came to be understood to have so greatly affected "us." In local as well as national news coverage, this story ultimately was less about the Amish than it was about the English, to whom "something good could rise."

# II

## Lessons Learned From Life Stories

# 4

## LIFE AND DEATH IN A SMALL TOWN
### Cultural Values and Memory in
### Community Newspaper Obituaries

When he died of pancreatic cancer in 1995, 91-year-old Porter Harvey was remembered for bungee jumping at 90, for his monthly poker games and his love of old-time monster movies. "But his favorite pastime always was finding news and writing it up," according to the obituary published in the newspaper he founded and edited for more than 50 years, the *Guntersville* (Alabama) *Advertiser-Gleam* (Harvey, 1995).[1]

His obit was one of nine published that day. Lucille Hart, 87, had been "bedfast for almost two years." Her obituary noted: "Before she got real sick, she planned her own funeral, specifying that her son would preach it and her grandchildren—both boys and girls—would be active pallbearers. Her family followed the plans to the letter" (Hart, 1995). The late James (Cull) Harris was one of Guntersville's best baseball players. At one time he "played on 5 teams at once, both baseball and softball, day and night" (Harris, 1995). And Josie Love had worked for 30 years in nearby Albertville, Alabama, at a laundry "which sent a bus each day for employees who lived in Guntersville" (Love, 1995).

These obits—each unique, though with common purpose—provide a fascinating peek into the lives of the people of Guntersville, a town of roughly seven thousand in the Tennessee River Valley of northern Alabama. For readers on that March day in 1995, and on nearly every other day the twice-weekly published that year, obituaries did much more than report the news of death. They celebrated life, and so represented a kind of "ideal," offering important information about community values.

Porter Harvey knew the importance of obituaries; his own noted that the *Advertiser-Gleam*'s used "a lot more detail than most papers use." In those details readers could learn what the newspaper and families wanted to remember about the lives of the deceased, in addition to details about the deaths. Taken collectively, these obituaries paint a kind of portrait of the community. This chapter analyzes 738 obituaries published during two years, 1965 and 1995, in the *Advertiser-Gleam*. The purpose is twofold: to show how individual citizens' lives were publicly commemorated, and to add to our understanding of the important role obituaries can and do play in community newspapers.

## COMMUNITY NEWS

The *Advertiser-Gleam*, in many ways a typical community newspaper, has received some national attention and praise for the loyalty it inspires in readers. A 1996 article in *American Journalism Review* said: "It is a paper that would make city editors at daily papers the country over laugh, yet its circulation (12,000) is greater than the population of its town (7,000). Virtually nobody in this corner of the world would think of doing without it" (Shephard, 1996, p. 32). Part of the attraction was the newspaper's focus on local news, on covering everybody in town. After Harvey's death, Bill Keller, executive director of the Alabama Press Association, said: "The *Advertiser-Gleam* moved years ahead of most other newspapers in treating its readers the same, whether rich or poor, black or white, male or female" (S. Harvey, 1997, p. 249).

This philosophy naturally extended to the obituary page. In the memoir *High Adventure: Porter Harvey and the Advertiser-Gleam*, Porter Harvey's son Sam Harvey wrote: "On most newspaper staffs, obituaries tend to be an afterthought, a chore often passed on to clerks or handled in desultory fashion by reporters. Porter had always tried to contact relatives to get more than the bare facts provided by funeral homes. ... Porter could find something interesting to say about almost anybody" (1997, p. 192). The *Advertiser-Gleam*'s obituaries were the focus of a 1993 Associated Press feature, which noted their popularity and their almost gossipy nature (p. 192). The newspaper clearly made obituaries a priority. Thus, it is not the purpose of this chapter to argue that the *Advertiser-Gleam*'s obituaries are typical, but rather, because of the newspaper's attention to detail and its inclusiveness, to suggest that they offer a way to learn something about the cultural values in this community, and about the potential of the obituary page at a small newspaper.

Of course, obituaries have long been part of the content of community journalism. Frederic Endres, in a historical study of small nineteenth-century frontier newspapers, found that almost everyone in their communities, regardless of age, gender, or station in life, "deserved some sort of meaning being given to their lives" in published obituaries (Endres, 1984, p. 54). Journalism textbook authors in the twentieth century wrote in anecdotal ways about the importance of obituaries in community newspapers. In 1961, Kenneth Byerly noted in *Community Journalism* that an obituary "is often clipped and placed in the family Bible where it may remain for 50 years, so writing it properly is of great importance" (p. 40). In 1974, Bruce Kennedy, in *Community Journalism: A Way of Life*, wrote: "A death in the community is a death in the family. Strangers are few; nearly everyone is a celebrity of sorts, and a death, no matter whose it is, touches a small town. ... An obituary is important news with high readership, and each one deserves careful, respectful writing" (p. 17). And in 2000, Jock Lauterer's *Community Journalism: The Personal Approach* argued that obituaries are "a test—of accuracy, humility, enterprise and journalistic craft" (p. 51). The obituary page, if made a priority, could help small-town newspapers fulfill their mission not only to cover the news, but also to connect readers and maintain community (pp. 8–10).

## OBITUARIES AND CULTURAL VALUES

Newspaper obituaries have received some scholarly attention, though to date much of the focus has been on large, mainstream daily newspapers. The historical study *Obituaries in American Culture* (Hume, 2000) examined more than 8,000 published between 1818 and 1930 in a variety of national and regional newspapers. These obituaries revealed an American society slowly becoming more inclusive. They illuminated other cultural changes as well, in American attitudes about dying, about religion, about patriotism, about industry and wealth, and about the way individual lives are valued in a society that supposedly embraces egalitarianism (p. 14). Obits linked everyday citizens with the American past by telling stories of relationships between the deceased and historic events or icons such as George Washington, Daniel Boone, or Wild Bill Hickok (p. 150). Publication of an obituary in the mainstream mass media constitutes a rare instance when an average person can become part of collective thought, part of what Americans might believe in common about their past and about the worth of a life (p. 163).

Indeed, though on the surface a simple news story, the obituary has a resounding cultural voice. Beyond identifying the deceased, giving a "cause of death" and sometimes telling readers details of a funeral, it offers a tiny picture of a life, a synopsis of what is best remembered about a person's history. It is a type of *commemoration,* representing an ideal, and because it is published or broadcast, that "ideal" is magnified for a mass audience. Barry Schwartz called for an understanding of two distinct aspects of remembering—chronicling and commemoration. He wrote:

> The events selected for chronicling are not all evaluated in the same way. To some of these events we remain morally indifferent; other events are commemorated, i.e., invested with an extraordinary significance and assigned a qualitatively distinct place in our conception of the past. … Commemoration celebrates and safeguards the ideal. (1982, p. 377)

Of course, not everyone who dies gets an obituary, especially in a major metropolitan newspaper. A study of obituaries published in Boston and New York newspapers found a clear pattern of masculine preference, giving "subtle confirmation of the greater importance of men" in twentieth-century American cities (R. Kastenbaum, Peyton, & B. Kastenbaum, 1976–1977, p. 351). And not every attribute is included for those who are remembered. The obituary "ideal" filters through a variety of screens, both cultural and journalistic. For example, books written to help community journalists learn their craft offer suggestions about how to cover the deaths of local citizens, promoting a formulaic approach, though most encourage enterprise reporting as well (see Byerly, 1961; Kennedy, 1974; Lauterer, 2000). Obituary writers at community as well as metropolitan newspapers deal with economic problems of space and often must nail briefly the virtues of a person's life. This would have an impact on what is publicly remembered about individual lives.

It follows, then, that obituary pages do not offer a clear, complete, and accurate reflection of a society, but they provide a small window through which to view and better understand social values. For example, the "accuracy" of an obituary might come into question because, in some newspapers, facts can take a back seat to sentiment in coverage of someone who has died. Still, obituaries can provide a valuable resource. An obituary distills the essence of a citizen's life, and because it is a commemoration as well as a life chronicle, it reflects what society values and wants to remember about that person's history. Thus the systematic examination of obituaries provides a useful tool for exploring the values of Americans of any era. Such an examination can help in understanding an important aspect of their culture, the public memory of citizens.

## MEMORY AND MEDIA

Obituaries contribute to the vitality of American society by highlighting the importance of its individual members (Warner, 1959, p. 150). The traits and actions of individuals, remembered and idealized, become part of collective consciousness. But Lowenthal warns of the importance of understanding "the screens through which historical information and ideas are commonly filtered" (1989, p. 1264). The obituary is a type of screen, filtered by the media and by families and friends of the deceased. A good example of this is how the *Advertiser-Gleam* reported suicides:

> Relatives were generally glad to tell the *Gleam* in considerable detail just how the departed left this world. Not so in the case of suicide. Traditionally, when someone took his own life, the paper said so, as part of telling the news. But Sam and Porter finally concluded they were causing too much pain for people who were already going through enough pain. They decided in 1993 that they would withhold the cause of death in suicides if the family requested it. (S. Harvey, 1997, p. 195)

As Maurice Halbwachs wrote, "Since a past fact is instructive and a person who has disappeared is an encouragement or an advertisement, what we call the framework of memory is also a concatenation of ideas and judgments" (1992, pp. 175–176). Each obituary would preserve some of those "ideas and judgments" so elusive for historians and chroniclers of values and culture.

This chapter seeks to answer the question: How did obituaries published in 1965 and 1995 in the *Guntersville Advertiser-Gleam* portray the lives and deaths of the deceased?

Though any year might have been appropriate for this kind of study, the years 1965 and 1995 were selected based on the life and death of editor Porter Harvey, who made obituaries a priority at the newspaper. He and others at the *Advertiser-Gleam* began focusing on feature-style obituaries in the 1960s, and he died in 1995. The 30-year span should provide an opportunity to compare and contrast changing cultural values in this small Alabama town. This chapter is meant to provide a starting point for more research. Future studies might focus on different regions, or compare obituaries in rural versus suburban weeklies. This chapter simply focuses on obituaries in one community newspaper recognized for its obituary quality and inclusion.

In all, 738 obituaries were examined, 271 in 1965 and 467 in 1995. These obituaries were photocopied from the microfilm collection of the *Advertiser-Gleam*, located in the Guntersville Public Library.[2] The intent was to gather all obituaries published during these two years, including 105 issues in 1965 and 104 in 1995. In 1965 obituaries for 160 men (59 percent), 91 women (34 percent) and 20 children (7 percent, 14 boys and six girls) were included. The 1995 *Advertiser-Gleam* included 231 men (49.5 percent), 225 women (48 percent) and 11 children (2.5 percent, six boys and five girls). Analysis includes cause of death and occupations but focuses primarily on the personal attributes of the deceased adults. Each cause, occupation, and attribute was listed to determine major themes or categories, as well as threads that were less significant in terms of percentages, but that provide cultural insight. Most obituaries for infants and children included only news of the deaths and information about pending funerals.

## CAUSE OF DEATH

In 1965 the *Advertiser-Gleam* sometimes left out the cause of death altogether, even for a relatively young person. More often, the cause was described for both men and women as a long or extended illness, or as a short illness or as happening "suddenly." Lengths of illnesses were reported—at three months, four weeks, 12 days, or two years. Obituaries in 1965 included more detailed accounts of the eleven deaths by automobile accidents and three suicides (likely because police reports would have been available), but they also offered descriptions of heart attacks, which were the most commonly listed specific cause of death. J. Early Nix, for example, died suddenly watching a football game on TV. The obituary noted: "He apparently died so peacefully that Mrs. Nix at first thought he was asleep" (Nix, 1965). Others died from strokes, an accidental shooting, drowning, burns, a fall, a tractor accident, and freezing. Cancer was reported as the cause of death for only two people in the 1965 sample, indicating that at least some of the extended or short illnesses were likely cancer, but for some reason were not reported as such.

By 1995 cancer ranked as the leading cause of death listed for women, and was the second most common cause of death, after heart problems, for men. Only rarely were the terms "long illness" or "short illness" used. According to these published newspaper obituaries, more men and women died from heart problems, cancer, strokes, and kidney failure than from other reported causes such as emphysema, aneurysm, Alzheimer's, diabetes, blood clots, pneumonia, bleeding ulcers, Lou Gehrig's Disease, liver cirrhosis, and a rare disorder called progressive supranuclear palsy. There were six deaths by car accident and three reported suicides, and three Guntersville residents were killed by a tornado.

As in 1965, heart attacks seemed to warrant extra attention in these 1995 obituaries. People had them while driving, walking the dog, deer hunting, or "unloading corn at the hog barn," to name a few (Watwood, 1995; Parker, 1995; Schrimsher, Herman, 1995). Many obituaries reported the deceased had not been sick at all before the attack (see, for example, Barnett, 1995; Cooper, 1995; Kennamer, 1995; and Vanzandt, 1995).

So there were changes in the way the *Advertiser-Gleam* reported causes of death in the three decades after the newspaper began to focus more attention on its obits. The newspaper was more likely to list medical causes in 1995 than in 1965, when Guntersville citizens had more often died of short or extended illnesses. A theme common in both years was the sudden and random nature of heart attacks, a leading killer of both men and women. Even with no official police reports to aid in the coverage (as would have been available with suicides, murders, automobile crashes, tornadoes, and drownings), the newspaper did extra reporting to give detailed accounts of heart attacks, indicating a fascination with, or a sense of unease about, these deaths.

## OCCUPATIONS

An examination of the occupations of those whose deaths were reported in the *Advertiser-Gleam* in 1965 and 1995 paints a dynamic picture of the working lives of the people in this small Alabama town—and indicates a major cultural change during this three-decade span, particularly for women.

Only eight of the 91 women's obituaries in 1965 listed occupations. These included work at a Piggly Wiggly (a Southern grocery store chain), a poultry plant, and a pharmacy. Two women were remembered for being teachers, one a nurse, one a school secretary, and one a domestic worker for a local family. The work lives of the other 83 women were not considered important enough for commemoration in their newspaper obituaries. Six of the women's obituaries published in 1965 listed the husbands' occupations.

In sharp contrast, obituaries in 1995 reported a long and varied list of women's occupations, including many farmers, teachers, store clerks and managers, cooks, waitresses, nurses, and workers in the area's cotton mills and textile plants. One was a portrait artist, another an electrical designer for NASA. One woman drove a chip truck for the Charles Chips snack food company. Another cleaned the offices of a U.S. senator. Still another was a behavioral psychologist. Ninety-one-year-old Naomi Regan's obituary recalled that in 1924 she had to give up her teaching career because the law would not allow married women to teach (Regan, 1995). Vera Caldwell "worked at 4 textile or garment plants and she outlasted them all" (Caldwell, 1995). A number of obituaries listed "housewife" and "homemaker" as women's occupations. Though not every obituary listed an occupation for women (and 49 listed their husbands' work), overall the obituaries published in 1995 celebrated women's work of all kinds and deemed it something worth remembering publicly as an important aspect of a life.

Nearly all the men, of course, were remembered for their work, and in both years farming was the occupation most often reported. Obituaries noted the number of years farmed and the kinds of crops grown. Often farmers did other things, too, like drive trucks, build houses, or work at area plants.

Most men's jobs reflected some kind of service. They were mechanics, construction workers, engineers, carpenters, truck and bus drivers, machinists, electricians, fire fighters, a commercial fisherman, a logger, a state trooper, painters, brick masons, a butcher, maintenance men, lawn service workers, postal workers, a doctor, welders, draftsmen, a newspaper editor, pharmacists, teachers, a coach, and security guards. One man was remembered for being a chicken catcher.

Industry in and near Guntersville was well represented too, including Redstone Arsenal, NASA, the Tennessee Valley Authority, sawmills, textile, poultry and other types of manufacturing or processing plants. Men also sold cars, tires, boats, bait, furniture, real estate, children's Bibles, groceries, hardware, ice cream, insurance and sandwiches. Several preached, and some were public officials, including a four-term mayor, county coroner, fire chief, judge, and school superintendent.

Occupations listed in men's obituaries during 1965 and 1995 did not reflect a major cultural shift, as did the women's. The men of Guntersville just kept on working, most in very physical blue-collar jobs, providing either some type of service in the community, or labor for area industry. Often, one man's obituary would include several different jobs, and numerous obituaries in 1965 and 1995 listed how many years the man had worked as a fact worth remembering publicly.

## COMMUNITY CONNECTION

Community connection was among the major themes reflected in the obituaries of both 1965 and 1995 in the *Advertiser-Gleam*. Over and over again, citizens were remembered for the number of years spent in their communities. Particularly noteworthy were those who spent a lifetime in the same house, or in near proximity. Floyd Ayers, for example, lived "within rock throwing distance of where he was born," as did Azzie Cherry Ramsey, who died "only about 500 feet from where she was born" (Ayers, 1995; Ramsey, 1995). Hometowns were listed, places where the deceased were born or spent their childhoods, and reasons were given for moving either into or out of Guntersville. Annette McCombs and her husband, for example, had vacationed on Guntersville Lake and moved to town to be near it full time (McCombs, 1995).

For men, membership in a Masonic lodge was worthy of note in both years examined, and men in 1995 were remembered for memberships in a variety of community associations including Lions Club, Moose Lodge, Civitans, Kiwanis Club, and Rotarians. Fewer women's obituaries from 1965 noted such associations, though two were remembered for being part of a patriotic organization and one for heading the March of Dimes, for being a charter member of a book club and a member of a music club (Bishop, 1965). By 1995, women were remembered for their associations with the Business and Professional Women's Club, Pilots Club, university alumni associations, League of Women Voters, or Retired Teachers' Association, and for being either a member or an officer in the Daughters of the American Revolution or the United Daughters of the Confederacy.

Both men's and women's community service was worthy of commemoration. I. B. Hyde had been in public office continuously longer than anybody else in the history of the county (Hyde, 1965). Dovard Oaks had helped build the levee that kept Guntersville from flooding; Jake Talley helped get water lines installed in the area; and Waymon Darden donated land for a fire station (Oaks, 1995; Talley, 1995; Darden, 1995). Janet Veazey's obituary offered a long list of public service, including service as vice president of the local school board and volunteer work in numerous service and charity organizations (Veazey, 1995). Several women were remembered simply for helping others, by sitting with the sick or cooking.

Finally, both men and women who died in 1995 were remembered simply because they enjoyed being with other people in Guntersville. One woman loved to walk with her neighbors. M. J. Lambert looked forward to going to town on Saturdays "because of all the people he'd see" (Lambert, 1995). Both men's and women's obituaries in 1995 noted they enjoyed activities at the community senior center.

## CHURCH

Church was another major theme in *Advertiser-Gleam* obituaries during both years examined. In 1965, 33 men's obituaries (21 percent) and 47 women's obituaries (52 percent) listed membership in specific churches or affiliation with particular denominations. That number was 92 in 1995 for men (40 percent) and 121 for women (54 percent). And membership was only part of the picture. In 1965, some men were remembered for leadership roles, as deacons, or simply for being active in church affairs. One man's obituary noted he had been a church member for 43 years. Women were remembered for regular attendance, and for being active.

Obituaries in 1995 provided a much richer picture of church activities. Women taught Sunday school, sang beautifully in the choir, played organ, and enjoyed church leadership and work. One was commemorated for being the oldest member of her church and another for her work in her church's Women's Society for Christian Service (Gray, 1995). Men were remembered for being charter members of their churches, or at least long-time members. They were known for service, including one man who did not charge for it but regularly mowed grass in area church yards and cemeteries (Killed in wreck, 1995).

Religious values were expressed not just through church service or affiliation. One man was remembered for hand-copying the entire New Testament 22 times and the Old Testament seven times. He bound the copies in leather and gave them to his children and friends (Donaldson, 1995). Another had five given names, each one for a preacher at a "camp meeting" his parents had attended (Guthrie, 1995).

## FAMILY

It is not surprising that family was another major category in obituary coverage during both sample years examined, particularly since family members were likely the major sources of information. Most obituaries listed, at the end, the deceased's immediate family as "survivors." Though these lists might provide interesting insights into changing definitions of families and their dynamics, they were not analyzed as part of this study. Family affiliations are mentioned here only as part of the descriptions of attributes and contributions of the deceased.

Spouses were the most often listed family member for both men and women, though many obituaries also listed parents by name, even the deceased parents of elderly citizens. As noted earlier, a number of women's obituaries included their husbands' occupations, though more pointed out when their husbands died. Women in Guntersville, it seems, often outlived their spouses. Men's obituaries mentioned wives, and noted, much more often than women's obituaries, the number of years they were married (likely because their widows provided information for the newspaper). Names of children were seldom listed in the narratives of the obituaries (apart from the survivor lists), but often women and men were remembered for being great-great-grandparents. And those with big families received special attention, particularly those with eight or 10 siblings or many descendants. One man was remembered for leaving 73 descendants in five generations, and another for 131 descendants (Schrimsher, 1995; Tucker 1995; Wiley, 1995).

But obituaries, particularly those in 1995, remembered much more than names of spouses and numbers of siblings or offspring. They offered hints into relationships. Rilla West's husband, a one-armed carpenter, only called her by name one time during their entire marriage, and that was when the house was on fire. He always called her "sweetheart" (West, 1995). Obituaries also reflected family connections. For example, one woman was the oldest of 10 children, all of whom lived within 10 miles of their father's home. Another woman and her twin sister married brothers and lived next door to each other (Bryant, 1995). At the end of their lives, many of the deceased lived with their children, siblings, nieces, or nephews. They enjoyed or loved spending time with their grandchildren. One man walked to Guntersville nearly every week with his sister (Carter, 1995). Odell Moore was remembered for helping rear her niece, the first black majorette at the local high school (Moore, 1995).

## SERVICE TO COUNTRY AND PUBLIC MEMORY

Obituaries linked the deceased to American history, particularly men with the nation's wars. While only one woman was remembered for being a veteran, many men were noted for their war service, including 11 World War I veterans (one of whom had received the Purple Heart medal) and eight World War II veterans in 1965. War service was commemorated in more detail in 1995, when 43 World War II veterans, eight Korean War veterans, and two Vietnam War veterans died. (Eleven other men were remembered for being veterans, with no particular wars named.) Location of service was often mentioned for World War II, and some obituaries noted the men had been combat veterans. Some of the obituaries told stories. Billy Dyar "was one of 13 survivors when his destroyer was sunk"; another man was stranded on a Pacific island for several months; another fought in the hedgerows at Normandy; and another survived the Battle of the Bulge (Dyar, 1995; Harris, Grover, 1995; Hill, 1995; Barnett, 1995).

Women's connections to history were also noted. Flora Klueger "barely escaped Hitler and the Nazis in Austria, and it was eight years before she and her children were reunited with her husband in

America" (Klueger, 1995). One woman lived on a farm during the Great Depression, another worked in a gunpowder plant during World War II. Remarkably, one man and two women were remembered for being children of Civil War veterans, including 97-year-old Annie Lemley, whose father had been a Baptist minister and a Confederate soldier (Yarbrough, 1965; Lemley, 1995). Alice Taylor's obituary noted that her family fought on both sides during the war: "one grandfather fought for the South and the other one fought for the North" (Taylor, 1995).

Obituaries published in the *Advertiser-Gleam* linked Guntersville citizens and their families with national history and collective memory. While close community connections were important, so too were regional and national ties. In this Southern town, Civil War memory was still strong.

## PASTIMES

Perhaps the biggest difference between the obituaries published in 1965 and 1995 was in the inclusion of favorite pastimes of the deceased, the things they loved to do. Only a scant few of the men's obituaries in 1965 mentioned the deceased's keen interest in stock car racing or sports (see, for example, Thomas, 1965). By 1995, obituaries for men and women celebrated their many passions. For men, fishing and hunting were the most popular hobbies (Bobby Dabbs's obituary actually included a photograph of him holding up two fish), and for women it was growing flowers and quilting or crocheting (Dabbs, 1995). Viola Dunn, for example, "crocheted 700 Christmas ornaments for members of her family just this year," and Horace Cranford was "one of the country's best coon hunters. ... He coon hunted right up until he went into the hospital for the last time" (Dunn, 1995; Cranford, 1995).

Women in 1995 were remembered for pastimes that made use of their hands. In addition to quilting and crocheting, these women sewed clothing, knitted, did embroidery, worked in ceramics, made pillows, painted, shelled pecans, played piano, and cooked big meals for their families. One woman canned more than 4,000 jars of fruit and vegetables and "never failed to share with other people" (Eller, 1995). They enjoyed activities that took them out, too, in addition to the creating the beautiful flower gardens. They grew vegetables, traveled, watched birds, walked, boated, attended gospel sings and dances, camped, golfed, and bowled. Many obituaries mentioned reading as a favorite activity.

When they were not hunting or fishing, Guntersville men followed sports, either on television or in person, and several were remembered for playing baseball, softball, basketball, or football, and for coaching

Little League or Pee Wee sports. Obituaries noted their passion for college football, particularly when the deceased was a diehard Alabama, Auburn, or Georgia fan. These men also liked tinkering with motors, whether from cars, tractors, or lawn mowers. They cooked (and ate), traveled, gardened, did yard work, read, painted, played and listened to music, rode trails, and collected baseball cards, guns, knives, grandfather clocks, and antique cars. One man took up woodcarving and made fireplace mantels for his friends and family (Hood, 1995). A few had more unique hobbies. E. Wade Cox raised "game chickens" and shipped them around the world to places where cockfighting was still legal (Cox, 1995). Another flew planes and was remembered for flying one under a bridge, "which was probably against the law." (This amateur pilot was so tall he once "rode through town in an ambulance with his feet sticking out the back window") (Burdette, 1995).

Though they had a strong work ethic, the people of Guntersville were remembered, too, for passions outside of their jobs, for their creativity and energy.

## INDIVIDUALITY

While these broad trends in causes of death and qualities of the deceased provide telling information about the culture of a community, so too do some of the unique attributes of those who died. "Firsts" became important, as did nostalgia. Joe David (Shank) Moore, who died in 1995, was remembered for being the first black employee of the Guntersville Post Office (Moore's, Shank, 1995). Henry Richardson "had the first flour and grist mill ever in Guntersville" (Richardson, 1995). Sarah Savannah Buckelew swapped a milk cow for her first radio (Buckelew, 1995). Kathleen Harper's father had operated the last horse-drawn hearse in the area, but her obituary noted she "went to her grave in a modern hearse, now called a funeral coach" (Harper, 1995). David Price, 36, known as a cowboy, had "said many times he wanted to be taken to his grave in a mule-drawn wagon. That's just how they took him" (Price, 1995).

Obituaries for elderly citizens offered hints of the difficulties of aging. For example, Royce Armstrong had to give up his cows at 85 because he was afraid of being knocked down (Armstrong, 1995). Yet sometimes the oldest Guntersville residents provided inspiration for staying young and active. Minnie Bishop "mowed her yard well into her 80s, fished into her 90s, and quilted after she was 100" (Bishop, 1995). Ervin Brothers took up motorcycle riding late in life (Brothers, 1995). Maudie Lathan was remembered for looking younger than 99 (Lathan, 1995).

Sometimes the obituaries simply related something unusual. When Nannie B. Jones died, her obituary pointed out that the "B" in her name didn't stand for anything (Jones, 1995). When he signed up for service in World War II, the Army made R. V. Childress call himself Robert, even though his name really was R. V. (Childress, 1995). Joy Bridges was remembered for her love of cats; when she died she had 10 grown ones and seven kittens (Bridges, 1995). Edna Cunningham won second place in the state Miss Nursing Home contest (Cunningham, 1995).

## DISCUSSION

Viewed collectively, the 738 obituaries published in the *Guntersville Advertiser-Gleam* in 1965 and 1995 do paint a kind of portrait, representing certain cultural values in this small Southern town. Taken individually, each obituary is more than just a news story about a death. Each also describes a life, portraying what was valued about an individual member of the community. These "commemorations" were shared with an audience larger than the town, legitimizing these memories and values to a much broader audience than simply the families and friends of the deceased.

What these published memories reveal is a people with strong ties to place, family, church, and to others in the community. These ties were more than simple affiliation; they included service as well. Obituaries reflected men, and later women, with a work ethic. Guntersville area citizens took joy in simple pastimes such as fishing or quilting. Their obituaries showed individuality, humor and energy. They revealed links American history and memory as well, particularly to wars—even the Civil War.

These obituaries also revealed some cultural changes between 1965 and 1995. The strongest example was in the commemoration of women's work, which barely existed in 1965 but was a strong component of 1995 obituaries. Of course, this does not mean that women were not working in 1965, just that their work was not publicly acknowledged and remembered in the way it would be in decades to come. In a letter written in January 2006, Sam Harvey, who took over the newspaper after his father's death, talked about how that policy has changed. "Most women who died in 1965 had never worked outside the home," he said. "Today a large proportion of them have. But in any case, if a woman has been primarily a homemaker, we now say so, recognizing that this is at least as noble a pursuit as many of the things that men do. Back then I guess it was just taken for granted that a woman was a homemaker unless noted otherwise."[3]

Published causes of death offered hints to other cultural changes, as well. According to Sam Harvey, editors at the *Advertiser-Gleam* had worried about the stigma of suicide and reported such deaths with care. But was there an unacknowledged hesitancy in reporting cancer, or other kinds of causes, in 1965? Looking back, Harvey wrote in 2006, "Part of that was a reluctance of families in the past to say what it was, especially if it was cancer. We still run into that on occasion today. The cause of death has to come from the family in most cases, since funeral homes won't say." Thus, when the newspaper and families reported deaths from an "extended illness," the silence surrounding the cause is telling.

Indeed, it is important to remember the silences on obituary pages. Women's work and particular causes of death are perhaps just two examples. Obituaries tend to reflect only dominant cultural values. The question becomes: Who and what were left out? Represented in only 34 percent of obituaries in 1965, it is likely that some women who died that year were not commemorated. Sam Harvey provided a partial explanation. He said it was the newspaper's policy to publish an obituary for any man who might have worked in its area of coverage, even if he lived elsewhere at death. That would account for some of the discrepancy in numbers, but perhaps not all. "It's an intriguing question for which I have no answer," he said. The *Advertiser-Gleam* included obituaries for African Americans in both years, but likely in very small numbers in 1965, when only a few obituaries identified the deceased as "colored" (see Hundley, 1965; Lovelady, 1965; Weatherly, 1965). These obituaries published the same kinds of information as those for Caucasian residents, and they were given equal placement. So why were there so few? Was there subtle discrimination at the newspaper, or did African Americans themselves not place any value on a published obituary? Part of the reason, according to Sam Harvey in 2006, was that African Americans in Guntersville in the 1960s "traditionally used the services of the funeral homes in Huntsville or Gadsen that catered to blacks," and so gathering that information was more difficult. The newspaper, he noted, tried other methods. "To try to keep from missing a black death, we had a resident of the black community whose sole task was to let us know when someone had died, so we could then check it out. I believe we gave him a free subscription in return. But we still missed some." In 1995 the newspaper did not identify race, so percentages of inclusion are impossible to determine. Yet the newspaper's policy of running photographs of the deceased when available revealed a number of black faces, and the affiliations with traditionally black churches indicate that African Americans were regularly included in 1995.

Of course, obituary pages are limited only to those who died, and so their reflection of the community is naturally skewed. Though people of all ages were included in 1965 and 1995, most obituaries were for people over 60, and many were for people in their eighties, nineties, and even a few over 100. Thus, the cultural values represented here are those of an older community. Values of youth remained largely silent.

Yet despite these limitations, obituaries did contribute to the vitality of the community and helped the newspaper perform its mission not only of reporting news but also of connecting readers. Obituaries connect families, friends, co-workers and neighbors in shared commemoration of not only the deceased, but of his or her love of hometown, church, associations, families, and simple pastimes. In legitimizing these powerful death stories for a wider audience, obituaries become not only reflective, but instructive as well.

It follows, then, that inclusion is the most important attribute of an obituary page. This is vividly apparent in the *Guntersville Advertiser-Gleam*, which focused resources on its obituary page—in space allocated and staff time spent—and made it an important part of the coverage of its community. Not only were more people included in 1995 than in 1965, but these obituaries provided a much richer portrayal of the values of community, family, church. Writing about his father, Sam Harvey said in 2006: "Until the late 1960s, he ran all deaths on the front page. His rationale was that some deaths needed to be there, and the only fair thing was to put them all there. We moved them inside shortly after I came on board in 1967 simply because there were getting to be so many that they were taking up too much of the front page. It's not unusual today to have nine or 10 deaths in an issue." Whether this coverage adds to the circulation figures or popularity of the newspapers is unknown, but the *Advertiser-Gleam*'s founding editor, the late Porter Harvey, believed in the importance of such coverage. And this legacy was remembered, commemorated and legitimized in his own obituary, which noted the national reputation of his obituary page, and Harvey's love of "finding news and writing it up" (Harvey, Porter, 1995).

# 5

## "IT TAKES A SINNER TO APPRECIATE
## THE BLINDING GLARE OF GRACE"
### Redeeming the "Dark" Celebrity

Celebrity deaths now routinely receive a great deal of press attention, and some become "media events," akin to national funerals that people "attend" through the media (Couldry, 2003; Dayan & Katz, 1992; Kear & Steinberg, 1999; Mazzarella & Matyjewicz, 2002; Walter, 1999b). Previous research has found that popular figures' lives are retold in a remarkably uniform narrative that draws moral lessons from a star's life difficulties but, in the end, usually forgives and celebrates him or her. That plot, which has emerged consistently in celebrity-death coverage over the past half century, includes an unhappy or very difficult childhood; exceptional talent or beauty; the lucky break or "discovery"; genius or beauty misunderstood; surrender to temptation followed by public disfavor and midlife crisis; recovery and comeback; and the ironic cruelty of death just when the person was being appreciated anew (Kitch, 2005).

This chapter considers how a similar tale was told in journalistic eulogy for male celebrities who died within roughly a two-year period: Johnny Cash (September 2003), Ray Charles (June 2004), Marlon Brando (July 2004), and Richard Pryor (December 2005). Thematically united by their well-known misbehavior and/or tragedies in life, these were the kind of public figures whose stories would have to undergo some sort of narrative repair in order to come to an uplifting conclusion. They can be seen as "dark" celebrities: one a "Man in Black" who publicly empathized with criminals; another whose skin was black and who sang gospel music with lyrics about sex; a third whose dramatic roles epitomized misery, from pathos to brutality, and whose final years were spent in isolation; and a fourth whose own experiences as a black man fueled his controversial comedy routines about American racism. Furthermore, these celebrities were eulogized within journalism steeped in memorial and against the broader backdrops of therapeutic popular culture and faith-based political conservatism that has coincided with an increase in religious or spiritual news content (Furedi, 2004; Hoover, 1998; Silk, 1995). Coverage of their deaths was remarkable in the extent to which temptation, sin, and the possibility of redemption were openly discussed in journalism, and to which each celebrity's struggle with his demons was understood as representative of modern American life.

Few would be surprised that Johnny Cash's life story was told in these terms; it also may seem predictable that the popular, smiling Ray Charles would be well remembered at death. Marlon Brando and Richard Pryor seem to be obvious contrasts—one an eccentric recluse who sneered at public opinion, and the other a confrontational performer who once set himself on fire while freebasing cocaine. Yet these hypotheses would be based on what we "know" about the celebrities through media coverage. In terms of their professional and personal life trajectories, these four men actually had a great deal in common. The differences in the ultimate cultural meaning of their respective lives and deaths—and the question of whether or not their sins were forgiven—lay, in the end, in the narratives and object lessons through which they were remembered in popular journalism.

Building on the work of cultural critics such as John Caughey (1984), Leo Braudy (1986), Richard Dyer (1986), and Joshua Gamson (1994), a growing body of literature has examined the role of celebrities in modern public life. This work has addressed the nature of fans' imaginary relationships with such people; it also has considered the function of celebrities as symbolic figures into whom both media producers and audiences project notions about ideal American life, the process through which celebrities become "negotiated symbols in a human shorthand by which we process the world" (Braudy, 1986, p. 588). "Stars articulate what it is to be a human being in contemporary society," claims Dyer (1986, p. 8). Joshua Meyrowitz writes that we think of certain stars as "media friends," explaining:

> We follow celebrities through various phases of their personal lives and public activities, and their life stages often become some of the key signposts we use to mark and recall the different periods of our own lives. With the help of programs such as

*Entertainment Tonight* and publications such as *People* magazine, we keep up with their romances and problems, their good years and bad years. (1994, pp. 63, 66)

Celebrity coverage also can be seen as an example of the journalistic use of personalization to discuss social and political issues (for instance, Larson & Bailey, 1998) and of the routine invocation of typicality in explaining heroism in a post-September 11 culture. As Gamson (1994) has explained, since the early twentieth century, celebrity heroes, while praised for their special qualities, have been validated in journalism through a construction of their ordinariness. Such a construction comes not only from the Hollywood publicity machine but also from those most often accused of attacking the famous: in her study of tabloid journalism, S. Elizabeth Bird (1992) found that while such publications frequently focus on celebrities' problems, they are increasingly likely to portray them in a sympathetic light. The illumination of a "real person" behind a manufactured image is an appealing story in what Frank Furedi calls our "culture of emotionalism," a climate in which confession of faults by public figures is not only welcomed but expected and "offers a route to public acceptance and acclaim" (2004, p. 42). At the same time, this sharing strengthens the illusion that the celebrity is not so different (and perhaps is even worse off!) than you and I—and, conversely, that none of us is so far from fame.

The "typical" problems of celebrities are revealed in plotted tales that seem merely to unfold over time in news media. Of course, they do not merely unfold; especially when crafting a "life story" told in retrospect, journalists necessarily play an active role in how such figures are assessed. This study focuses on one journalistic medium that has had perhaps the closest and longest relationship with celebrity culture. Magazines have reported on fascinating public figures since the emergence of modern mass media a century ago (Gamson, 1994), and they are a regular forum for the public dissection of celebrities' experiences.

The material discussed in this chapter comes from all the coverage of the deaths of the four subjects appearing in four major American celebrity/entertainment magazines—*People, Entertainment Weekly, TV Guide*, and *Rolling Stone*—and the two leading newsmagazines, *Time* and *Newsweek*, which, as James Baughman (1998) and others have documented, have turned their attention increasingly toward celebrity culture in recent decades. The analysis primarily considers the content and structure of text, though it also notes how photographs were used to underscore certain characterizations of the subjects. The evidence includes all stories published immediately following their deaths.

Except to the extent that the memorial tributes reprinted or drew on earlier reporting, this study does not include coverage of these celebrities in previous or subsequent issues of these magazines.[1]

The four celebrities are discussed below not in the order they died, but rather in what the analysis reveals to have been their levels of salvation, from lightness to darkness.

## JOHNNY CASH: "ALL THE VARIOUS LOST CAUSES OF THE HUMAN SOUL"

In many ways, Johnny Cash had scripted his own memorial story, having spent much of his life engaging in and singing about sin, weakness, regret, and recovery, and having, after a midlife crisis, openly embraced the Christian beliefs of his second wife, June Carter Cash. Certainly it also helped "the story" that he performed dressed entirely in black and openly talked about salvation and grace. As *Newsweek* noted, "his obsessively forthright self-presentation and chronic self-examination" were part of his public image (Gates, 2003, p. 98). *Entertainment Weekly* made the same point while putting the metaphors into play: "Johnny Cash's soul had been the battlefield for plenty of celebrated skirmishes over the decades. Usually, the inner conflict was a clear-cut as his near-mythic stature in country music: drugs or sobriety, rage or peace, God or the other guy" (Willman, 2003, p. 310).

Eulogy for Cash used these kinds of religious terms, as well as concepts such as darkness and death, extensively, and not always with the acknowledgment that Cash himself had created his celebrity persona around them. Leading the rhetorical excess was not a gushy celebrity publication, but the newsmagazine *Time*. The following several quotations all are from *Time*'s tribute cover story (Corliss, 2003), which also was the source for the title of this chapter:

> Demons found him even when he wasn't looking for them. He dressed like a hip coroner and sang like a gunman turned Pentecostal preacher. His haunting songs perfectly matched his haunted voice. ... His songs played like confessions on a deathbed or death row, but he delivered them with the plangent stoicism of a world-class poker player dealt a bum hand. (p. 62)

> Cash sang of specific injustices and eternal truths; he was the deadpan poet of cotton fields, truck stops and prisons. He was a balladeer, really, a spellbinding storyteller—a witness, in the Christian sense of the word. Here was a man who knew the Commandments because he had broken so many of them. (pp. 62–63)

Inside Cash, the churchman and the outlaw were having a brawl. (p. 64)

As is typical in the telling of most celebrity life tales, the coverage emphasized Cash's difficult childhood, though it also established that, from the start, he had a "gift" and the love of a good woman. *Rolling Stone* contained this anecdote: "Apart from his mother's unshakable belief in his musical talent—'God has his hand on you son,' she told him when he was a boy, 'don't ever forget the gift'—little in Cash's impoverished background suggested that the extraordinary life he would lead was possible" (DeCurtis, 2003, p. 72). *Entertainment Weekly* characterized his origins similarly, calling him "the Arkansas dirt farmer's son who might almost have taken the closing words of *The Grapes of Wrath* as a grist for a real-life, guitar-slinging sequel and mutual love affair with the working downtrodden" (Willman, 2003, pp. 32–33).

Cash's own disadvantages were seen to have uniquely qualified him to be, as singer Kris Kristofferson told both *TV Guide* and *People*, "a champion for people who didn't have one," a spokesman for "the underdogs, the downtrodden, the prisoners, the poor" (Man in Black, 2003, p. 43; Smolowe & Dougherty, 2003, p. 82). In *Rolling Stone* Bob Dylan claimed: "If we want to know what it means to be mortal, we need look no further than the Man in Black. Blessed with a profound imagination, he used the gift to express all the various lost causes of the human soul" (Remembering Johnny, 2003, p. 74).

In this life story, then, Cash's "gift" was not merely musical talent, but the insight and empathy to speak for others in dark circumstances, a special access to truth that excused his own bad behavior. *Rolling Stone* called him "part rural preacher, part outlaw Robin Hood [who] was a blue-collar prophet," going so far as to claim that, as "this dark figure who never really fit ... the quintessential outsider," he was a role model for "all these bad-boy [rap] artists who are juggling being on MTV and running from the law" (DeCurtis, 2003, pp. 72, 73). *Entertainment Weekly*'s cover story opened with an almost apocalyptic conceptual photograph of Cash standing in an overgrown graveyard, under a leafless tree and next to a crooked, wooden cross, playing a guitar and singing with his eyes closed as wind whipped back his hair and coat (Willman, 2003, p. 30).

Yet Cash was not really "bad," because, as he fought his demons, he offered up testimony and confession. The musician Marty Stuart told *People*, "What kept him credible with people was that when he made mistakes, he was the first one to raise his hand and say, 'I did it. I messed up.' He had a humble nature, and you couldn't not forgive him" (Smolowe & Dougherty, 2003, p. 84). In *Rolling Stone*, the singer Merle Haggard recalled having seen Cash perform in San Quentin Prison while he himself was incarcerated there: "He chewed gum, looked arrogant and flipped the bird to the guards—he did everything the prisoners wanted to do. He was a mean mother from the South who was there because he loved us" (Remembering Johnny, 2003, p. 74). He also recounted Cash's advice when he appeared on Cash's ABC variety show: "Haggard, let me tell the people you've been to prison. It'll be the biggest thing that will happen to you in your life, and the tabloids will never be able to hurt you. It's called telling the truth" (Remembering Johnny, 2003, p. 74).

While surely this can be seen as canny career advice, it is presented in eulogistic testimony (and it is interesting how we come to know of Cash's failings and repentance primarily through the testimony of others he helped or guided) as proof of his willingness to repent and his desire to be saved from himself. Here, as the story was told, the crucial plot development was the love of another good woman. Overlooking the circumstances of their union (both left their spouses, with whom they had children), the magazines uniformly presented June Carter as the "miracle" whose Christian faith saved Cash's life (when he was addicted to painkillers in the 1960s) as well as his soul. "His salvation was literally waiting in the wings," wrote *People* (Smolowe & Dougherty, 2003, p. 84), while *Entertainment Weekly* used a quote from the singer Reba McEntire to create this picture of the sinner saved by the hand of Providence: "For him to have had such a rough life, then to be paired up with such a strong woman, I think that was God's way of saying 'Buddy, I think you need a little help'" (Willman, 200, p. 33). The successful outcome of this intervention allowed the story to end with Cash's sobriety and late-in-life comeback, through which he presumably influenced a new generation. The narrative closure also enabled *Time* to end its cover story with this:

> ... if some felt shock at the news of Cash's passing, they could segue into celebration over a difficult life made exemplary, an outlaw redeemed by a woman's devotion. Besides, if you believe, the Man in Black is now garbed in white, and the doting husband has eternity to spend with his beloved. (Corliss, 2003, p. 66)

### RAY CHARLES: "SHEER EROTIC JOY"

Such language returned in journalism nine months later when Ray Charles died. It is likely that he would have received more coverage in the newsweeklies had he not died the same week as former President Ronald Reagan. Yet in the entertainment magazines (one of which,

*People*, also reported extensively on the Reagan ceremonies), there was a great deal of coverage, in the same kinds of dramatic tribute language the magazine had used for Cash, and with similar metaphors of good and evil, light and dark.

In several ways, the life stories of the two men really were parallel. Born two years apart into Southern poverty during the Great Depression—"with his [Charles's] family being even poorer than most, 'nothing below us 'cept the ground,' as he put it" (Farley, 2004, p. 90)—both nevertheless had musical gifts and, according to the story, mothers with unshakable faith in them. *Rolling Stone* recounted of Charles, "His mother insisted that there was nothing he could not do if he set his mind to it, telling him, 'You're blind—you ain't stupid'" (DeCurtis, 2004, p. 98), while *Time* contained this anecdote: "Ray's mother told him, before she died when he was 15, 'You might not be able to do things like a person who can see. But there are always two ways to do everything. You've just got to find the other way'" (Farley, 2004, p. 90). Noting his mother's death and his 17-year drug addiction, *Entertainment Weekly* wrote, "It's a wonder that Charles didn't, to quote one of his best-loved songs, drown in his own tears," called him "an American Hero," and asked, "Does any artist better embody the great American dream of success against overwhelming odds than Charles?" (Sinclair, 2004, p. 44). "Through it all," wrote *People*, "he sang with such drive, passion and perfection that he was nicknamed 'the Genius'" (Ray Charles, 2004, p. 59).

As with Cash, Charles's "overwhelming odds" combined with his "genius" and his "passion" to explain his unorthodox approach to music that brought black traditions into the mainstream while offending the respectable Southern black community. As *Newsweek* explained, Charles got his start "scandaliz[ing] good church people by appropriating the conventions and inflections of sacred music, and helped invent what we now know as soul music," a genre that drew on religious passion to express "sheer erotic joy" (Gates, 2004, p. 75). This tension provided the lead for the majority of the stories about his death, and it gave him authority as a musician. *Rolling Stone*'s tribute article opened this way:

> The battle between sin and salvation, between Saturday-night revels and Sunday-morning sanctity, rages at the heart of American popular music. But for Ray Charles, those combating urges were one and the same, and he made the music to prove it. Beginning in 1954 with his R&B hit "I've Got a Woman," Charles set tales of desire, longing and lust to the propulsive rhythms of gospel, breaking the ground for what would soon be called soul music. (DeCurtis, 2004, p. 97)

Ironically, it was this storyline, and the language used to tell it, that cast Charles as a pseudo-religious leader, even though he never had the kind of faith, let alone conversion, experienced by Cash. The music itself gave him almost a holy status. *Time* claimed that Charles "showed us that soul was good for the spirit" (Farley, 2004, p. 90). This was one of three magazines to call him, in either title or text, "Brother Ray" (Farley, 2004; Ritz, 2004; Sinclair, 2004): borrowing the lyrics of a Charles song, *Entertainment Weekly* declared, "It's crying time, again. Brother Ray has left us for good" (Sinclair, 2004, p. 43). As *Newsweek* noted, "blues and gospel formed the deepest layer of his sensibility" (Gates, 2004, p. 75), and, in the retelling of his life story, Charles's music became his redemption.

As he frequently had pointed out throughout his life, he did not particularly *seek* redemption, though only in *Rolling Stone* was this a significant subplot. In a secondary article, the ghostwriter of his autobiography recalled what Charles had told him in 1975, more than 10 years after he had stopped using hard drugs, "that every day he still drank lots of gin and smoked lots of pot ... that he had a huge appetite for women; that he wasn't even certain how many children he had fathered; that he was unrepentant about it all" (Ritz, 2004, p. 98). Yet this frank recollection closed with his comments from an interview given a year earlier, after he had been diagnosed with liver cancer:

> [Charles] "I used to think all that church praise, all that hooting and hollering, was overdone. Stop shouting. Be cool. Besides, if God is God, why does he need all this praise? Now I'm thinking it ain't God who needs the praise—it's us who need to do the praising. The praise makes us stronger. That's why I'm getting stronger."
>
> [interviewer] "What's the source of the strength?
>
> [Charles] "Used to think it was me. But now I see my strength has limits. I used to think that I'm in control of this whole motherfucking operation—my music, my band, my life, my ladies. But soon as you start thinking that way, brother, run for cover. 'Cause someone's about to kick your ass." (Ritz, 2004, p. 100)

This article was accompanied by the rare somber photograph of Charles, shown sitting in a chair with his head down. Far more common were pictures (and one in particular, at the piano) of him in performance, smiling broadly, with his head joyfully thrown back, an image of surrender and salvation. That shot appeared over the title of *Newsweek*'s tribute essay, titled "We Can't Stop Loving Him" (Gates, 2004, p. 75). *Time* closed its coverage by returning to the character of Charles's mother: "He did his mother proud. He found that other way" (Farley, 2004, p. 90).

## RICHARD PRYOR: "PROFANE AND PROFOUND"

Richard Pryor's mother also was an early inspiration, though of a different sort. All of the coverage after his 2005 death recounted the nature of his birth as the start of his tragicomic destiny. *Newsweek* reported: "He was born Richard Franklin Lenox Thomas Pryor. Pryor's mother was a prostitute, and each of the names apparently came from one of her johns. He was, in short, the personification of the idea that tragedy feeds great comedy" (Peyser & Samuels, 2005, p. 61). *People* noted that he was "raised by his grandmother, who ran the brothel where his mother, Gertrude worked; his father, Buck, was an occasional pimp and bartender. 'His comedy was born of pain and poverty,' says [a] close friend" (Espinoza, 2005, p. 88).

From this harsh entrance into a cutthroat world of urban poverty came Pryor's style as well as his material, as the story goes. "Pryor's comedy came wrapped in barbed wire," wrote *Newsweek*, describing

> his indelible cast of characters: junkies, hustlers, winos. They were angry, proud, secure, profane—people no one found funny before. But Pryor mined their stories for truth as well as humor, and he told their stories with a streetwise vernacular that verged on poetic performance art. … "His very presence gave black people a chance to laugh and feel good about stuff that usually pissed us off," says [comedian] Chris Rock. (Peyser & Samuels, 2005, p. 61)

The violence of his upbringing and his comedic subject matter spilled over into an out-of-control life, explained *Time*: "His no-holds-barred comedy was matched by a private life that seemed an unending soap opera—outbursts of violence, run-ins with the law, and drug abuse." Yet precisely because Pryor used his own life as material, the magazine contended, he became "America's most celebrated comic revolutionary" (Zoglin, 2005, p. 35). And, as suggested in the passage above from *Newsweek*, the authentic brutality of his youth, along with the color of his skin, gave him a special access to truth.

As with Johnny Cash, the kind of "truth" Richard Pryor told was a matter of witnessing the dark side of human existence; it was an acknowledgment of the pervasiveness of evil rather than a lesson about goodness. *Entertainment Weekly* quoted *Saturday Night Live* producer Lorne Michaels as saying that "the pressure on black comedians to be role models was tremendous when Richard was coming along. Well, Richard wasn't that. He tried. But he naturally moved into the role of truth teller." Michaels added that Pryor's appearance on *SNL*, a show including a skit in which Pryor traded racial insults with Chevy

Chase, "lent integrity and credibility to our show. His appearance as host defined the outer limits of what we could do. ... He made us, by association, more legitimate." Referring to Pryor's routines about racism, the magazine also quoted the comedienne Lily Tomlin: "The kind of laughter he evoked was the laughter of liberation." The article concluded: "That was Pryor: a humble introvert who boldly told truth to power—told truth to everybody, really, and perhaps most notably, told truth to himself, about himself, and at his own expense" (S. Brown, 2005, pp. 15–17).

And there—in Pryor's description as, ultimately, "a humble introvert"—was the narrative shift from street-savvy, profane, urban black man to an ordinary American just like any of us. "For all of his supposed fearlessness, what made him so magnetic, so familiar to his audience was his neurotic, almost sheepish vulnerability," wrote *Entertainment Weekly*, which called him "America's profane [Mark] Twain" (S. Brown, 2005, pp. 17, 14). While acknowledging his excessive use of drugs and alcohol, his seven marriages, and his four heart attacks, the magazines emphasized his emotional fragility. *Newsweek* claimed that, "like his bombastic characters, he also had a charming humility. 'I had some great things and I had some bad things, the best and the worst,' Pryor once said. 'In other words, I had a life'" (Peyser & Samuels, 2005, p. 61).

These qualities did not prevent Pryor from a midlife fall from grace, common to the life plot of the other celebrities as well. He "could never fully escape his demons," even at the height of his success in the 1970s, a time when "the tempting excesses of celebrity—coupled with the comic's long-standing attraction to the abyss—drew Pryor closer and closer to oblivion. His infamous 1980 self-immolation was the beginning of the end" (Espinoza, 2005, p. 88; S. Brown, 2005, p. 16). He rarely performed after he was diagnosed in 1985 with multiple sclerosis. *Entertainment Weekly* wrote: "By the time he was gone, in other words, he'd been gone a long time. And yet, last week, something precious and ineffable was lost" (S. Brown, 2005, p. 15).

Despite his absence from the public eye for two decades and his lack of a comeback, Pryor's death was still marked as a "loss" of something "precious." Certainly one part of that loss was, as the stories concluded, his ability to grasp the dark truth and to bring it to light while breaking taboos in popular entertainment. Most of the magazines acknowledged the debt of many young black comedians (all of them men) to Pryor's trail-blazing style. *Newsweek* claimed: "You can draw a straight line from his angry, impolite comedy to Eddie Murphy, Arsenio Hall, the Wayans brothers and Dave Chappelle." The magazine quoted the comedian Martin Lawrence: "He did for comedy what politicians do for movements. He passed a law that said it was OK to tell it like it is" (Peyser & Samuels, 2005, p. 61). *Time* proclaimed that "his ruthless honesty and performing brilliance set a standard by which every comic since must be measured" (Zoglin, 2005, p. 35).

Another part of the loss, however, was the example of his sheer survival and endurance, qualities described as both admirable and pathetic. Most of the magazines illustrated their tribute articles with photographs of Pryor either early in his career, when he appeared youthfully hopeful, or late in his illness, when he gazed at the camera with a frightened and almost pleading expression. *TV Guide* closed its article, titled "Tribute," with that note: "The later images of a subdued Pryor, debilitated by his struggle with multiple sclerosis and longtime substance abuse, are a stark contrast to the wild energy he once had on stage and screen. But Pryor's daughter Rain says that even at the end, 'his soul was as strong as ever'" (Battaglio, 2005, p. 13).

## MARLON BRANDO: "A LIFE OF ENORMOUS, ABUSIVE APPETITES"

Nearly the same conclusion might have been written about Marlon Brando when he died in 2004, also "a stark contrast to the wild energy he once had on stage and screen." But it wasn't. The lack of this forgiving spirit was anticipated by the actor Jack Nicholson, who began his own tribute to Brando in *Rolling Stone* with this declaration: "Marlon Brando is one of the great men of the twentieth and twenty-first centuries, and we lesser mortals are obligated to cut through the shit and proclaim it" (J. Nicholson, 2004, p. 53). Nicholson's voice was the exception within a less than celebratory public assessment of Brando's life, after decades of reports of the reclusive actor's eccentricity and physical decline. Like Pryor, Brando had no late-in-life comeback, and the characters he played, similar to the characters who populated Pryor's comedy routines, were wounded and violent. Yet Brando did not exhibit the public vulnerability that Pryor (and Cash and Charles) had; indeed, he expressed open contempt for public opinion.

His life story paralleled those of the other men in several ways. He had had a difficult start, which *Time* referenced succinctly and parenthetically in its mention of his "troubled and rebellious past (cruel and drunk father, wistful and drunken mother)" (Schickel, 2004, p. 73). *People* wrote that "his own bruised, inarticulate genius [was] fueled in part by unhappy memories of an alcoholic, often absent mother, Dorothy, and a brutal father, Marlon Brando Sr., a traveling salesman"

(Gliatto, 2004, p. 83). *Entertainment Weekly* reported that he suffered from "a deeper torment than even the hard-luck tales from his early days could explain: His parents were alcoholics (his father abusive, his mother a frustrated actress); he was kicked out of military school for insubordination, and sidelined from the draft by a bad knee" (Schwarzbaum, 2004, p. 23). Paralleling the other men's drug-fueled trouble with the law, Brando endured public personal tragedy when his son murdered his daughter's lover and the daughter subsequently committed suicide (though the difference is that this was not Brando's own "sinning" on the public stage). And like Charles, he had "an untold number of other children born of various wives and non-wives" (Schwarzbaum, 2004, p. 28).

Brando broke the boundaries of his profession by creating a new kind of acting that departed from existing styles and genres. Certainly the same can be said of the music of Cash and Charles, but in Brando's case, his unusual talent was remembered as alienating (as was true of Pryor's early comedy). "Brando was touched by genius," explained *Time*, "by which we mean that he did things in his art that were unprecedented, unduplicable and, finally, inexplicable"; to make its point clearer, this essay (labeled "Appreciation") was titled "A Hostage of His Own Genius" (Schickel, 2004, p. 73). *TV Guide* recalled Brando's "genius" as a challenge to American moral standards of the mid-twentieth century: "Sweating, bawling and absolutely electrifying, he became a dangerous new icon of masculine sexuality" (Fox & McDonagh, 2004, p. 6). *Entertainment Weekly* used a sexually charged adjective to make the same point, observing that "never was a talent more potent but Brando squandered his intensity…" (Schwarzbaum, 2005, p. 26).

It is this last quote that hints at the narrative departure in Brando's story, or, rather, at the reason for a lack of cohesive narrative. When Brando's career faltered at midlife, he "squandered" not just his career but his looks, and this theme dominated coverage of his death. "He created the modern Hollywood ideal (or is it an anti-ideal?) of sexually dangerous, antiauthoritarian, anti-glamorous masculinity … but he let his once beautiful face and body balloon in later life as if he despised his very flesh," declared *Entertainment Weekly* (Schwarzbaum, 2004, p. 26). *People* began its coverage of his death, "At the end of his life, Marlon Brando was a broken-down colossus, his body giving out after a life of enormous, abusive appetites," and went on to call him "one of Hollywood's saddest examples of talent waylaid and wasted" (Gliatto, 2004, p. 80). *Time* described Brando in his early acting days as a "stud, possibly the most gorgeous (and authentically sexy) male the movies had ever seen" but later in life as being "encased in fat and cynicism," a change that was "sad and to some of us infuriating" (Schickel, 2004, p. 74). *Newsweek* wrote that "his ballooning weight seemed like a fortress to keep the world out" (Peyser, 2004, p. 73).

In this sense, Brando (or at any rate, journalistic characterizations of him) can be understood less as a hero than as what Jack Lule, in his typology of mythic characters in news, identifies as the "trickster," a character from folklore: "the Trickster is driven by physical appetites, lust, and desire. He has no control over his impulses ... [he] serves as an exemplary model in reverse ... the Trickster archetype shows what happens if the rules laid down by society are not observed" (2001, p. 124). Though at first we (audiences and journalists) knew what to make of the young actor, his lack of impulse control made a mockery of the public image through which, as a "genius," he had begun to make some narrative sense: Brando "let himself balloon into an unsettlingly eccentric, supersized version of the handsome, muscle-bound star who first electrified Hollywood" (Gliatto, 2004, p. 82).

As implied in the defense mounted by Jack Nicholson (himself arguably another trickster), the line between trickster and hero is a fine one. Dominated as these stories were by the theme of Brando's weight, there were tributes of sorts, and even gestures toward forgiveness and immortality. *People* quoted Brando's sister as saying, "I'm glad he's free now," and concluded, "Brando could be said to have freed Hollywood, paving the way for at least two generations of actors. ... Without Brando, there would most likely be no Al Pacino, no Robert De Niro, no Jack Nicholson, no Sean Penn or Johnny Depp" (Gliatto, 2004, p. 82). *Time* remembered Brando as a generational icon whose art ultimately justified his heroic status:

> ... if you were young and impressionable in the '50s, he was forever Our Guy—a man whose inarticulate yearnings, whose needs and rages somehow spoke for a silent generation, privately nursing our grievances at the bourgeois serenity of our elders. We would get mad at his fecklessness, but we never quite lost our faith in him. ... Now that he's gone, that faith abides. ... The work will abide—while the often foolish and more often misspent life that these performances mysteriously drew upon will fade away, lost at last in the hum and buzz of our infinitely distractible media age. (Schickel, 2004, p. 74)

## WHO GETS SAVED?

This last quote contains a touch of unintended irony, in its suggestion that *Time* magazine—or, more broadly, "we," the public—has access to truth (about celebrities) somewhere beyond the borders of "our infinitely distractible media age." Yet, as can be seen in several of the excerpts above, this is only one of a number of remarks that provide a second layer of meaning to this kind of journalism, a meta-commentary on the life-story summary within the summary itself. It is from these cues that we are to know not only the facts of the person's past, but also the lasting cultural meaning of his life, a lesson more important than the trivia of celebrity gossip ("the hum and buzz" or "the shit"). Indeed, that bigger truth, as *Time* suggested, can make the actual facts not that important. That must be one conclusion of this study, since, when one considers the facts of these four performers' lives, even as they are divulged in these accounts, one notices the similarities as much as the differences.

Of course, all four were men, and their sex is no doubt one explanation for their life stories being retold as a battle against temptation (with the implication that boys will be boys); it is hard to imagine a female celebrity publicly engaging, for decades, in the substance abuse and sexual promiscuity of either Ray Charles or Richard Pryor, and then being remembered so fondly. S. Elizabeth Bird confirms that there remains a double standard in the ways celebrities' life choices are explained in media. She notes that "prowess with women" is one element in the heroic tale reported after the death of a famous man, and that a life of multiple relationships with women merely underscores that prowess rather than detracting from the man's character: while affairs and divorces might be reported as scandals during a male celebrity's lifetime, after his death they become folded into his life story as inevitable consequences of his masculinity (Bird, 1992, p. 182).

It is further worth noting that women play similar supporting roles in these men's stories. In all four cases, the male celebrity had a sympathetic woman at his side at (or close to) the end, a daughter or sister, or "the right" wife who finally understood him.[2] Even more striking is the role of mothers in the stories. All of these men lived long, troubled lives, yet only two of them regained professional success and public esteem, while the other two were seen as unable to get up again after the blows life had delivered to them in middle age. Resilience and redemption were reserved in these narratives for the two men—Cash and Charles—who had begun their lives with good (as opposed to drunk and immoral) mothers who loved them and believed in them unconditionally.

Beyond stereotypical gender ideals, the specific parallels in these four men's life stories—the childhood poverty or neglect, the many wives and lovers, the unorthodox talent, the abuse of drugs and alcohol, the public fall from grace—do raise the question of why their eulogies took such different shape in journalism. The answers do not seem to lie in obvious identity markers such as race or class. Indeed, these factors seem almost irrelevant, given that the two white men received the best and worst eulogistic portrayals, and that the only one who was not born into abject poverty, the white Brando, suffered the worst portrait of all. If race and class were a factor in these stories, they were, like gender, unifying narrative elements that lay a potential foundation for these men to enact the American dream of success despite the odds. (Region as related to class, however, may have been a factor in these plots, since the two men seen as most admirable were those who transcended Southern, rural poverty.)

Johnny Cash's narrative was by far the most flattering of the four. He was explained as a tortured soul who felt deeply for others, who faced "demons" (his sins were described in passive terms, as things that happened to him, rather than things he chose to do), and who was saved by sobriety, religion, and the love of a good woman. The latter three aspects of his life seem to have been quite real, though they were well-known "facts" in part because he kept singing and talking about them. It is not the purpose of this discussion to suggest that the positive tone of his eulogy was inappropriate—just that it was probably inevitable, and that it was due partly but not only to the retrospective narrative choices of journalists.

All four men took up political and social causes during the 1960s and 1970s, and these were mentioned to varying extents within the coverage. In the cases of Cash (performing for and identifying with prisoners, including murderers), Pryor (directly addressing white racists in his comedy routines), and Charles (refusing to perform in segregated concert halls), their activism was seen as part of their empathy and access to "truth," whereas Brando's affiliation with the Native American rights movement was seen as evidence of his increasing marginality and eccentricity, a distraction from his real work.

Both Charles and Brando were described as "geniuses," though only Brando's genius was seen as "inexplicable." In striking contrast, *Newsweek* wrote of Charles (referring to his shift, later in his career, toward country-western and pop music): "The purists had long ago forgiven him for selling out, if that's what he'd done—and even shrugged off his Diet Pepsi commercial—because who are you to tell a genius what to do with his gift? You say thank you" (Gates, 2004, p. 75).

All four men committed sins of excess, sins of the flesh, though only in Brando's case did this fault literally result in excess flesh, and only in Brando's case was "appetite" given as cause of death. More direct links between substance abuse and cause of death could have been made for

Pryor, Charles, and Cash. Yet it was Brando who had committed the worst sin of all in America: getting fat. Brando's softness was a significant departure from the masculinity of the celebrities' shared narrative, especially within a popular culture in which the celebrities most vilified for weight gain are female (Elizabeth Taylor, Kirstie Alley, and Wynonna Judd are just three examples from this time period),[3] and in which popular reality television shows include *The Greatest Loser*, a weight-loss program charting ordinary people's return to "normal" life through intensive dieting and exercise. Moreover, the loss of Brando's looks may have, paradoxically, resulted in the loss of audiences' sense of him as a "real" person with whom they could, or wanted to, identify; in the end, he was *not* how Americans would like to see ourselves. The corporeal aspect of Brando's demise may have seemed the most visible gesture that he did not seek public forgiveness of his personal and professional lapses.

That outreaching wish was the primary narrative difference in eulogistic coverage of these four men. In these stories, significant attention was paid to the celebrities' varying levels of willingness to share their feelings in public ways and to seem "open" to audiences. Frank Furedi describes this aspect of the "culture of emotionalism" by explaining that "public figures are regularly judged by the way they feel rather than by their deed or the outcome of their action" and that such a person's choice to keep his or her problems private is "pathologised and denounced as cold and inhuman" (2004, p. 37).

Cash confessed and repented, repeatedly. Charles did not repent, but confessed to sinful urges through music that had the rhythms and fervor of gospel. Pryor seemed to have been sufficiently punished by the humiliation and lasting disfigurement from his cocaine accident plus his battle with multiple sclerosis, all of them very public forms of atonement for previous sins. Brando continued to indulge his appetites and shut himself away from the public; though he had been admired for creating film characters who spurned the world, he was reviled, or at best seen as "inexplicable," when he did it himself.

In the resulting set of life-story narratives, Pryor and Brando both fell from grace, the first as a tragic victim of his own demons, the second as a swaggering and eventually gluttonous hero whose innovative brilliance was squandered. In contrast, the life stories of Cash and Charles were told as journeys toward grace, as tales of lifelong struggle between good and evil finally resulting in redemption. In the popular journalism surveyed in this study, Ray Charles was forgiven ("we can't stop loving him"), Richard Pryor was understood and grudgingly admired ("America's profane Twain"), and Brando was at least pitied ("a hostage of his own genius"). Yet it was Johnny Cash who was saved. Eulogized in *Rolling Stone* as "a legend who never stopped being a common man" (DeCurtis, 2003, p. 70), it was Cash who, ultimately, stood for the American experience, and for a secular articulation of the traditionally Protestant notion that "grace" is available to all of us.

The presence of the concepts of sin, repentance, forgiveness, and redemption in this kind of reporting supports scholars' assertions that journalism can be understood as a form of cultural narrative, and that myth-making in journalism is a layered, narrative process that occurs over time. The extensive, almost excessive use of religious language in these particular articles also may illuminate broader, early twenty-first-century social trends in a politically conservative America unusually concerned with memorial, therapeutic spirituality, open expressions of faith, and public tributes to heroes—trends also underlying coverage of the seemingly much more serious topics of this book's other chapters.

At the very least, the coverage described in this chapter is evidence that entertainment reporting today conveys something more than just gossip. In his argument as to why popular culture deserves serious critical attention, George Lipsitz noted that what may seem like "a sideshow can sometimes be the main event" (1990, p. 20). He was writing about music, but the same case can be made for *People* and *Rolling Stone* and other publications that anoint the famous and analyze their meaning. In their pages, the Man in Black and Brother Ray live out moral fables, reenacting not just their own experiences but ours as well, within a secular celebration of forgiveness and salvation. These stories are not merely entertainment; they are, for many people, the central tales of an ideal American life.

# 6

## "WE CAN'T KEEP LOSING OUR KIDS"

*Fear, Blame, and Mourning in Press Coverage of Teen Deaths*

In January 2006, *USA Today* reported that college freshmen are "uniquely vulnerable" to death, that "students away from home for the first time are more likely to die of accidents or illness" (Davis & DeBarros, 2006, p. 1). *Current Events,* a magazine geared for middle and high school readers, warned in a cover story: "Car Crashes Are Top Teen Killer," and noted that "about 10 American teens age 16–19 years die in teen-driven car accidents every day" (E. Johnson, 2005, p. 1). *Newsweek* in May 2004 reported that teenagers "are twice as likely to get hurt on the job as adults" and provided its readers a grim statistic: About 70 teens die each year "on the job, mostly in farm and retail work." Teenagers, by nature, bring considerable risk to the workplace, as the article explained: "A working teenager can be a perfect storm of eagerness and inexperience" (Scelfo & Springen, 2004, p. 61). In August 2005, *People* told its readers about an "extreme form of risk-taking among troubled youth" who play choking games intentionally to lose consciousness. The article focused on a 13 year old found hanging from her closet door, but noted her death was not particularly unusual. "The practice is responsible for the deaths of a number of children across the country. … In fact, say child psychiatrists, many of the kids experimenting with suffocation are trouble-free youths unlikely to try illegal narcotics" (Fields-Meyer, Sheff-Cahan, Swertlow, Pera, & Egan, 2005, pp. 141–142).

In reporting trends, each of these nationally circulated publications focused on the deaths of particular teenagers—the 13 year old found hanged, a 16-year-old country club employee who ran a golf cart into a deck and punctured his heart, another teen who crashed his new black Mazda into a tree, a 19 year old who died of alcohol poisoning following a fraternity drinking ritual. The magazines did what journalists do: they used feature writing and human interest-style reporting techniques to seek maximum impact for their stories. The deaths of these teenagers were presented as "lessons" for readers, and each article quoted experts who called for solutions—for new laws protecting teens, or at least for more parental awareness of dangers facing them.

But when a teenager dies, even if it is part of a perceived national trend, the event is first a local story. Local media write the initial draft, and they too use the deaths of teenagers in prescriptive ways, even as breaking news occurs. They participate in a kind of public mourning ritual, which by its nature seeks a larger purpose or meaning for tragedy. This chapter examines how the deaths of teenagers were covered in four contemporary mainstream daily newspapers from 2003 through 2005, to determine how these stories were framed, how the teens were remembered, and what those portrayals might reveal about the complex relationship between the press, teenagers, and American cultural notions about death.

## THE PUBLIC DEATH STORY

The psychology professor Robert Kastenbaum wrote in 1972 about "the kingdom where nobody dies." His landmark essay (Kastenbaum 2000), reprinted in Kenneth J. Doka's edited *Living with Grief: Children, Adolescents, and Loss,* pointed to a cultural misperception that children and adolescents are somehow protected from death. The essay was meant to guide caregivers as they worked with children experiencing grief, but his words offer insight into the sense of public shock and loss felt when a young person dies. In an era when the life expectancy for an American is 77.6 years,[1] the death of a teenager seems a terrible aberration. Yet the press regularly reports the deaths of teenagers, especially those who die suddenly in accidents.

This chapter argues that, in part because of the cultural unease surrounding the deaths of young people, press coverage of those deaths serves a critical symbolic function. More than simply relaying the facts, news stories about teenage deaths seek to explain, commemorate, and even unify. This symbolic function is particularly important because the death of a child is unnatural, and thus "crystallizes our need to deal with grief whether in private or public forums" (Jorgensen-Earp & Lanzilotti, 1998, p.157). As will be shown here, these news stories also assign blame, often to the deceased, and serve as warnings for readers about the dangers caused by and facing young people.

How the press deals with teen deaths is an important topic for scholarly attention. This chapter highlights the familiar story forms used by newspapers when teenagers die and seeks to determine what they might represent in terms of issues or ideals, and what exemplary models they offer.

Unfortunately, no one has studied media portrayals of the deaths of individual teenagers. Studies have focused on incidents that involved multiple deaths and garnered national news coverage, such as the 1999 Columbine High School shootings in Littleton, Colorado. Regina G. Lawrence and Thomas A. Birkland (2004) studied how media coverage of Columbine drove certain issues to the top of media and government agendas. Erika Doss made a different observation regarding media reaction to Columbine in her study of "the commemorative dimensions of death, dying and bereavement in contemporary America as embodied in visual and material culture." Media coverage of Columbine, she said, focused on "the public expression of grief, not discussion of social causes or public policies or political circumstances" (2002, p. 71). She noted with surprise the lack of media attention to the religious contexts of the event and the "death-shrines" erected in its aftermath. Yet the media, she wrote, hardly failed to frame the site itself as a shrine, as "sacred ground" (p. 72).

Jonathan D. Fast analyzed responses to the Columbine killings at the national and community levels, and noted that people created "a community of bereavement," by undertaking grief projects and by creating and raising memorial objects. "Sudden deaths," he wrote, have unique characteristics that induce unique responses. "Sudden death survivors are more prone to experience a sense of unreality, of helplessness, heightened feelings of guilt about having failed to avert the disaster, and a strong need to blame someone for the crisis" (2003, p. 485). Although their focus was not on teenage accidents, Susan M. Conner and Kathryn Wesolowski did examine newspaper framing of 278 automobile crashes in four Midwestern cities, particularly the framing of public health messages. They found that newspapers "assigned blame in 90 percent of crashes covered, under-reported restraint use and driver's risk of death, failed to reflect the protective value of restraints, and misrepresented the roles played by alcohol and teen drivers" (2004, p. 149). The coverage, they argue, "did not accurately reflect real risk," but presented crashes as "dramas with a victim/villain storyline" (p. 149). Newspapers "over-represented the involvement of teens in fatal crashes. While only 14 percent of all fatal crashes in these communities involved a teen driver, 22 percent of the crashes covered … involved teen drivers" (p. 151). The newspapers, for better or worse, viewed the deaths of teens as particularly newsworthy.

This chapter seeks to answer the question: How were the deaths of teenagers portrayed in *The Denver Post, The Seattle Times, The St. Louis Post-Dispatch*, and *The Columbus* (Ohio) *Dispatch* from 2003 through 2005? Metropolitan daily newspapers were chosen, rather than national publications, because a teenage death is first a local story, and the goal here is to shed light on the storytelling techniques of local newspapers, important reflectors of cultural values. The sample was gathered via LexisNexis Academic, using the keywords "teen," "teenager," "death," and "dead," in 2003, 2004, and 2005. In all, 102 articles were examined.

## SUDDEN DEATHS

The teenage deaths reported in these four metropolitan daily newspapers were what Jonathan Fast called "sudden deaths." In fact, only one article in the 102 examined reported a death that was not "sudden." It mentioned a 17 year old who died of liver cancer, yet that article was published not at the time of her death but later when a camp for grieving children had been named after her (King, 2004, p. F1).

The largest category in these sudden deaths was automobile accidents, including 40 articles, some reporting multiple deaths. Alcohol was reported to have been a definite contributor in a couple of these accidents, but speeding and other risky activities such as "car surfing," "drifting," "drag racing" and "hill jumping" were included in 17 articles.

*The Denver Post* defined "car surfing" as "standing atop a moving car," and reported the death of a 15 year old who fell off the car and hit her head (Wyo. Teen charged, 2004, p. B2). The driver, a 17 year old who reportedly called an ambulance and then left the accident scene, was sentenced to two years' confinement for vehicular homicide (Teen sentenced, 2005, p. B2). "Drifting," is "slang for revving a car as fast as possible while making tight turns. The object is to balance the car on two wheels," the *Post* reported in July 2004 in an article about teenage risk-taking that featured deaths of 10 teenagers in a variety of automobile accidents (Deam, 2004, p. F1). *The St. Louis Post-Dispatch* warned about "hill jumping" in its coverage of the death of a 15 year old who was "speeding fast enough to launch his car into the air at the top of a steep rise in the road" (Sunset hills, 2003, p. 7). The article noted he was at least the eighth teen to die in such a manner, and reported on government efforts to level the stretch of the road where the boy died.

A *Denver Post* article on the dangers of drag racing followed a fatal accident involving "a car filled with teens." A source who lived near the crash site told the newspaper, "'You actually see 10 or 15 cars parked on a side street' and someone with a red bandana signaling the start of the drag race ... 'They race all night long'" (Olinger, 2004, p. B1). *The St. Louis Post-Dispatch* told its readers that eight teenagers had been killed in drag-racing incidents over an 18-month period, including an innocent girl returning home from the library who was killed in a race that "went out of control" (Ratcliffe, 2003, p. A1). Underage driving was listed as a cause in three accident stories, including the crash of a pickup truck driven by a 13 year old on a rural county road, the crash of a speeding car driven by an unlicensed teen, and the wreck of a car, with five teenagers "hurrying back to school from lunch," driven by a 15 year old (Kirksey, 2003, p. B3; Ratcliffe, 2003, p. A1; Schrader & Kirksey, 2003, p. B1).

Suicide was the next mostly frequently listed cause of a teenage death in the sample examined. Eleven articles included details of eight suicides, including one 16 year old whose body was found leaning against his high school as his peers began arriving for Monday classes (Halverson, 2003, p. B5) and a 13 year old who shot himself in front of classmates (Huy Vu, 2004, p. B3). *The Seattle Times* reported that 94 youths had killed themselves in Washington state in 2002, and listed "myriad warning signs adults need to watch for, including teens drastically losing weight, cutting or burning themselves and withdrawing from friends and family" (Huy Vu, 2004, p. B3). *The St. Louis Post-Dispatch*, in its article on the suicides of two teenagers, pointed to the need to raise awareness of mental illness among teenagers. It noted that "children with mental illness are often 'punished' for their disorders in ways no one would dream of treating 'teens with other diseases" (Hesman, 2005, p. A1).

Other causes of these sudden teen deaths included drug overdose, alcohol poisoning, shooting, drowning, fire, aneurysm, sudden asthma attack, heat exposure, reaction to an insect bite, leap from a cliff, head injury inflicted by a skateboard, and a closed head wound that caused a young man to collapse during a football game.

## PROBING CAUSE, GAUGING RESPONSIBILITY

The articles about teen deaths examined for this study did more than list the "cause," or manner, of the deaths. They probed deeper into underlying reasons and discussed responsibility and blame in prescriptive ways.

Teens who committed suicide suffered from depression, social alienation, volatile dispositions, and anxiety (Huy Vu, 2004, p. B3;

MacDonald, 2004, p. F1). Most of these descriptors were generalizations about teenage suicide, not targeted at particular victims. An exception was one 16 year old who was described as "fun, outgoing and creative," yet the article noted he "struggled with anger, depression and frustration" (Teen commits suicide, 2004, p. B3). A letter to the editor of *The Seattle Times* warned particularly about high suicide rates among homosexual teenagers. It asked: "How many gay and lesbian teens would rather die than face a life of discrimination, hate, rejection and condemnation?" (Sondheimer, 2005, p. D5). *The St. Louis Post-Dispatch* wrote of a teen who had committed suicide: "All anyone could say with certainty was that [he] had an illness that shrouded him in the deepest darkness, a black hole from which he never fully emerged" (Hesman, 2005, p. A1).

Many articles reporting traffic fatalities of teenagers laid the blame and responsibility squarely on the teens involved. They either implied or stated outright that teenagers were inherently risk takers who could not or would not listen to reason. One article warned: "Teens must bear responsibility for causing crashes. ... Deliberate risk-taking emerges as a distinction between experienced drivers and teens" (Schrader, 2004d, p. B1). Other articles noted the teen driver's lack of experience in making good split-second decisions. As one patrolman said in a *Denver Post* article about a drag-race fatality, "Obviously he is an inexperienced driver who is trying to drive like a race-car driver on a highway. ... It's really sad" (Mitchell, 2004, p. B1). In another article about a teenage drag-racer who crashed and killed her sister, a law enforcement spokeswoman said, "We are concerned with the conduct of young people that can lead to such disastrous consequences" (Schrader, 2004c, p. B5). Another quoted a state patrol officer: "We know that inexperience, distractions, risk-taking, and all those things that these teenagers are doing have been causing some of these fatal crashes" (Frates, 2005, p. B1). *The St. Louis Post-Dispatch* warned that "peer pressure trumps everything. Kids are showing off for their friends" (Ratcliffe, 2003, p. A1).

Several articles brought up the possibility of alcohol or drugs as a factor in traffic accidents, even if that information was not available. Such articles stated simply that "it is unknown" whether they were involved (Frates, 2005, p. B1; Kirksey, 2005, p. B2; Kouwe & Frates, 2003, p. B6). Sometimes the newspapers implied that the teens were speeding, even if such information had not been released (1 teen, 2004, p. B3), or that the teens were not wearing seat belts, even if that fact had not been determined (Logan County, 2005, p. B2). The reason for such speculation likely was that, according to these newspapers, alcohol, excessive speed and lack of seat belts had regularly contributed to teen deaths. For example, the *St. Louis Post-Dispatch* told readers that most teens that die in crashes do not use safety belts. The article quoted a police chief who said: "Combine this low safety belt use with research that shows teenagers are more likely than older drivers to speed, run red lights, make illegal turns, ride with an intoxicated driver and drive after consuming alcohol and you have a recipe for disaster" (Gustin, 2004, p. C1).

Other articles also pointed to careless driving, recklessness, distractions, and peer pressure (Deam, 2004, p. F1; Schrader, 2004b, p. B5). One noted an "all too familiar pattern for teenagers … 'They get into a lot of accidents because of the risks they take. … It's the belief that nothing can happen to them" (Mitchell & Depperschmidt, 2004, p. 2D). Another quoted a witness to an accident who said she hopes "teens realize they are not immortal" (Burnette, 2005, p. B3). An insurance executive quoted in another article said: "It's not that teenagers don't know the risks. They do. They know what they are doing is reckless and dangerous. … It's all about the moment, the risk-taking, the exuberance of youth" (Deam, 2004, p. F1). Even when noting the large number of crashes on a particularly dangerous stretch of road in the St. Louis area, the newspaper quoted a police commander who again blamed the teenage driver: "I don't think the road itself is causing it. It's someone pressing the gas pedal that causes it" (Ratcliffe, 2003, p. A1).

Two articles in the sample examined looked to outside influences on teenagers. As *The Denver Post* noted:

> Police said some teens are being influenced by video games and Hollywood into making dangerous decisions. "The video games and movies that are promoting this activity [drag racing] are done under strict conditions on closed roadways, and these aren't closed roadways or professional drivers. … Unfortunately, these are people, and not just kids, who are making two-second decisions that impact their lives forever. (Kouwe & Frates, 2003, p. B6)

Another article quoted a dead teen's brother: "Teenagers can't separate the fiction they see on TV from reality" (Schrader, 2004d, p. B1). Yet the articles did not call for media reform. Rather, some reported efforts to institute more legal restrictions on teenage drivers, as one Colorado state representative said: "You all need to remember when you were a teenager, and what that was like, driving" (Hughes, 2005, p. B2).

Articles about other kinds of sudden deaths also seemed to blame the teens involved and their poor judgment. One high school sophomore dared another teen to strike him on the head with a skateboard. As the article noted: "'The other kids there say that he claimed he could take the pain, and they took it as a joke, a dare. ... The other kid grabbed the skateboard and whacked him on the head with it. [He] dropped to the ground, convulsing'" (O'Neil, 2003, p. B1). A 19 year old who "died from exposure to 110-degree heat in the Arizona desert" had disappeared during a dirt bike excursion. The article noted that he had not taken any water with him to the remote, hot area (Kelly, 2004, p. B5). One teenage girl knew that animal dander was a trigger for her asthma attacks. "When she attended a party at a New Mexico ranch ... she thought she'd be safe as long as she stayed away from animals ... She'd forgotten her rescue inhaler" (Quinn, 2004, Health & Fitness p. 3). Another teen jumped 150 feet from a bluff into a pool of water at an abandoned quarry—the fence around it was broken in spots and easy to pass through, the article noted (Hampel, 2004, p. B1). An article about an accidental drowning wondered "what compelled [the teen] to walk down to the creek and how he ended up in the water" (Kohler, 2004, p. B2).

Even the article about a young athlete who collapsed and died during a football game due to a closed head injury blamed the victim. School officials, the article noted, were looking into whether the teen had been "injured in an earlier practice or game and didn't tell his coaches or family" (Meyer, 2004, p. B1). The teen's mother implored others to "listen to their bodies and tell coaches and parents when they don't feel right," and a school district spokeswoman said, "It's common for kids to believe they're invincible" (p. B1). And a lengthy article titled "Wasted Lessons" probed the death by alcohol poisoning of a 19-year-old college student, who had spiraled from a "vivacious blond to the alcohol casualty who stopped breathing in a frat house hook-up room" (Briggs & Dunn, 2004, p. A1). The article described the young woman's drinking habits in detail and noted, "in life and death she remains a role model" (p. A1). It quoted the local police chief: "All college kids think they are invincible, and this is a great lesson that proves they're not." Yet, the article reported, a month after her death "her friends decided to celebrate her life by throwing a party—a drinking party" (p. A1).

## PUBLIC MOURNING AND REMEMBRANCE

In their coverage of the deaths of teenagers, *The Seattle Times, The Denver Post*, the *St. Louis Post-Dispatch*, and *The Columbus Dispatch* participated in a type of public mourning. They did so by including remembrances of some of the teens who died, and by covering the commemorative activities at schools and in the communities.

Some teens were remembered for particular activities, or positive traits of character, in commemorative ways. Most often, these were teenagers who died in traffic accidents, or in other "sudden deaths," that either were not their fault or were not deemed the result of their own risky or reckless behavior. *The Columbus Dispatch* wrote about a 16 year old killed while riding a motorcycle he had received as "a reward for the four summers he spent washing windows with his uncle." He was described as sweet, helpful, a hard worker, and "kind of like a teddy bear—very kind and considerate and friendly" (Gray, 2003, p. C3). *The St. Louis Post-Dispatch* remembered one teen, whose car crashed while he was returning home with Italian food, as intelligent and self-confident. He was "maturing into a kind, courteous adult" (Anthony, 2004, p. 1A). A 16 year old who was the innocent victim of a drive-by shooting was "a good kid," "strong and tall," "quiet and serious" (Green, 2005, p. B1). His grandmother planned to leave his portable stereo on the kitchen table, where he had left it the night before he died. She said: "That's where it's going to stay. Something to remember him by." A 17 year old who died in a car crash on a fishing trip was "a great guy" (Lane, 2005, p. C1), and a teenage girl was described as having an "important" life (Schrader, 2004, January 18, p. B3). Most articles reporting teen deaths caused by the deceased's own risky or reckless actions did not include pejorative statements about their character; they simply were not described beyond the details of the accidents and the behaviors that caused those accidents.

Schools the deceased teenagers attended often became sites for the community to gather to share grief, or for students to receive counseling, and the news coverage of the deaths provided this information for readers (Halverson, 2003, p. B5; Nicholson, Espinoza & Duran, 2004, p. C3; Schrader & Kirksey, 2003, p. B1). *The St. Louis Post-Dispatch* announced plans for a triple funeral that would be held in the high school gymnasium. Explained the mother of one of the deceased: "We wanted to keep the boys together" (Shinkle, 2003, p. C2). Another high school, part of a Hmong community of 5,000 people, canceled after-hours activities and opened its doors for those who were grieving the death of one teenager and the serious injuries of four others. The newspaper quoted a survivor's uncle:

We are a very tightknit community, and we are so small that this is a tragedy that takes its toll on all the Hmong right now. … I was at the deceased person's parents, and there was a lot of commotion. There was a lot of sadness. There was a lot of crying and grieving at this time. (Schrader & Kirksey, 2003, p. B1)

Students at one high school "wore white shirts ... emblazoned with the number 40, memorializing a classmate," and a moment of silence was held at their Friday night football game (Meyer, 2004, p. B1). Students at another high school held a benefit concert and car wash to raise money for a scholarship in the name of their deceased classmate. The article noted: "Such activities benefit the grieving teens as much as they do the family. ... It's better to be in a group than alone" (Lane, 2005, p. C1). This article, published in *The Columbus Dispatch*, was the only one in the sample examined that tried to paint a more flattering picture of teenagers in general. Of the students involved in the benefit, the deceased teen's mother said: "These kids have been great. Teens get such a bad rap these days, and they have shown so much character. We've just been overwhelmed with the generosity. The parents of these children should be so proud."

*The Denver Post* described a typical "makeshift shrine" erected by the roadside where four teenagers were killed:

> Four white crosses are pressed into the ground. Teddy bears, matted from recent rains, and signed baseballs lie in the grass. Strips of car trim still litter the ditch. A patch of scorched dirt marks where the teenagers' car burst into flames. A nearby metal utility box has become the message board to the dead: "Tony," reads one scrawled note ... "Thanks for being such a great friend. I'll miss you." (Deam, 2004, p. F1)

Such shrines seemed commonplace following automobile accidents. One article told of a mother who brought her 9-year-old daughter to place a bouquet ("purple flowers adorned with bands of purple sequins reminding her of a prom queen's crown—and a homemade card") at the site where an 18-year-old prom queen and cheerleader crashed and died, a site already crowded with balloons, tea lights, photographs, and ribbons (Kee, 2005, p. E1).

Yet the community was warned about at least one of these spontaneous shrines because of poor judgment of the teens gathering there. Near St. Louis, "flowers, balloons and written messages" were placed along the highway where two 16-year-old boys were killed, and many students began gathering at the site to remember and commemorate the deceased. The *Post-Dispatch* wrote:

> As police continue to investigate the crash, they expressed concern for the students who had been visiting the makeshift memorial at the crash site, some running across lanes of Highway 94 to get

there. "That is a really dangerous area to be parking and to be getting out of your car, walking anywhere on Highway 94," said St. Peters Police Sgt. Dave Kuppler. (Weich, 2005a, St. Charles County Post Section p. 1)

The boys' high school, in response to the outpouring of grief and to the danger, made plans to construct a memorial site at the school and sent letters to parents to discourage their children from going to the site of the wreck.

Makeshift shrines were not the only type of public memorial presented in these newspapers. An athlete's teammates wore stickers on their helmets and painted his jersey on the weight-room wall at the school gymnasium (Frankel, 2003a, p. B1). Friends of the college student who died from alcohol poisoning decided on a more permanent commemoration—they got black-and-blue tattoos showing an ace of spades playing card, with the deceased's nickname, "Sam Bam," etched in the center. The card, they said, was the emblem of a fund established to educate students about the dangers of excessive drinking, though they were not willing to give up alcohol themselves (Briggs & Dunn, 2001, p. A1). Students at a St. Louis area high school raised money and made bracelets and posters to commemorate a dead classmate. As the story noted: "There is a lot of talk among the students of the senselessness of this—why did it happen? … Kids do impulsive things, and sometimes there are tragic consequences. Students are trying to act out their feelings in positive ways" (O'Neil, 2003, p. B1).

Even more private memorials became public following recognition in these daily newspapers. Classmates of a high school junior who died in an automobile accident bought a class ring for his family and "filled up his school account with electronic messages" that he would never read (Kee, 2005, p. E1). One teen's family donated his organs, and later met the recipient and felt his heartbeat. They were presented a silver heart ornament with the inscription: "Two Families, Two Children, One Heart & Two Lungs, Joined Forever, 11-6-03, God Bless You" (Frankel, 2003b, p. B1).

The teenagers who did not seem to be memorialized in these kinds of public displays were those who committed suicide, at least according to one mother quoted in *The St. Louis Post-Dispatch*: "You can talk about it if a student dies in a car accident. You can talk about it if a student dies of cancer. You can honor them. You can plant a tree in memory of them … but with suicide (the attitude is) you can't talk about it" (Hesman, 2005, p. A1).

## CLIMATE OF FEAR, FRUSTRATION

The actual smashed car involved in a teen fatality became a different kind of memorial. As *The Denver Post* announced: "The crumpled silver 2000 Chevrolet Impala that carried three … students to their deaths in February 2003 now will carry a message about making smart choices behind the wheel" (Schrader, 2004d, p. B1). The car was to tour the state of Colorado as part of a "safe-teen-driving exhibit." The newspaper noted:

> Accompanying the car will be photos of the teens and words written by their parents about what their dreams for the future were and what the parents have lost. "We don't want the young drivers to just see the crashed car. We want them to think, 'This could be me; this is what could be taken from my family.'" (p. B1)

The mother of a teenager killed in a car crash participated in a similar program called "Prom Talk," which urges students to drive carefully on their prom nights, and "often includes a mock fatal accident" (Weich, 2005b, St. Charles County Post Section, p. 1). Students at still another high school wore black rubber bracelets with the words "Enough IS Enough" after two students died in separate accidents. To receive the bracelet the students had to sign a safe-driving pledge (Rice, 2005, Jefferson County Post Section, p. 3). These public commemorations remembered the deceased, but in fearful ways, meant to warn the teenagers and the public about the potential for further tragedies.

Indeed, fear and frustration were a theme common to these articles about the deaths of teenagers. One state patrolman said: "We can't keep losing our kids" (Schrader, 2004d, p. B1). A grieving relative put it succinctly: "'I don't know if you have kids, but getting that phone call would be the worst thing imaginable,' he said, fighting back tears" (Mitchell & Depperschmidt, 2004, p. D2). Articles wrestled with the pros and cons of education, particularly regarding teen suicide. *The Seattle Times* asked:

> What, if anything, can prevent youth suicide? Does education on the topic lead depressed students to get help? Or do discussions instead run the risk of pushing some students closer to attempting suicide? (MacDonald, 2004, p. F1)

The article noted that many newspapers do not report suicide because of this fear.

Several articles told about proposals for changing laws, and some reported memorials aimed at education. Yet even efforts to teach teens about the dangers of reckless driving were reported with pessimism. As one grieving mother said: "You think they will make the connection … but for some reason they just don't. It just doesn't sink in." That seemed to be true, too, for friends of the college student who died from alcohol poisoning. "Denial—like vanilla vodka and Keystone Light—continues to flow freely," the article noted (Briggs & Dunn, 2004, p. A1).

## DISCUSSION

The 102 articles examined for this chapter did show common frames— repeated themes and narratives—in press coverage of the deaths of teenagers. The stereotyped images, sources of information, and clusters of facts and judgments provide, if not an archetype, then certainly a vivid image of the deceased teens as chronic risk takers almost incapable of rational thought and judgment. All but one article in the sample examined focused on "sudden deaths." The teens who died from other causes, such as illness, in Denver, Seattle, St. Louis, and Columbus, Ohio, during 2003, 2004, and 2005 were all but ignored on news pages. Fast (2003) noted in his study of reactions to the Columbine school shootings that sudden deaths induced unique community responses, including a sense of unreality, helplessness, guilt, and a strong need to blame. Blame in coverage of teen traffic fatalities was placed squarely on the shoulders of the deceased, or of other teens involved; guilt of others surfaced more in articles about suicides and alcohol poisoning; and many articles seemed pessimistic, even hopeless, about reported efforts to affect change.

Doss (2002), in her discussion of Columbine, expressed surprise at the absence of religious rhetoric in press coverage. Articles examined for this study, which focused on deaths of particular teens, also lacked any reference to religion, apart from the scant mention of crosses at a memorial site. Journalists struggle with coverage of the spiritual aspects of death, and of religion in general. Journalists tend to frame stories in traditional ways, disregarding the deeper and more complex spiritual or religious context (Beckerman, 2004, pp. 28–29). Yet Clark and Franzmann, in their study of roadside memorials, argue that the construction of such a memorial represents a pulling away from traditional religious or secular traditions that had been inadequate for the expression of grief following unexpected deaths. Use of crosses, they argue, was "little more than an attempt to find culturally appropriate symbols to express death and the sacred" (2006, p. 591).

Yet journalists, in their coverage of death, did important cultural work. They provided a public space for the expression of sadness and anger, and for commemoration. These articles published remembrances of some teens, and they allowed readers to share in a kind of public mourning through their reporting of rituals such as community gatherings and memorials. Such coverage unifies audiences in communities of grief or concern and allows for public testimony, which can aid in recovery. At the very minimum it acknowledges loss, which scholars have noted helps provide psychosocial care for those affected (see, as an example, Raphael, 1986, p. 245). It also teaches a community particular public ways of grieving, so that roadside shrines and touring wrecks become commonplace and even expected.

Yet even the commemorative aspects of the coverage were prescriptive in nature. In news coverage of the traffic fatalities, only the teens who did *not* engage in risky or reckless behavior were remembered for attributes of character—for being sweet, or helpful, or hard workers. These "good" teens, the antithesis of the risk takers, were mature and serious. Those teens whose behavior threatened the social order were treated differently, their attributes ignored other than the behaviors that led to tragedy. The one exception was the lengthy article about the college student who died of alcohol poisoning. This long-form feature, written not as breaking news but well after her death, focused on multiple aspects of her personality and said her death represented "wasted lessons." At least some of the public memorials and "grief projects" became more about warnings and caution than about remembrances. Monuments historically have served to "'advise' and 'instruct' the public about the future at the same time that it 'reminds' them of the past" (Jorgensen-Earp & Lanzilotti, 1998, p. 151). In the coverage of memorials to teens who died, the larger purpose seemed to be representation of fear; the teens became exemplary models of irrationality.

Frank Furedi, who writes about risk taking and the modern "culture of fear," notes that humans need "a vocabulary" to help make sense of unexpected events that cause pain and suffering, and that vocabulary "almost always contains the implication that someone ought to be blamed" (1997, p. 11). He warns that those who think they can avoid all risks "invariably find that what they acquire instead are obsessions" (p. 13). Coverage of these teen deaths blamed the victims and used fear as a communication tool to try to warn communities that such tragedies could and would happen again. The question for communication scholars (as well as educators and other community leaders) becomes: Does this type of prescriptive coverage work? For better or worse, these stories became metaphors for cultural fear—potent, even obsessive reminders that teenagers are "uniquely vulnerable" to death, and that they do not reside in a "kingdom where nobody dies."

# 7

## MOURNING "MEN JOINED IN PERIL AND PURPOSE"

*Working-Class Heroism in News Report of the Sago Miners' Story*

On January 2, 2006, 13 miners were trapped by an explosion in the Sago coal mine near Tallmansville, West Virginia. Over the following 44 hours, television and print news media covered the rescue effort and its backdrop, focusing on the miners' families and friends who gathered at a Baptist church, and reporting the miscommunication from a rescuer to the families that the men had been found alive, when in fact only one had survived.

During its early portion, the Sago story promised to replicate the saga of the rescue of nine miners from the Quecreek mine in Sipesville, Pennsylvania, in July 2002. The Quecreek story had been an uplifting tale, a redemptive drama enacted in a rural area 10 miles from the site of the crash of United Flight 93 on September 11 less than a year earlier. *Dateline NBC* reporter Hoda Kotbe summed up that story: "For a deeply religious community that refused to give up hope, this time around there was a happy ending to a story about human faith, the power of miracles and rebirth" (*Dateline NBC,* 2002).

The January 2006 Sago accident failed to yield an uplifting tale; indeed, because of the early false report of survival, it initially shifted to a story of betrayed mourners who were denied their "miracle." Within just a few days, though, news coverage of Sago took yet another narrative turn, becoming a collective portrait of an ideal small town, populated by brave men and bereaved women who were the backbone of the country during a time of war. Journalists performed "news repair," a process requiring them to "take an active role in normalizing the story … rewriting the story in more familiar terms as new 'facts' are disclosed" (W. Bennett, Gressett, & Haltom, 1985, p. 53; also see Tuchman, 1978). This much grander narrative transformed the Sago story into one that *did* confirm the story of Quecreek—a nostalgic parable of a blue-collar way of life, representing the best qualities of America.

Katherine Fry (2003) argues that geographic regions "are embedded with meanings or identities" that are specific and yet that contribute in their own ways to "the cultural strength of the nation as a whole" (p. 37). The term "heartland," she writes, "conjures up images of trust and simplicity" and "exists as a repository of fundamental American values—religion, agriculture, and family" (p. 42). Her definition of the symbolic meaning of region in news echoes Herbert Gans's enumeration of "values in the news," including "small-town pastoralism," a "good life" defined by "cohesiveness, friendliness, and slow pace" (1979, p. 48).

In its simplicity, such a characterization is inherently conservative and forgetful, a product of "selective memory and soothing amnesia" (Kammen, 1991, p. 656). Woven into this nostalgic geographic ideal are stereotypical ideas about class and gender, a vision in which the blue-collar worker and the women around him (mothers, wives, and daughters) embody "traditional" ideas presumed to be nearly lost in modern American life. As Deepa Kumar (2004b) notes in her study of the Jessica Lynch story during the Iraq war, gender stereotypes are especially useful in performing news repair that reasserts the strength of the American character amid danger.

In a separate study, Kumar also discusses how the family is used as a symbol of the nation in news coverage of labor strikes, arguing that in such reporting, "[t]he national family brings together business, consumers, workers, and the state in a harmonious relationship" (2005, p. 147). She is one of several scholars who have examined media portrayals, fictional as well as factual, of the working class and the poor, and almost all of this literature concludes that such characters do not fare well in media, if they are represented at all (also see Eisler, 1983; Harry, 2004; Parenti, 1986; Phillips, 2004; Puette, 1992). Some such critics contend that because news organizations are part of large corporations, it is inevitable that they will be biased toward owners or will ignore labor interests (see, for instance, Kumar, 2004a; Martin, 2004; Mazzocco, 1994; Parenti, 1978; Zweig, 2000). Other scholars are less negative, seeing media representation of the working class as "a complex assortment of people and beliefs" (Bodnar, 2003, p. 219) yet acknowledging the predominance of nostalgic stereotypes. In his study of images of coal miners in a century of novels, theater, film, and poetry, David C. Duke contends that writers, while sympathetic, "have viewed mining people as 'the other,' as objects waiting to be defined rather than subjects capable of defining themselves" (2002, pp. 3–4). Duke further observes that "[t]he fact that coal mining is a dying industry tends to relegate it, like cattle drives, to the past and render the entire process even more unreal, thereby increasing the distance that exists between us and them" (p. 125).

In news, of course, such nostalgic and stereotypical constructions are made from real people who have experienced real events in a real place. These characters seem to represent a genuine vernacular culture, people "intent on protecting values and restating views of reality derived from firsthand experience in small-scale communities" (Bodnar, 1992, p. 14). Paradoxically, at the same time that their regionality (their difference) validates them as an authentic culture, it is the perceived realness of these news characters that allows them to "serve as potential points of identification for the audience" (Hartley, 1982, p. 12) and allows the audience to feel implicated in the event and its outcome.

The evidence for this study comes from: the major television news networks, CBS, NBC, and ABC; the three major U.S. weekly newsmagazines, *Time, Newsweek,* and *U.S. News & World Report*; Associated Press reports; National Public Radio; and seven newspapers. The newspapers include the nation's top-five circulation papers, (in order) *USA Today, The Wall Street Journal, The New York Times,* the *Los Angeles Times,* and *The Washington Post* (Audit Bureau of Circulation, 2006). The Sago mine is geographically in the middle of the cities of the other two newspapers, the *Pittsburgh Post-Gazette* to the north and *The Charleston* (WV) *Gazette* in the state's capital to the south, and both of these dailies covered the Sago story as a local one.[1]

The evidence includes all reports on the Sago incident published or aired through the end of August 2006, with particular attention to the first two weeks of coverage, from January 2, 2006, the day of the explosion, to January 16, 2006. The latter date—the day after a joint memorial service for the miners (following their funerals), a public service attended by 2,000 people (Gately, 2006, January 16, p. A9)—marked the end of daily, national attention to this West Virginia community, but there was sporadic subsequent coverage of government hearings on mine safety and of the condition of the sole survivor of the accident. A total of 761 newspaper articles, newsmagazine articles, and broadcast reports was examined. For context, this study also draws on several reports by the same news organizations on the Quecreek mine rescue.

## "TRAGEDY IN THE MOUNTAIN": RECLAIMING
## THE QUECREEK TEMPLATE

Despite the fact that what happened at the two mines were very different kinds of accidents (flooding versus an explosion), the Sago setting was likely to bring to mind the Quecreek rescue three and half years earlier. The mines are less than 150 miles apart on the same seam of bituminous coal running through the Allegheny Mountains, and the two communities are similar: both are rural, low-income, and politically conservative regions, and in both cases major characters in the story spoke openly of their Christian faith. The Pittsburgh Post-Gazette had quoted a minister's sermon on the morning of the Quecreek rescue: "It happened because of prayer—people around the world knocking on heaven's door asking for one more chance" (Pro, 2002, p. A4).

That earlier storyline was summed up well by the opening of television journalist Jane Pauley's report on July 28, 2002:

> The numbers were stacked against them, nine men, 240 feet, 77 hours. But numbers alone could not account for the blood, sweat and skills of the rescue crews above the ground, nor the iron wills of the miners below. Tonight, the story of a rescue, how hundreds of people in a rural county of Pennsylvania came together to create a miracle in the mountain.

Also on this show, rescued Quecreek miner Blaine Mayhugh told Pauley, "I couldn't even imagine how many people was out there behind us. I mean, that just tells us what kind of country we live in. I mean, we always pull together" (Dateline NBC, 2002). This story was less about the miners than it was about "the indomitable human spirit," in the words of Meet the Press (2002) host Tim Russert, who was on air on the Sunday morning of the rescue.

During the period while the Sago miners had not yet been located, Good Morning America anchor Diane Sawyer interviewed Dennis Hall, another rescued Quecreek miner, who remembered: "The families didn't know whether we were alive. That was probably the hardest thing for me, thinking that I knew that I was alive, but they didn't know that. But you always have to think positive. Never give up. Never give up" (2006a). This theme set the stage for the initial news coverage of the West Virginia accident.

On January 3, 2006, the day after the Sago mine explosion, NBC anchor Brian Williams began his report by reminding viewers of the Quecreek "miracle" and by saying "it's our nature as a people to be hopeful" (NBC Nightly News, 2006a). The following night, Williams explained how the newer story had unexpectedly gone very wrong, in a report that included the kind of rhetoric that would characterize the coverage of the following two weeks:

> For several hours last night, millions of Americans from the East Coast to the West started hearing the word, from deep underground in that small town in West Virginia, one miner was dead, but they had found the other 12 alive. It was instantly branded a miracle. The church bells rang out, families celebrated, and the media reported the whole giddy scene on live television. But it was wrong. Thy joy turned to sadness and then anger. Twelve good men were gone, and a town was crushed. (*NBC Nightly News*, 2006b)

Williams's opening suggested that a sense of betrayal had been experienced not only by the miners' families in West Virginia but by all of America, presumably awake in the middle of the night waiting for "word from deep underground." On the same program, reporter Tom Costello noted, "Newspapers rushed to press with the incredible development," and his segment included clips from the cable television news networks, Fox News and CNN.

What was already at work here was news repair, initially necessary because the families' anger seemed directed as much at the media as at the mine owner. The brother-in-law of one of the dead miners conflated the company (which did not speak with reporters at the "survival" stage of the story) and the media in his comment that "they straight out lied to millions of people watching" (*All Things Considered*, 2006). Another distraught family member cried out, directly into a news camera, "now I just found out that my granddaddy is dead because people has lied on the TV. … We had a miracle, and it was taken away from us" (*NBC Nightly News*, 2006b). It was the last part of this statement that created the greatest need for narrative repair. The problem was less a matter of an incorrect news report than the loss of the "miracle" template—the theme that had been meant to make this local story, about death in a dangerous profession, into a national story about faith and community.

Subsequent coverage reveals the characters and themes through which that more positive national story was preserved. This was made possible in part by a shift in the status of the story from news to feature, and by the descriptive language in so many of the reports that cast their subject as something timeless. With the same wording that *Dateline NBC* (2002) had chosen for its special episode on Quecreek, ABC titled its hour-long *Primetime Live* show "Tragedy in the Mountain" (2006), as if "the mountain" were a concept rather than a place. "The mine" was used similarly: *U.S. News & World Report* ran its title "Prayers for the brave men in the mine" (Roane, 2006, p. 10), while a *Today Show* report began, "Back in West Virginia, the small towns that make up the coal country are mourning the men who died in the mine" (2006b).

Such colloquialism was common in press characterizations of the area where the miners had lived, a region of several towns described by *The New York Times* as "hamlets" (Gately, 2006a, p. A14), the very same word *NBC Nightly News* (2002) had used to describe the towns around the Quecreek mine. The normally formal language of ABC's *Nightline* (2006) lapsed into phrases such as "just down the road a piece," while *CBS Evening News* (2006) reported that "Fred Ware's home and heart was (*sic*) tucked inside this coal-mining community for 59 years." The host of National Public Radio's *Weekend Edition* (2006) program offered this: "Just as veins of coal lace through the Appalachian Mountains, coal dust flows through the veins of the men, women and children who live in the hollows and towns that dot those rolling hills." In an article that also quoted the owner of "the General Store in Hinkleville," *USA Today* provided a folksy setting: "Many of the 5,700 people of Buckhannon, the county seat, linger in coffee shops and corner stores to gossip and swap stories. Everybody knows everybody—and news travels fast. It also means that when tragedy strikes, it touches everyone" (Bazar, 2006a, pp. 1A–2A). A similar picture was painted even by a West Virginia reporter in *The Charleston Gazette*:

> After the funeral, a procession of about three dozen cars and trucks twisted through the countryside to the cemetery, the smell of wood smoke coating the air. The procession passed by pastures with cows grazing on brown grass, across a one-lane bridge, through stands of pine. ... On the outskirts of Pickens, the road climbed, and a gray-haired woman stood at the end of her gravel driveway, keeping warm beside a barrel fire, watching as the hearse passed. The woman had her right hand pressed across her heart. (Eyre, 2006, p. 1A)

Notions of community and family were at the center of the regional characterization of West Virginia itself, as they had been in the press portrayal of rural western Pennsylvania three and a half years earlier. Joe Manchin, the state's governor, told reporters: "We're really family here in West Virginia. And we're pulling together, and we're still very hopeful" (*The Early Show*, 2006a). The day after the public memorial service for the miners, the governor repeated these statements in an interview with NBC reporter Lester Holt, and then segued into a broader theme, praising

[t]he strength ... that these people have, the inherent danger that they face and the pride that they have of providing a living for their family, the pride of the state of West Virginia that they carry with them, the pride of the energy that they produce that has made this country strong and keeps this country strong. (*Today Show*, 2006c)

Conversely, *The Charleston Gazette* described a feeling of family directed inward, from strangers toward the mining community, due to "the offers of help that poured into Upshur Country from all over the world. 'We discovered this week that Upshur County is our community, West Virginia is our community, and America is our community,'" a local fireman told the paper (Finn, 2006a, p. 1C). In this view, people nationwide were imagined as connected to the unfolding tragedy. *Today Show* host Matt Lauer told Anna McCloy, wife of the only surviving miner, "I hope you know that the prayers of just about everybody in this country are with you and your family and your husband" (2006a).

The dead miners were eulogized as family men, especially as fathers, evident in the many newspaper photographs that showed them holding babies (Barringer & Goodman, 2006, p. A1; Grady & Dao, 2006, p. 18). *NBC Nightly News* reporter Lisa Daniels chose this theme as well: "Terry [Helms] was Judy Shackelford's baby brother, only somehow, he never seemed to get his role right [i.e., he took care of her]. ... For Jerry Groves, coal ran through his veins, but it was his new role he cherished the most: granddaddy" (2006c).

## "A DIFFERENT BREED OF MEN": STEREOTYPES OF HYPERMASCULINITY AND FEMININE GRIEF

As the news story evolved after the miners were found dead, their fate was explained as preordained, an inheritance from a long line of male relatives before them, in phrases that wove together the narrative threads of family devotion and rugged masculinity. Here are some examples: "It wasn't uncommon to find fathers and sons, uncles and brothers, following one another into the deep tunnels" (Jones & Tyson, 2006, p. A8); Marty Bennett "followed his own father into the mines. ... His only son, Russell, worked at the Sago Mine on the shift after his dad's" (A tribute, 2006, p. 1C); "It's a profession handed down from grandfather to father to son" (Huffstutter & Simon, 2006, p. A12); "They were the sons of miners, the brothers of miners, and by and large they married miners' daughters" (Dao, 2006b, p. A19).

Such continuity was understood not as a matter of economic or educational limitations, but as a "calling" (a word actually used by *NBC Nightly News* anchor Brian Williams [2006c]), a somebody-has-to-do-it choice like those made by firemen, policemen, and soldiers. Mining was, according to *Primetime Live* (2006), "a tough, proud way of life." "There's a closeness in the miners that's unexplainable," the owner of a local store told *USA Today*. "They're a band of brothers" (Bazar, 2006a, p. 2A).

As such language suggests, the miners were celebrated in the press as hypermasculine. Covering a memorial service, *The New York Times* reported: "They were praised as men who had a work ethic that would not quit, who hunted and fished and followed NASCAR races when they were not in the hollow of a mountain" (Gately, 2006b, p. A9). Although he was 50 years old when he died, *The Pittsburgh Post-Gazette* described miner Terry Helms as a "6-foot-1, 240-pound former high school football player" (Hard work, 2006, p. A1).

Women interviewed by reporters testified to their men's bravery and fatalism despite the danger, and to the burden of being with a man who risks his life every day but remains devoted to his "calling," even wed to it. One miner's wife, Pam Winans, told CBS, "He has these feelings. You know, that's just your risk you take going in the mines" (*The Early Show*, 2006a). The same network reported, "Fred Ware Jr. and his fiancée Loretta were planning a Valentine's Day wedding, but the 59-year-old Ware would always be married to his job, according to his daughter. [Ms. Peggy Cohen:] "He even said, 'I'll die in the mines. I'm not retiring. I'll die in the mines'" (*CBS Evening News*, 2006).

News stories emphasized women's traditional roles. *The Washington Post* described "the swift chain reaction that crisis triggers in a small town's heart. First came the women with platters of fried chicken and baked hams and pies from their kitchens" (T. Jones, 2006a, p. A4). *Newsweek* wrote that "Della Mae Tallman and the other 33 women of the Homemakers' Club were engaged in a coal-country tradition—preparing a feast of chili, macaroni salad and raised rolls for the Monday funeral of Martin Bennett" (Wingert & Campo-Flores, 2006, p. 45).

Photographic coverage of the Sago incident was dominated by the anguished faces of women and girls. On the front page of *The Pittsburgh Post-Gazette*, an unidentified elderly woman sobbed on the shoulder of West Virginia's governor (Breakdown, 2006, p. A1). The governor also appeared in a *New York Times* photograph that was actually a portrait of grief: its real subjects were a middle-aged woman appearing stricken with fear and disbelief, gazing outward past the governor, and a girl, hanging her head, beside her (Dao, 2006a, p. A1). Middle-aged and young women were similarly paired in other photographs taken at candlelight vigils and funerals. In some cases, the grieving women were not even relatives of the dead: an Associated Press photo featured a mother and teenage daughter, huddled together in tears at the altar of the Sago Baptist Church, with a caption explaining that they had come from Louisville, Kentucky, "to pay their respects … [to] the 12 coal miners who died" (Breed, 2006, p. A3).

Females shown alone tended to be teenagers or young women, symbolizing innocence lost. Daniele Bennett, a granddaughter of one of the dead miners, appeared shocked and furious in a large picture on the front page of *The Washington Post*, a snapshot of the "betrayal" moment when the families learned that the miners had not, in fact, been found alive (Jones & Tyson, 2006, p. A1). A few days after the accident, *USA Today* featured a front-page portrait of 22-year-old Amber Helms, daughter of victim Terry Helms, showing her in profile with her head bowed, in front of the crossed coal chutes that in television coverage had come to represent the mine site. The article led with this all-female scene:

> Sandra Lockwood and Cindy Ware weep when they speak of their 12-year-old niece Katelyn.
> Katelyn's dad, Jesse Jones, was one of 12 coal miners who died in the Sago Mine this week. Like most next of kin, Katelyn spent a long night in Sago Baptist Church, riding the wave of emotions of raised hopes and, grimly, dashed dreams of a miracle rescue. Now, she is left fatherless.
> "What they did to my niece, there are no words to describe," said Ware, 44, choking through tears. (Bazar, 2006a, p. 1A)

A week later, the same newspaper pictured Katelyn Jones in a front-page article—titled "'I never caught up with them,'" a quote from miner Owen Jones, who had been unable to rescue his brother Jesse—that combined two gender tropes. A small photo showed Katelyn, with her head in her hands, gazing downward; the larger picture above showed Owen, his closely-cropped face covered with soot, his eyes tired and pale, his mouth set grimly (Bazar & Vanden Brook, 2006, p. 1A). It was a picture of a man powerless to change his fate (and the fate of men like him) but willingly facing it nevertheless. This was the masculine ideal describing the dead miners across news coverage, and it painted a portrait of regional and class identity as well.

Covering the miners' funerals, *USA Today* quoted a local minister: "Butcher, who comes from a coal mining family, said the miners who perished were members of a unique brotherhood. 'Coal miners are a different breed of men,' he said. 'They don't have any fear'" (Bazar, 2006b, p. 1A). *The New York Times* contained the same remark and quoted the Rev. Donald Butcher's eulogy for miner Jesse Jones: "God gives us people who are heroes, and we don't even realize it. ... America is great because of this profession and because of men like Jesse, who put their lives on the line" (Gately, 2006a, p. A14). In a story featuring West Virginian Rick Price, a "pastor now in a little church in the mountains ... [who] longs to go back underground," *The Los Angeles Times* claimed:

> Men change when they're that far underground; some become gruff or crude, but others gain an almost mellow calm. Price said he found an unexpected contentment in the single-minded focus on clawing coal from the earth, on finding the fuel that that powers America ... . (Huffstutter & Simon, 2006, p. A12)

## "A TRADITION OF SACRIFICE": LABOR AS PATRIOTISM

In such vignettes, news media explained the miners' work as a matter of patriotism, a value system in which taking care of a family (or carrying on a family tradition) was a form of civic duty. In a segment using the music of Johnny Cash as a partial soundtrack, *Good Morning America* reporter Chris Cuomo proclaimed the miners' larger meaning:

> The 12 men who *were taken* [emphasis mine] by the explosion in the Sago mine were much more than victims. They were part of a rich tradition. The coal miner has often been the model for the blue-collar, hard-charging American worker. ... It is much more than a job for them. For more than a century now coal miners have scraped at the earth's deepest reaches, fueling this country. A hard life, a hard living. A job that isn't about money for a miner, but a bond, a special connection between men joined in peril and purpose. ... They say that every time they leave their families they know they might not come back. ... [T]hese men [are] part of something that is bigger than just themselves. It is a tradition of sacrifice that truly helped build this country.

The report included testimony from other miners: "We watch out for one another. We eat one another's food, we care for one another, if one of us is hurt, we take care of them"; "he's your buddy. ... he looks for you and you look for him" (*Good Morning America*, 2006b).

CBS reporter Randall Pinkston interviewed Richard Baisden, one of hundreds of people who came to the funeral services even though they did not know the miners, who said:

> You feel like it's a loved one, and you feel like not just that they're going to go through a healing process, but this is our family and we're going to go through a healing process, too. ... They're our heroes, they're our warriors. They're on the front lines, and I think that they did an outstanding job of standing up for who we are. (*The Early Show*, 2006b)

As overly dramatic as this news-story quote may seem, it directly identifies the mythic themes contained in so much of this kind of journalism. In her study of news coverage of Midwestern floods, Katherine Fry explains how national lessons emerged through images of churches and of the American flag, "signal[ing] the nation's patriotic religion as well as its unity in sacrifice ... representing twin religions. ... It is no surprise that the use of the war metaphor was so prominent" (2003, pp. 63–64). In the Sago story, visual imagery of broadcast and print journalism similarly featured public grieving rituals containing references to these "twin religions" of church and nation, as well as to war.

On a two-page spread, *Newsweek* used a photograph of dozens of townspeople holding candles at a nighttime vigil in front of a church (Wingert & Campo-Flores, 2006, pp. 44–45). News coverage of the dead miners repeatedly referred to them as "fallen," as though they had been killed while fighting for a cause (see, for instance, Breed, 2006, p. A3; Frank, 2006, p. 3A; Gately, 2006a, p. A14) and as "brothers," not only to each other but also to their neighbors, as *NBC Nightly News* reporter Lisa Daniels suggested in this report: "Mourners gather today for prayers; tomorrow they will bury their brothers" (2006d). *Good Morning America* anchor Charles Gibson began an obituary tribute by saying: "They were 12 men, bound together by a brotherhood of the mines" (2006b). *USA Today*'s use of the phrase "band of brothers" (Bazar, 2006a, p. 2A) tied them to early twenty-first-century nostalgia (much of it expressed through media) for "the good war" of World War II.

Newspapers published photographs of a memorial created in the town of Phillippi, West Virginia: a row of crosses—each with a dead miner's name on it and with an American flag planted in front of it—onto which miners' helmets had been set, in imitation of military ritual. One photograph of this scene showed a state trooper bending down to place something in front a cross, amid flowers, candles, and pictures of the miners (Urbina, 2006a, p. A17). *The New York Times* (Harris, 2006, p. A13) published a photograph of black ribbons, their streamers blowing in the wind, tied to a chain-link fence crossing an open field, with small American flags stuck into the ground below. These greatly resembled photographs taken at both the World Trade Center site in New York City and at the temporary (and still standing) memorial on the site of the crash of Flight 93 in Shanksville, Pennsylvania, after the events of September 11. The journalistic attention paid to ritual objects at Sago also paralleled newspapers' ongoing use of many photographs of yellow and black ribbons and American flags on display outside the homes of, and at shrines to, American soldiers killed fighting the "war on terror" in the Middle East. Such images placed the Sago miners' deaths within a visual rhetoric of patriotic sacrifice with national meaning.

## "A SYMBOL OF HOPE HERE": THE SURVIVOR'S STORY

Despite (or perhaps because of) their sacrifices, the Sago story also featured a survivor, a "hero" saved: Randal McCloy, who was taken to the hospital in critical condition. During the time he was in a coma, journalists presented a likely scenario leading to his survival: that the other men had protected McCloy with their bodies because, at 26, he was the youngest. Some relayed McCloy's father's belief "that the older miners had given his son their oxygen canisters, knowing that he was the father of two young children" (Grady & Dao, 2006, p. A18).

Like the other men, Randal McCloy was pictured holding his infant daughter, and the press repeatedly underscored his wife's devotion. Photographed initially as one of the weeping potential widows, Anna McCloy appeared in a front-page photograph a month after the accident looking serene and determined, with the caption: "'We Go Home Together': Anna McCloy refuses to go home until her husband is well enough to go with her" (Bazar, 2006c, p. 1A). This did happen in late March 2006, when McCloy was released from the hospital, described by *The Los Angeles Times* as "thin but grateful" (Thin but grateful, 2006, p. A11). The press labeled him the "Miracle Miner" (*Good Morning America*, 2006c; Lash, 2006, p. A1; *World News Tonight*, 2006) and noted that one of his doctors had "likened his ongoing recovery to a resurrection" (Lash, 2006, p. A1; also Thin, 2006, p. A11).

Coverage of McCloy's homecoming contained several contradictions to the initial media story of his survival, and of the miners' supposedly stoic acceptance of the sacrifice required by their calling. His eventual description of what had happened underground contradicted the theory that the other men had protected him. More jarring was his own account of the event, his description of the scene as one not of strength and heroism but of chaos, fear, and anger at the mine company; as he put it in his interview with *Today Show* host Matt Lauer: "You're running like a goose in a damn mine, and you don't even know where you're going. ... We knew ... we was going to end up taking the bullet on that one" (2006d). He gave a similarly inglorious account in the letter he wrote to the dead miners' families, subsequently excerpted in many newspapers: "One person sitting near me collapsed and fell off his bucket . ... I continued to sit and wait, unable to do much else" (Bazar, 2006d, p. 1A).

He also made it clear that he would never go back to mining: "No, I done learned my lesson, the hard way," he said on *The Early Show* (2006c). Three and a half years earlier, Blaine Mayhugh, the youngest of the rescued Quecreek miners, had said the same thing to NBC's Jane Pauley: "I'll never go back underground" (*Dateline NBC*, 2002). Both miners referred to their work not as a calling, but as something they had done only because they needed the money and they had few other opportunities.

Yet these counter-themes were details buried within the happy story of a hero's homecoming. Calling him "a symbol of hope here," ABC's *World News Tonight* (2006) opened its report from Simpson, West Virginia with the image of "[a] jubilant thumbs-up from a four-year-old Randy McCloy, old enough to understand his father is back home, too young to realize his dad beat incredible odds." An Associated Press report printed in *The Washington Post* led with a similar vignette: "It wasn't a fancy homecoming. Just a few dozen balloons, handmade signs, a whole lot of hugs and his wife's homemade lasagna" (Associated Press, 2006, p. A3). The *Pittsburgh Post-Gazette* extended the scene:

> As his giggling son and nieces chased one another on the new wood ramp outside, Randal McCloy Jr. tinkered with a karaoke machine and sank into his living room couch for the first time in nearly three months. In the kitchen, his wife, Anna, assembled the making of a lasagna feast. ... Around them and outside on newly named Miracle Road, relatives and friends grinned, hugged and chatted in the spring sunshine about accompanying Mr. McCloy on trout fishing trip and jaunts in the cherry-red Ford Mustang his wife has ordered for his birthday April 14. (Lash, 2006, p. A1)

Through the themes of fatherhood and marriage, McCloy's final story dovetailed with those that had been told about him while he was in a coma. At the end of the *Today Show* interview, Lauer asked Anna McCloy why she thought he had survived, to which she replied: "I know his determination and his willpower, and I know his love for me and them kids, and I knew that if anybody was [alive], it was going to be him" (2006d). Reporting from the same interview material three nights later on *Dateline NBC* (2006), Lauer's summary was more mythic: "As we learned when we visited with Randy and his wife, Anna, the miracle of his survival is really a combination of things, a medical mystery, yes, but also a story of determination, faith, and maybe most of all, love."

### "NO ONE WAS UP ABOVE LISTENING FOR THEM:" COUNTERNARRATIVES IN LOCAL COVERAGE

*The Charleston* (WV) *Gazette* devoted far more coverage to the Sago story and its consequences than did any other news organization, and it continued to report well beyond the end of the funerals, when the other news media turned their attention elsewhere. Much of this reporting echoed the themes described above, especially those of community, gender roles, and family values. As a previously quoted example reveals, local reporters also described the West Virginia mountains in poetically rural terms. And in its coverage of the eventual government hearings about the accident, the newspaper led with women's suffering, naming one widow or daughter after another: "Peggy Cohen wants to know what happened ... Charlotte Weaver wants someone to explain why ... Debbie Hamner can't understand how" (Ward, 2006b, p. 1A). Yet the *Gazette* provided greater detail on those hearings, reminding its readers of the failure of the miners' equipment and the mine company's slow response. The paper quoted the son of one of the dead, who summed up the miners' final hours: "'They pounded on a bolt, and wasted precious air, and no one was up above listening for them,' he said" (Ward, 2006b, p. 1A).

An op-ed piece published in the *Gazette* even overtly made the military connection merely suggested in the other news media, beginning, "Am I the only one here in West Virginia this week who is seeing the similarity between coal miners and our soldiers?" Yet this writer proceeded to make her case in specifically regional and economic terms missing from the other media metaphors. Noting that the state's beautiful landscape "doesn't allow for much in the way of economic activity," she wrote,

> generation after generation, young people looking to make a way in the world go in two directions: the coal mines and the military. ... Soldiers lose their lives because their armor protects only their chests and backs or their vehicles lack sufficient armor plating.

They die because the brass wants to get somewhere in a hurry ... miners die because they lack simple safety equipment. ... In both cases, making war and mining coal, important people in a hurry for results economize on their human capital. (Rodell, 2006, p. 4A)

This was a rare media perspective, one that understood the Sago miners as representatives of a larger group of people whose socioeconomic status made them perpetually vulnerable, depending on the interests and decisions of those in power.

The West Virginia newspaper (and, to a lesser extent but far more than the other papers, the *Pittsburgh Post-Gazette*) also gave considerable attention to mine safety, unionization, regional economics, and government regulations and investigations.[2] As part of its evident commitment to telling the Sago story as the story of a preventable accident (as opposed to a family tragedy), *The Charleston Gazette* also ran several lengthy features recalling other major mine accidents stretching back a century. Its overall point in doing so was that Sago was *not* an extraordinary story: mine accidents had occurred regularly, with far higher casualty numbers, and always followed by vows of improved safety standards (see, for instance: Tuckwiller, 2006a, 2006b, and 2006c; Ward, 2006a; and Williams, 2006).

The other striking difference in local coverage is that (perhaps merely in its closer attention to every facet of the story) it included narrative subplots, not found in mainstream news coverage, that threatened to mar the picture of the West Virginia families as good, simple, mountain folks. The *Gazette* reported that, while her husband was still in a coma, Anna McCloy—who consistently was depicted in mainstream news media as shy and unassuming—not only sued the tabloid *National Enquirer* for running a picture of the hospitalized Randal McCloy but also sued her husband's brother for providing it to them (Sago survivor's wife sues his brother, 2006; McCloy's wife sues *National Enquirer*, 2006). It included a feature on the high rate of domestic violence in coal mining communities, especially in times of rising unemployment (Berry, 2006). And unlike the other news media, the West Virginia paper included one detail in its coverage of the miners' memorial ceremonies that narratively problematized the comforting role of religion in this story, reporting that, across from the community service, "members of the Kansas-based Westboro Baptist Church held a demonstration ... [and] carried inflammatory signs proclaiming that the 12 miners were in hell because America tolerates the existence of gays and lesbians ... [and] sang a slur-filled version of 'Take Me Home, Country Roads'" (Finn, 2006b, p. 1A).

## DISCUSSION

The hardships of life in a rural mining community were acknowledged in national news coverage as well. Seen from a distance, though, this place—"in the mountain"—was a destination of reminiscence, a land where lost American values were discovered anew, through simple people living close to the earth, dedicated to God, country, and each other. Within this story of regional nostalgia were gendered subplots in which men stood for America's lost strength (as well as its potential resurgence) while women embodied loss and grief (as well as loyalty and faith despite the odds). These news characters combined to form an imagined, ideal community characterized, ultimately, in terms of military sacrifice.

Thus the final narrative performed news repair not just to fix the incorrect report of the miners' survival, but also to create a better story—the "loss of a hero" story. This second narrative enabled the Sago story to have the same kind of inspiring ending the Quecreek story had provided so soon after the September 11 attacks, a lesson about the enduring American spirit embodied by rural people with "real" values. The ultimate journalistic story of Sago was not one about a deadly industrial accident, but one about the life-affirming power of sacrifice through commitment to family and about the survival of long-held national values in regional identity.

Especially in its references to patriotism, the Sago coverage confirms media critics' belief that the press functions to preserve the political status quo and to provide reassurance when national unity is in question. Certainly this story was conservative in its symbolic uses of women and girls as signs of loss, its descriptions of rugged masculinity, and its folksy characterizations of rural life. Yet something else was at work here as well. The Sago coverage supports Michael Schudson's contention that myths "do not tell a culture's simple truths so much as they explore its central dilemmas" (1995, p. 164), and that those dilemmas are evident in journalism.

News' eulogy for the miners corresponded with the widespread reverence, in public ceremony as well as journalism, for American soldiers killed in Iraq, and both of these phenomena have echoed popular-culture tributes to firefighters who died at the World Trade Center. The dead in all of these cases were working-class people, nearly all male, physically strong, but with limited incomes and options. These kinds of news characters have emerged as the most admirable of all American heroes in various kinds of sacrificial-death stories in post-September 11 media—a development that raises interesting questions about the cultural meanings and political uses of class in national identity today.

While news media are a primary forum in which ideas about class are conveyed, those ideas also emerge in the broader public sphere, and the public is implicated in their construction. Much of the national media audience are themselves working-class, and the symbolic valorization of others in their own occupations may serve at least potentially as an affirmative rather than manipulative message (confirming Jack Lule's [2001] suggestion that myth in journalism contains challenges to the status quo even as it works to uphold it). Others in the news audience may identify with what they imagine to be working-class values because they retain their own nostalgic ideas about their parents' and grandparents' lives, a backdrop against which their own lives stand as proof of the American dream of upward mobility.

Indeed, when *The Charleston Gazette* ran letters it received from all over the world, several contained this theme; one began, "I may live in Detroit, but West Virginia is dear to my heart. Some of my fondest memories are of sitting on either of my grandparents' porches watching the trains go by loaded with coal" (Sobolewski, 2006, p. 3C). For this audience, the news theme that the miners (or soldiers or firemen) come from a long line of men in the same occupation is especially resonant, though its appeal to middle-class audiences is ironic: these men are available as heroic symbols only because they have *not* experienced upward mobility (of course, because they are portrayed as fathers, there is always narrative hope for their children).

Although its daily realities are unenviable, working-class life has a powerful symbolic appeal to Americans, and it allows journalists to paint heroic portraits with broad strokes—ideal, nostalgic pictures that nevertheless are legitimized because their present-day subjects *are* so inarguably real. As many scholars (for instance, Bird & Dardenne, 1997; Borman, 1985; Carey, 1987) have noted, the personalization of news naturalizes its themes. If we come to understand, through news coverage of tragedy, that its victims are just like us because they are "families," then their challenges are seen as individual obstacles we applaud them for trying to overcome (by going to work in the mines for the sake of their children), rather than systemic societal problems such as economic inequity and unsafe labor conditions. Illustrating Roland Barthes's (1972) contention that myth "depoliticizes" speech, the Sago coverage naturalized the political backdrop against which this tragedy unfolded.

The political circumstances were not ignored by journalists, though they were defined only in terms of mining. All of the newspapers (less so the television news programs) devoted at least some coverage to mine-safety issues and to the government's failure to collect the fines that already had been imposed on owners operating unsafe mines.[3]

They noted the weakening of the Mine Safety and Health Administration and the erosion of safety standards under the Bush administration. Yet these stories had the same narrative effect as their format: they were sidebars to the main story, which was coherently constructed as one of human bravery, sacrifice, survival, and, ultimately, hope for the future.

From early in the coverage, that forward narrative of hope was told in terms of family. Six weeks after the Sago explosion, *USA Today* published a trend piece on how coal companies have been successful in recruiting new miners despite several recent fatal accidents in West Virginia and Kentucky. Datelined "Core, W.Va.," the article began with this vignette: "Every night, just before his coal-miner class begins, Ryan Boyd marks the date in his notebook. Next to that, he writes 'Levi Hunter,' the name he and his wife, Miranda, chose for their newborn boy. 'That reminds me why I'm here,' says Boyd, 22" (Vanden Brook, 2006, p. 1B).

# III

## The Journalism of Ritual and Tribute

# 8

## "PORTRAITS OF GRIEF"
## AND STORIES THAT HEAL
*The Public Funeral for Victims of September 11*

The events of September 11 presented an unprecedented political, social, logistical, and spiritual challenge to Americans. They also presented a challenge to journalists faced with the task of explaining the seemingly inexplicable. Yet during the first few months after the disaster, a set of themes emerged through which Americans "understood" what had happened: the victims had been typical Americans with family values and a passion for life, the same qualities that would see America itself through this crisis; and, through faith and "pulling together," the country would heal, even learn, from the personal sacrifices made on that day. These themes took shape within a cultural discourse constructed in schools and churches, in businesses and civic events, and, most of all, in news media.

This chapter traces the discussion in journalism of these presumably shared values and the rituals through which journalists offered consolation and closure, and found lessons in circumstances of chaos and horror. It surveys two prominent examples of this process, each a series of articles published throughout the fall of 2001 by media based in either New York City or Washington (two sites of the disaster) yet read nationwide: the "Portraits of Grief" obituary series published in *The New York Times* and the coverage provided by the three major American newsweekly magazines, *Time, Newsweek,* and *U.S. News & World Report.* The analysis traces the ways in which news media helped to create sense and consensus by conducting what was, in effect, a national funeral ceremony.

## PORTRAITS OF GRIEF, REFLECTORS OF VALUES

In the aftermath of September 11, 2001, *The New York Times* began publishing a remarkable series of "Portraits of Grief," small sketches commemorating the lives of individuals lost in the terrorist attacks. Those involved were quick to note that the portraits were not typical obituaries or profiles. In fact, as *New York Times* reporter Barbara Stewart explained in *Columbia Journalism Review,* the portraits "skip most items required in standard obituaries: survivors, lists of colleges, degrees earned, jobs held, descriptions of newsworthy accomplishments." Stewart, who wrote many of the portraits herself, called them "impressionistic sketches, or as one of the metropolitan editors who created them says, 'little jewels.' Like a quick caricature that captures a likeness, they are intimate tales that give an impression, an image of a person" (Stewart, 2002, p. 66).

The portraits began running four days after the World Trade Center collapse and continued as a regular feature until December 31, 2001, when the newspaper suspended their daily publication but promised to continue them sporadically. And they did continue, often filling pages in weekend editions, even as late as the one-year anniversary of the attacks. Response to the portraits was swift and strong, according to published accounts (see R. Clark, 2002; Scott, 2001; Stewart, 2002). *New York Times* Metro Editor Jon Landman, quoted in the *New Yorker,* said: "Nobody involved in this had any idea early on that this would turn into some kind of national shrine" (Singer, 2002, p. 30).

Though on the surface a simple news story, the obituary has a resounding cultural voice. Beyond identifying the deceased, giving a cause of death and sometimes telling readers details of a funeral, it offers a tiny picture of a life. It is a type of commemoration, representing an ideal, and because it is published or broadcast, that "ideal" is magnified for a mass audience.

The "Portraits of Grief" differed from regular obituaries in certain important respects. First, the portraits were not meant to celebrate elites. The newspaper made a real effort to include as many of those who died in the terrorist attacks as possible, according to published interviews with some of the approximately 100 writers and editors involved (see N. Adams, 2001; Clark, 2002; Scott, 2001; Singer, 2002). Most information was gathered through telephone interviews with family members and friends of the deceased. Stewart explained: "Though a few people have not wanted a profile or have been too upset to be interviewed, the majority have been eager to talk about the people they loved" (2002, p. 66). Thus, "inclusion" was not an issue, at least in terms of *who* was portrayed. The portraits also veered from certain journalistic conventions; as Stewart noted, although they were "meant to be accurate, they are clearly not objective" (2002, p. 66). In the portraits, the cause of death, normally an important part of traditional obituaries, was essentially a mass death. More than 3,000 people died almost at a single moment, from the same "cause." The portraits were also much shorter than most *New York Times* obituaries, most averaging about 300 words whether the deceased was a corporate executive or an immigrant laborer.

The portraits remembered victims individually. Yet published together on full pages, with photographs and under single dominant headlines, they made a powerful statement collectively. The portraits also have been published as *Portraits 9/11/01: The Collected Portraits of Grief from The New York Times*, and a few selections were broadcast in a documentary on the Discovery Channel on September 11, 2002.[1] Obituaries historically have served as a type of model of ideal values in a society (Hume, 2000), and these portraits, because of their commemorative nature, would have served as their own type of cultural model. They, too, provide a fascinating glimpse into social values in the days and months following the attacks, a tragic and anxious time for New York and the United States.

The first study in this chapter examines 427 "Portraits of Grief" published between September 15, 2001 and December 31, 2001 in *The New York Times*. The sample was drawn from the newspaper's Web site, including every fifth portrait published on each day as indicated in daily indexes on the site. Analysis focuses primarily on the personal attributes of the deceased. Five major themes, or categories, emerged in these 427 portraits, as well as a number of threads that were less significant in terms of percentages but provide some cultural insight. The major themes include devotion to family; passion, talent or interests outside work; a work ethic; generosity, humor and humanity; and good health or energy.

In the sample examined, 349 (82 percent) of the portraits were of men and 78 (18 percent) were of women. Occupations of the deceased were naturally reflective of jobs housed within the Twin Towers of the World Trade Center, of those who might have had cause to be in the buildings on the morning of September 11, and of police and firefighters who arrived at the disaster site to help and were killed in action. A few portraits in the sample were of those who died in the airplanes hijacked in the attack. In addition to emergency service providers, occupations included brokers, traders, risk management specialists, insurance executives, numerous corporate vice presidents and other officers, accountants, human resources specialists, chefs, government workers, clerical workers, engineers, computer specialists, mechanics, a sculptor, a wine master, photographer, waitress, retired geography professor, maintenance worker, and fire and building safety directors. Thus, this study does not argue that these portraits reflect a cross-section of New York, New Jersey, and Connecticut society. However, in some respects the portraits were more reflective of a diverse population than the obituary pages of many metro dailies and the *Times*, as they included immigrants, clerical workers, and waiters on equal footing with corporate executives. Causes of death were implied rather than stated, the word "died" seldom used, and funeral arrangements rarely mentioned, likely because most of the bodies had not been recovered at the time the portraits were published.

## DEVOTION TO FAMILY

Devotion to family was by far the attribute most often featured in the sample of "Portraits of Grief" examined for this study, a number likely influenced by the fact that family members were the sources most often used. Eighty-two percent of men and 72 percent of women were remembered for familial associations. And rather than listing family simply as "survivors," as do so many traditional modern obituaries, these portraits included much more active and social connections between the deceased and spouses, children, parents, grandchildren, grandparents, nieces, nephews, and cousins.

Relationships between parents and children were vividly portrayed. The men coached and cheered their children's soccer, track and football teams and attended dance recitals, rode horseback or motorcycles with children, or simply took weekend drives or shopped with them for groceries (see, as examples: Always making, Family first, Golf, Manners, and One office, all 2001[2]). Women, too, cheered at their children's athletic events, took bicycle rides and trips, attended concerts, played games, dressed up for Halloween with the kids, and participated in school activities (see, as examples, Donna Marie Giordano, Family costume, Handling, Jeannine M. Laverde, Linda Rivera, A maximum, and Time for her sons). John Patrick Gallagher played hooky from work on the Friday before his death "so he could treat his wife, Francine, and 2-month-old son, James Jordan, to a day at the Bronx Zoo" (John Patrick Gallagher, p. B6). Venesha Richards "couldn't wait" to see her daughter's first step (Venesha Richards, p. B8). Firefighter Raymond York "was a Little League coach, he was a scout leader—when it came to his kids, he was there for everything" (He always, p. A10).

Many portraits focused on the bond between the deceased and wives or husbands, often reminiscing about the earliest moments of the relationships. For example, more than 40 of the male portraits and 12 of the female ones presented nostalgic snapshots of how the couples met, one in a Staten Island pub, another on the subway, one at Macy's, another at a university alumni meeting, or on a hiking trail in New Hampshire, or when he cut in front of her in a line (see Arthur Warren Scullin, Craig Montano, Frederick Rimmele, His bright, and Love at first). These meetings often had a fairy-tale quality about them, as when David G. Carlone announced on their first date that he would marry his wife, Beverly (Catching up). And the idyllic unions continued. Equities trader Joshua Aron often sent love notes to his wife (Joshua Aron). Noel J. Foster and his wife Nancy were "extremely in love" and had just celebrated their tenth wedding anniversary (Blue eyes, p. B11). Donald H. Gregory, 62, kissed his wife at the start and end of each day (A family man's, p. B11). Indeed, the social value of the ties between husband and wife, parent and child was so strong that some portraits even celebrated that value in single people. Gerard P. Dewan, for example, had always planned to have children, and found a substitute home and family after renting the basement apartment of friends (Gerard P. Dewan). Michael Tarrou had never asked his girlfriend to marry him, but his portrait assured readers: "No one doubts that would have happened" (Wanting, p. B9).

Other family relationships were important, too. For example, Ysidro Hidalgo-Tejada cooked dinners for his extended family and cared for his 90-year-old diabetic mother (Ysidro Hidalgo-Tejada). Michelle L. Titolo sipped afternoon tea with her sister (Michelle L. Titolo). One corporate vice president installed a garage door opener for his sister, while another organized multi-generation "tomatofests" when the extended family gathered to can enough tomatoes to last the winter (Joseph Sacerdote, Always in demand, and Salvatore F. Pepe). Giovanna Poras was "like a second mother to her nephews" (Living the life, p. B13) and Manny DelValle Jr. "was the one in the family who always sent a card and gift to siblings, half-siblings and cousins" (Carpe diem, p. B11).

Yet the portraits often hinted at how difficult it was for these mostly professional, white-collar men and women to find time for such strong familial relationships. Often the portraits would point out how the deceased "managed to find time" to come home, or perhaps had taken a less demanding job for family reasons, as did one engineer who "had carved out a 'Father Knows Best' kind of life, with him coming home at six every evening, choosing to know his family well rather than to work longer hours for more money" (David Kovalcin, p. B8). One father sent his children online messages from work because he left home before they got up for school (The perfect); another would juggle his schedule, eating lunch with his family if he had a dinner meeting. The article quoted his wife: "I think it was shocking to his clients who would call to find out that he was gone for an hour but he would be back from reading in his daughter's class" (David B. Brady, p. B8). A few pointed regretfully to missed opportunities with families, but always ended on a positive note (see, as examples, A long and A way). Indeed, most of these portraits made clear that family was a priority, even for a successful corporate executive. Tom Burke, remembered as the "quintessential Wall Street man," exemplified this trait:

> "He was successful, but that's not what made him happiest," said his sister, Nancy Salter. "It was his family." That was the part the young guns did not see, the part not learned in college. Tom Burke's mother always had a happy birthday. Tom Burke's family never wondered where Daddy was. Tom Burke's friends never lay sick, alone. (Bonds, p. B12)

## PASSIONS OUTSIDE WORK

In addition to strong family relationships, terrorist attack victims featured in the "Portraits of Grief" were remembered for having passions, talents, or interests outside the office. Such passions were mentioned in 50 percent of the men's portraits and 46 percent of the women's.

For the men, the most often listed interests were sports, particularly the New York professional teams, and world travel. For the women, travel topped the list. Travel for one woman was a "yearly ritual: pick a part of the world and explore it" (Exploring, p. B9). Another man would "every year grab his passport and head as far as his savings would take him—Spain, Italy, Nice, Monaco, Ireland" (He traveled, p. B11). Both the men and women were remembered for engaging in all kinds of physical activities, both indoor and outdoor. The most popular of these for the men were golf, fishing, hunting, skiing, sailing, scuba, dancing, and cycling. The women, too, rode horseback, skied, hiked, and kayaked. Food and cooking, theater, music, and movies were popular passions for both genders, as were shopping and gardening or home improvement. Susan L. Schuler, for example, had "transformed her standard-issue, quarter-acre backyard in Allentown, N.J., into a dazzling botanical paradise" (Susan L. Schuler, p. B7). A number of men and women were noted for church affiliations and for religious faith. David Brady, for example, was "a devout Catholic" who "attended Mass almost every day and occasionally wrote prayers" (David B. Brady, p. B8).

The portraits indicate that the deceased had been actively involved in their passions, not just passive observers. They were artists, or craftswomen, readers, writers, chefs, history buffs, photographers, and carpenters. One man loved bull riding (Thomas Foley). Another was "nutty over lighthouses" (Feeling Maine's). Still another loved inventing and had "built 40 fully functioning crossbows, most of them patented" (Simon V. Weiser). The men were passionate about cars, particularly red ones, and both men and women loved their motorcycles (see, as examples, Always making, Dominick Pezzulo, Edward R. Vanacore, Joe Romagnolo, and Michael A. Marti). Most of these passions were listed simply, letting the regret over the lost life remain implied rather than stated. However, occasionally a portrait would note the loss, as did the one for Susan M. Getzendanner, a corporate vice president. It said:

> Ms. Getzendanner, 58, had a great grin, and silver-gray hair that she never dyed. She lived on the Upper East Side and worked behind the scenes for the Blue Hill Troupe, an amateur group of Gilbert and Sullivan players. On weekends, she went to her cottage at the foot of Mount Riga in Connecticut, which, like her apartment, was filled with handicrafts and art from her travels. Her brother Tom Getzendanner lamented the fact that a woman who spent her life traveling foreign lands and trusting others was killed in an act of international terrorism. (Business, p. B11)

## WORK ETHIC

Despite the numerous passions for, or interests in, activities outside the office, individuals commemorated in this sample of *New York Times* "Portraits of Grief" had a strong work ethic. This attribute was remembered in 46 percent of the women and 43 percent of the men, and in fact, only one of the 427 portraits examined for this study admitted that the deceased did not enjoy his work (but it was quick to note he enjoyed his life) (Eugene Clark). Indeed, "loved" was the descriptor most often used when explaining how the deceased felt about their jobs. Many were remembered for how early they would get to the office and how late they would stay. "Peggy Alario's Bronco was always the first one in the commuter lot and the last out," her portrait noted (Time for, p. B15). Gary Shamay was often at work by 5:30 a.m., and Denise Elizabeth Crant would arrive at 6:30 and "then she would leave a voice-mail message for her brother, teasing him about his 'banker's hours'"

(Gary Shamay and Denise Elizabeth Crant, p. B10). Giving 100 percent at work was not enough. One trader gave 150 percent; a firefighter, 300 percent (Giving and Patrick J. Brown). Others were noted for their hard work, persistence, dedication, innovation, success, skill, responsibility, self-reliance, industry, determination, ambition, and drive. They were hard-driving go-getters who worked full throttle at careers that were exciting and fulfilling. For bond trader Patrick J. Buhse, "the yelling, screaming, posturing and power plays of the trading floor" were "his idea of nirvana" (Living large, p. B11). For Edelmiro Abad, a senior vice president, "The company was a second home ... and its staff another family" (One office, p. B15). And the building they worked in was special, too. Charles Henry Karczewski "loved 'that stupid trade center,'" according to his wife. "Every time they drove by the buildings, he would say, "I work there'" (Loved wine, p. B 11).

Firefighters and immigrants particularly were noted for dedication to their jobs. For example, many firefighters were remembered for volunteering to work at different stations when off duty from their main assignments. One had just returned to work, "a tremendous victory," after a long, difficult recuperation from burns suffered on the job (Back at, p. B13). Another did everything "over the top," and another "loved even the unromantic parts of the job, like fire inspections" (Fred Ill, p. B7). When it came to firefighting, Thomas Foley "said it was the best job in the world and he would never give it up" (Thomas Foley, p. B11). Immigrants were remembered for their difficult climb, for holding several jobs at once, and for the pride, even joy, they took in their work (see, as examples: Abdoul Karim Traor, A Dream, Never liked, Things were, and Yaphet J. Aryee). Lucille Francis, who moved to the United States from Barbados in 1986, "took immense pride in polishing the brass and vacuuming the much-trod carpets of Windows on the World on the 107th floor of 1 World Trade Center. She always insisted that her rooms be as perfect as the view" (Never liked, p. B8). Manuel Asitimbay, an immigrant from Ecuador and proud cook at Windows on the World, "took such joy in the food he prepared" (A dream, p. B11).

## GENEROSITY, HUMOR, AND HUMANITY

Working long hours was a valued quality among those who perished in the terrorist attacks, but according to their "Portraits of Grief," greed was not the reason for all that work. Forty-five percent of men and 35 percent of women were remembered for positive human qualities, including generosity. As the portrait for Patrick Buhse said: "What he liked even better than amassing money was giving it away" (Living large, p. B11). Trader Scott McGovern had "silent charities," and was a "secret Santa" for the son of a struggling single mother who did not know his identity until after his death (A secret, p. B11). One man "kept extra winter jackets in his Jeep in case he spotted a shivering homeless person" (Eugene Whelan, p. B6). Sometimes even family members learned of generous acts only after September 11. "Strangers who did not know his [one firefighter's] name came by with fruit baskets to tell of how he helped fix their fences or change their tires" (Michael Paul Ragusa, p. B7). Indeed, firefighters especially were remembered for generosity, as was Fred Ill Jr., who not only saved a man's life in a subway accident but "later stayed nearby as the man learned to walk on artificial legs, and he helped to find scholarships for the man's children" (Fred Ill, p. B7).

Yet even more prevalent than generosity in these portraits was sense of humor. Again and again, men and women were remembered for making others laugh, as did Charles Austin McCrann, a levelheaded and respected executive who "would surprise someone taken in by his straight appearance with a funny duck walk as he left the room" (A past, p. B11). Brothers John Vigiano and Joseph Vigiano "hatched pranks that were wicked in their creativity but gentle in their impact" (John Vigiano, p. B8). Individuals, too, were often remembered for distinctive laughs, for smiling, and for loving life, as was Moises Rives, who "imbibed life in big gulps" (Some kind, p. B8). The deceased were loyal, friendly, nice, kind, thoughtful, fun, decent, solid, trustworthy, optimistic, honorable, honest, genial, graceful, playful, respectful, warm, easygoing, tolerant, fair, and positive. Both men and women were remembered for being gentle and sweet and for having big hearts.

## GOOD HEALTH OR ENERGY

Perhaps because many of the victims of September 11 were so young, they were remembered for good health and energy, including 16 percent of the men and 18 percent of the women. They were runners who participated in races or marathons (see, as examples, Catching up, George C. Cain, and A strong). Many were remembered simply for working out, for eating right or being physically fit. Joseph V. Maggitti was "always a jock" (Joseph V. Maggitti, p. B8), and Donald Foreman was known for "playing basketball with kids young enough to be his grandchildren" (He kept, p. B11). One Port Authority property manager was not content simply to climb 110 flights of stairs during his lunch-hour fitness routine. "That would be wimpy. Instead, he would go all the way to the subbasement of the World Trade Center and begin his climb there. And it was also not enough to simply climb to the top. He would descend the stairs as well" (He would, p. B11). The deceased had energy, were natural athletes, and were strong, like Venesha Richards, "a one-woman power plant" (Venesha Richards, p. B8). The portraits reflect shock that such lives were taken so suddenly. As one grieving father said of his son: "We don't have anything but an urn. … He was a bundle of energy, and now there is no energy" (A bundle, p. B8).

## OTHER NARRATIVE THREADS

Several other themes appeared in these 427 "Portraits of Grief" and offer insight into cultural values. One was home ownership, mentioned in 29 of the portraits. Home was a sanctuary, fixing it up a hobby, entertaining in it a pleasure. "It's our dream house," one widow said (Death, and a new life, p. B11). Another theme was bravery, mentioned in 36 of the male obituaries, often in reference to firefighters, police officers, and other rescue workers, most of whom were believed to have rushed into the burning buildings or raced to work as soon as the alarm sounded (see, as examples: George Howard, Leonard W. Atton, and Robert Regan). But it was not just rescue workers who were noted for bravery. One engineer was last seen making sure no one was left behind in his office on the 64th floor; a hotel executive calmly helped with the evacuation and then was trapped with two injured firefighters (His motto and "Go ahead"). These men were not remembered as victims. Barry J. McKeon, who worked for Fiduciary Trust International, for example, surely died while helping others. Said his best friend: "I'm totally convinced if Barry had thought of himself on Sept. 11, he'd still be alive. … If he saw someone struggling, he'd be the last one out" (Barry J. McKeon, p. B8). Another theme was love of pets, remembered in fewer portraits but with vivid detail, often describing the pets as children. For example, Frankie Serrano was remembered for spoiling his 109-pound Neapolitan mastiff. His girlfriend said: "All the toys he bought him, you can't imagine. It was like his child" (Frankie Serrano, p. B8).

Several portraits dealt with coincidence and mysticism surrounding the deaths: a fortuitous phone call made to a mother, not on the regular day; a man known in his basketball-playing youth as a Twin Tower; a premonition in the form of a sleepless night; a recent love letter from someone not known for such sentiment (Lonny Stone, David Kovalcin, Love to fill, and An easygoing). One man labored for decades over filling and labeling photo albums. "The last photo he ever entered … was one of him in a helicopter flying over Lower Manhattan, staring at the World Trade Center" (Dennis L. Devlin, p. B8).

Finally, 29 of the portraits mentioned idiosyncrasies of the deceased, qualities that might once have annoyed family members, co-workers, and friends. Yet because the portraits were not meant to be objective, and because commemorations are by nature flattering, these qualities were presented in positive, almost bemused ways, as quirks. One man changed clothes a lot; another chatted with toll booth operators (much to his children's dismay); another was so quiet his wife once asked if he was in the witness protection program (Arthur Warren Scullin, Louis J. Minervino, and Peter F. Raimondi). One woman was a perfectionist who "often cleaned. Every last spot of dirt" (Determined, p. B11). One man's friends called him "Prozac" because "sometimes he needed to calm down a little" (Tarel Coleman, p. B8). Another man beat up his future wife's boyfriend "and took her. Caveman-like, pretty much" (A fight, p. B8). Another had a "parade of girlfriends" paying condolence calls, each wearing one of his firehouse T-shirts. His mother said: "They all think they're the only one that has one. … I'm dying the whole visit, hoping another one doesn't show up at the same time" (Jimmy Riches, p. B7). Such traits were presented with humor by family members or friends who wanted to remember the deceased not as saints, but as human beings.

## SHARED VALUES

The Portraits struck a chord with readers and journalists, and were part of the newspaper's 2002 Pulitzer Prize-winning coverage. They were discussed on talk shows and written about in publications from *Slate's* online "Chatterbox" to the academically oriented *Chronicle of Higher Education*, which noted that the Portraits "prompted some of the strongest reader responses in reader memory" (The democratization, 2002, p. B4). Though written for and about people mainly in New York, New Jersey, and Connecticut, these portraits reached the wider audience of *The New York Times*, communicating cultural values to readers beyond a limited regional community.

The Portraits also offer scholars and historians glimpses into the tensions between dominant cultural values. These New Yorkers struggled mightily to juggle their work and family ethics, their passion for life with their responsibilities. Time became the metaphor. Many obituaries spoke of families waiting for Mom or Dad to get home at a particular time, of children who were tucked in at night by a working parent and how special that daily moment was. Many portraits spoke of precious time spent with husbands or wives. In fact, the value of marriage and parenthood was so strong that even single people were remembered for spouses they might have married, children they might have had. The value of kindness and humor was so dominant that even personality idiosyncrasies were remembered with kindness and humor. No matter what major value—family, outside interests, work, generosity/humor and health/energy—the portraits remembered activity. Individuals were always on the move, whether working or traveling or even performing acts of kindness.

In the portraits, as in most traditional obituaries, there was no room for greed, or impatience, or laziness, or weakness or fear in those mostly young Americans whose lives were taken, omissions that brought some criticism that the Portraits were a "bland reincarnation" (Mallon, 2002, p. 7). Only the rarest of Portraits indicated any kind of sadness in the deceased's lives. In fact, these individuals were noted for loving life and for living it abundantly. There was an electricity about all of those portrayed, perhaps remembered so vividly because the losses on September 11 were so great and so sudden. Above all, then, the lives in these "Portraits of Grief" were remembered for being extinguished too soon.

## NEWSMAGAZINES AND SOCIAL RITUAL

While *The New York Times* was eulogizing the typicality of those killed on September 11, celebrating their ordinariness, the nation's three newsmagazines were painting a national portrait, one that united all Americans with the dead through journalistic ceremony, testimony, and, at times, extremely grand language. Heartbreaking details were underscored by an emphasis on optimism, a combination that, in both the *Times* and the newsmagazines, ultimately transformed the victims into heroes. In the broader story told by the newsmagazines, Americans in general—the readers—also played a major role: to embrace a kind of patriotic resolve that would ensure that the subjects of the Portraits series had not died in vain.

The second of the two studies in this chapter considers the more interpretive role of newsmagazine journalism by analyzing a total of 20 issues of *Time, Newsweek,* and *U.S. News & World Report,* including special issues as well as all regular issues published during the month after the attack; it also consulted the three magazines' year-end summary issues to see how, in their cohesive narrative, the story had "turned out" by the close of 2001.[3]

This collective coverage provided a remarkable example not only of the explanatory role of newsmagazine journalism, but also of the role of journalism in national ritual. Indeed, the summary and discussion provided by these three national magazines closely paralleled what anthropologists identify as the three themes of "transition rituals": separation, transformation (or liminality), and aggregation.[4] In that theoretical framework, the first stage is the initial tear in the fabric of society that the death creates, and the resulting shock and disbelief. The second stage is a transitional time when the wound is still raw, when anger and uncertainty upset the social order, when social values are challenged and debated, and yet when answers and healing are sought. The third stage is a re-forming of society with renewal of faith in social values and a commitment to get on with life as a group. Much of the mourning process occurs during the second stage, a "liminal" period in which social hierarchy is replaced by what Victor Turner calls "communitas." He explains that that liminality "can be seen as potentially a period of scrutinization of the central values and axioms of the culture in which it occurs" (1977/1969, p. 167) According to Arnold van Gennep, this examination leads to the third stage, "reunit[ing] all the surviving members of the group" (1960/1908, pp. 164–165). This study uses these three stages of transition rituals as a framework for understanding the evolution of newsmagazine coverage during the month after September 11.

## STAGE ONE, SEPARATION: "I SAW THINGS NO ONE SHOULD EVER SEE"

The newsweeklies' design choices signaled the gravity of the news of September 11—and the start of a funeral ritual. In their special editions published just three days after the attacks, both *Time* and *Newsweek* substituted black for their standard use of red on their covers (on *Time*, the cover border, and on *Newsweek*, the banner behind its logo), and all three magazines used black backgrounds for their pages. (From their first special issues through their year-end issues, *Time* and *Newsweek* continued to set apart their coverage of the disaster and its military aftermath with funereal page-design devices, *Time* using black-and-grey striped side borders and *Newsweek* running a black banner across the tops of pages.) These design choices were just one aspect of the role of visual communication in setting an emotional tone and allowing the reader to become a witness to the events and their aftermath.

Bearing witness and giving testimony were key to the first stage of coverage, which corresponded with what anthropologists call separation—the first stage of the funeral, which is the loss of the dead and the resulting rift in the social order. News coverage of a disaster begins by expressing shock and disbelief, yet also by documenting this rift with detailed testimony, some of it verbal and much of it visual.

*Time*'s first special issue (2001a), published three days after the attacks, consisted primarily of photographs. They showed the second plane hitting the towers, the towers burning, people falling from buildings, the towers imploding, bleeding victims running down streets, firefighters at the scene, debris scattered across the ground, bodies on stretchers, the faces of bystanders as they witnessed the disaster, and the remaining shards of the towers after their collapse. This first edition contained just two articles, one of them opening alongside a photo of the shocked and tearful faces of Iowa schoolchildren watching television coverage.

*Newsweek*'s first issue, also a special issue (2001a), contained many of the same documentary photos, and the same set of subjects and themes. Like those in *Time*, photographs in *U.S. News & World Report*'s first issue (2001a)—showing Manhattanites on the street, looking upward in horror—served to witness the act of witnessing. In her study of the role of photojournalism in Holocaust memory, Barbie Zelizer writes that "This aesthetic—showing witnesses without evidence of the atrocities—forced attention on the act of bearing witness. It froze the act of bearing witness in time and space, inviting readers to attend to what was being witnessed even if it was not shown" (1998, p. 104). As part of a newsmagazine, this process of witnessing witnesses involved the reader as well as the photographer, becoming a triple act of bearing witness to the horror.

*Newsweek* (2001a) included a report it characterized as "dispatches from the front," with a title drawn from one survivor's quote: "I Saw Things No One Should Ever See." This was one of several articles in the newsmagazines in which survivors and close observers provided eyewitness accounts. Most had the rough feel of immediate confession: "I saw it all, I saw it all. I ran. I saw people lying on the street screaming. One man had his face slashed open. There were little children. I didn't stop to help them. My only thought was to save myself"; "All I could see was all the fire and smoke and bits of building and paper floating around like confetti"; "Then the smoke cloud swallowed us all. We could barely breathe. I had ashes in my mouth" (I saw things, 2001, pp. 57, 62–63; Ground zero, 2001, p. 46).

*U.S. News & World Report* noted that the need to "testify" extended beyond survivors and witnesses and was part of the nation's initial disbelief: "Americans talked and talked, struggling to make sense of the carnage. They jammed phone lines, spoke to neighbors over backyard fences, sent emails, gathered around televisions in bars ... they used words to try to make sense of the senseless" (Whitman, 2001, p. 38). The newsmagazines themselves followed this urge. Their articles journalistically reported the day, yet (even if they were more polished) they had the same general tone of shock, anger, and uncertainty as did quotes from witnesses.

In *Time,* Nancy Gibbs wrote: "If you want to humble an empire it makes sense to maim its cathedrals. They are symbols of its faith, and when they crumple and burn, it tells us we are not so powerful and we can't be safe." She asked, "Do we now panic, or will we be brave?" (2001a, n.p.). In a back-page essay for the same magazine (the special issue published three days after the attacks), columnist Lance Morrow used what were perhaps the strongest words in all of the newsweekly coverage: "America needs … to relearn why human nature has equipped us all with a weapon (abhorred in decent peacetime societies) called hatred" (Morrow, 2001, n.p.).

Such anger, unusual in news coverage, is not unusual in grief, and it is part of the transition from the first stage of the funeral ritual to the second—the transformation, or liminal, period, when mourning rituals occur and when the social order is, if only briefly, disrupted. It is in this second stage of such a story that news media are most likely to participate openly in civil religion and to turn from the language of reporting to the language of grief. In this middle period, which was represented primarily in the newsweeklies' second week of coverage, journalistic reporting gave way to mourning and to the same kinds of textual and visual content that are symbolically central to the funeral itself.

## STAGE TWO, TRANSFORMATION (LIMINALITY): "LAMENTING DAY BY DAY"

The anthropologist Jack Goody noted that "the funeral is often an inquest as well as an interment, a pointer to revenge" (1975, p. 5). Morrow's angry essay in *Time* was not the only example of newsmagazine content that conveyed this need for revenge against a villain. Readers' letters printed in the magazines' second week of regular coverage echoed his point and tone: "Osama Bin Laden, you are a coward. … It is time we ended your reign of terror"; "It takes a lot to get us mad, but once you do, we do not rest until we have extracted the last ounce of retribution" (Segna, 2001, p. 8; Daly, 2001, p. 12). Both *Time* (2001b) and *Newsweek* (2001c) used head shots of Bin Laden in which he either was in a red light or the photo was digitally changed to make him appear red, like a devil; *Newsweek* used the image, closely cropped, as its cover. *U.S. News & World Report* (2001c) used his face under the crosshairs of a rifle sight as its second-week cover subject.

In their own language and in the quotes that filled the pages of the newsmagazines' second issues, angry statements also were made within ones expressing religious faith or resolve. *Time*'s cover story printed the lyrics of a hymn sung at the memorial service in Washington's National Cathedral: "And though this world, with devils filled, / Should threaten to undo us, / We will not fear, for God hath willed / His truth to triumph through us" (Gibbs, 2001b, p. 21). The article's author claimed that "the candle became a weapon of war ... for the rest of us who are not soldiers and have no cruise missiles, we had candles, and we lit them on Friday night in an act of mourning, and an act of war" (p. 19). Such writing wove the desire for retribution into the mourning process.

Accompanying the article was a double-page spread of hundreds of people in an Illinois town holding candles in the air at a night-time memorial service. The second-week issues of the newsmagazines included many photographs of spontaneously created shrines—at the sites of the attacks and elsewhere across the country—consisting of candles, flowers, and pictures of the dead. The magazines intertwined these representations of Americans' spontaneous services with their own funereal gestures. The *Time* cover story's title, "Mourning in America," ran across three pages (including a pullout page) and over a photograph of firefighters carrying a flag-draped corpse out of the World Trade Center wreckage; on the other side of this pullout page was a photo of posters showing pictures of the missing people (in effect, a triple act of portraiture), hung on a "wall of prayers" (Gibbs, 2001b, p. 19). In its "Commemorative Issue," published just over a week after the attacks, *Newsweek* included brief obituaries of 41 victims, with photos of them or their surviving relatives (some holding photographs or posters showing the victims) (Lost lives, 2001). *Time* also published brief obituaries of victims, and *Newsweek*'s second regularly dated issue of coverage provided anecdotes or relatives' and friends' quotes about the dead (The victims, 2001; Love and loss, 2001). That issue included a photo of a fire company's window display of portraits of 11 missing firefighters. Inside the station window, on either side of the pictures, were flowers and the American flag; on the outside, visitors had taped handwritten notes of thanks and tribute (as well as an illustration of Christ) to the display (*Newsweek*, 2001b, pp. 16–17).

*Time*'s second dated issue of coverage closed with a photo essay by its distinguished staff photographer James Nachtwey. Together, these images conveyed a situation still emotionally and politically unresolved: a bonds trader, wearing his usual jacket but an American-flag tie, standing dejected on Wall Street; yellow ribbons tied to a fence along the Hudson River; messages (including "Never again", "Feel the pain", "God bless us all") written in chalk on the pavement of a New York City park; a firefighter's face shown on a large television screen above Times Square; and the revised skyline of lower Manhattan seen through the bars of a fence at twilight (Nachtwey, 2001, pp. 88–93). The issue closed with a back-page photo, titled "Farewell," that showed a rear view of two firefighters standing on either side of a flag-draped coffin on a fire truck as it led a funeral procession through Manhattan; a black banner on the back of the truck read, "We will never forget" (Farewell, 2001, p. 114).

This sort of visual eulogy was as ceremonial, religious, and patriotic as it was reportorial, and it was an important component of the news-magazines' second stage of coverage, a way of providing visual tribute and consolation when words still seemed insufficient. The words that *were* included in these middle-stage issues included expressions of condolence from world political leaders and of consolation from religious leaders. The latter addressed the social precariousness of liminality: "'The greatest memorial is not to be afraid'" (Rev. Calvin Butts, Abyssinian Baptist Church, Manhattan); "'evil and death do not have the final say'" (Pope John Paul II); "'if we meet negativity with negativity, rage with rage, attack with attack, what then will be the outcome?'" (the Dalai Lama) (Words, 2001, pp. 74–75). *Newsweek*'s obituaries began with an introduction quoting the poet Henry Wadsworth Longfellow: "'The friends who leave us do not feel the sorrow / Of parting, as we feel it, who must stay / Lamenting day by day'" (Lost lives, 2001, p. 90).

That *Newsweek* introduction, however, also used the poet W. H. Auden's phrase "'let the healing fountain start,'" much as *Time* had included part of Alfred, Lord Tennyson's poem *Ulysses*: "'Tho' much is taken, much abides; and tho' / We are not now that strength which in old days / Moved earth and heaven, that which we are, we are'" (Lost lives, 2001, p. 90; 60 second, 2001, p. 13).[5] This combination of healing and resolution combined ideas about death and life, and about the phenomenon of "life out of death," as in this declaration in *Time*: "So much that was precious has died, but as though in a kind of eternal promise, something new has been born. We are seeing it in our nation and sensing it in ourselves, a new faith in our oldest values, a rendezvous with grace" (Gibbs, 2001c, p. 14). *Newsweek* was full of the same kind of rhetoric:

> Grief and love, rage and vengefulness, pride and defiance—a volatile set of emotions was let loose in America last week. They can be dangerous, but they can also be constructive. It hardly seems possible, or even fitting, to imagine that some good could come out of such horror. But it is not out of reach. (Auchincloss, 2001a, p. 18)

*Newsweek*'s "Commemorative Issue" was published around the same time as the magazine's second dated issue containing the passage above.

Perhaps because it was a glossy, book-like issue meant to be saved as a keepsake, more than any other issue in this study it combined themes of mourning and recovery. This transitional function was suggested by the two items most often featured in its many photographs: lit candles and American flags. The candles were a symbol of grief (separation), while the flags were a symbol of patriotism (aggregation). Yet the dominant symbol by far was the flag, and it was through patriotic gestures that the newsweeklies moved to a resolution of the story.

## STAGE THREE, AGGREGATION: "A NEW FAITH IN OUR OLDEST VALUES"

As a number of scholars (for instance, Firth, 1973; Zelinsky, 1988) have contended, when a tragedy is perceived as distinctly national in nature, the flag takes on civil-religious status. The bold and repeated use of this image on the covers and pages of the newsweeklies was part of a national ceremony that was conducted inside and beyond news media. It included news media in the ritual of flag display outside homes and businesses across the country.

Twenty photographs showing the flag—including the cover photo of a little girl waving one—appeared in *Newsweek*'s "Commemorative Issue" alone, which contained an article claiming that "if we've learned nothing else this year, we know that the idea represented by the flag can never be taken from us" (Alter, 2001, p. 80). For their issues dated September 24 (their second issues after the attacks), all three of the newsweeklies used the American flag on their covers. The letters in the normally red logo of *Time* were red, white, blue, and black, drawing further attention to the flag held up by President George Bush in the cover photo. *U.S. News & World Report* and *Newsweek* used cover photos of firemen raising flags. (The latter one—published under the coverline "God Bless America"—became the most widely circulated image of the patriotic-recovery narrative.)

All three magazines profiled and praised the "heroes," including survivors and firefighters, who had made sacrifices and had showed what *U.S. News & World Report* called, in one title, "Courage under Terrible Fire" (The heroes; McDonald; Stein, all 2001). This shift of focus from victims to heroes helped to effect a transition from death to life, and it coincided with the rhetorical shift from shock to sorrow to patriotism. The story of heroes was a story of hope rather than despair, and heroism and hope were described as aspects of the unalterable American character. Listing many of the same common values that emerged in the "Portraits of Grief," a writer in *Newsweek*'s "Commemorative Issue" declared:

In the aftermath of September 11, it became fashionable to say, "Nothing will ever be the same." That isn't true. … There are many strands in the national fiber. Bold ones like heroism and solidarity and sense of purpose, which were on such impressive display after the attack. And also more modest ones, like individuality, humor, frivolity and fun. … They will be back, and soon, because terrorists could not possibly destroy them. America is getting back to normal. (Auchincloss, 2001b, p. 18)

In their third regularly dated issues after the attacks, all three news-magazines, while retaining themes of witnessing and mourning, looked forward to recovery. *Time*'s cover story was illustrated by a photograph of visitors taking pictures at the World Trade Center site (yet another triple act of witnessing when it included the reader), and its title asked, "What comes next?" (Gibbs, 2001d, p.22). *Newsweek* contained a report on what sort of memorial might be built for the World Trade Center victims and ran a double-page spread photo of hundreds of Broadway actors and actresses filling Times Square and singing for the filming of a New York tourism advertisement called "Let's go on with the show" (McGuigan, 2001; Stepping out, 2001). The issue profiled families struggling to make ends meet after the death of a breadwinner, reporting serious problems but concluding with a quote from one widower: "'But I have faith in America. We'll pull through this as a country." The writer of this story had the last word, declaring: "A nation wishes them Godspeed" (McGinn, 2001, p. 53).

By their fourth regularly dated issues, there were indications in all of the newsweeklies that, while the ongoing war would remain news for some time, the "story" of the tragedy was coming to a close. *Time*'s double-page photo of "The Site" (2001, pp. 86–87)—an image that served both as news coverage and as a tribute—was the only reference to the New York aspects of the tragedy; the rest of the issue focused on the war and the possibility of future acts of terrorism, as did the other magazines.[6] Only 20 pages in *U.S. News & World Report* were about the attack and war, and, perhaps more tellingly, they were followed by a 45-page special section (with correspondingly themed advertisements) on online education (Special report, 2001); *Newsweek*'s issue the same week contained a 26-page section on "Fall health & fitness" (Special advertising section, 2001). The newsmagazines were literally back to business as usual.

Yet the closing of the story did not seem to be merely a construction of journalism; it was endorsed by "Americans" as well. Throughout their coverage, the newsweeklies had extensively featured anecdotes about, photographs of, and quotes from ordinary people like the readers—victims, survivors, witnesses, and mourners whose stories fit into the narrative evolving from despair to hope. These reader letters—printed in issues dated October 15, closing the first full month of coverage—were just two of many echoing the magazines' own language:

> Those who are working in the rubble teach us daily lessons in true grit. I will learn them. In the name of the fallen, I will walk justly, fear no evil and continue to sing America's songs. (Austin, 2001, p. 11)

> [from a New Yorker:] America needs to know that, for all the carnage, New York has not been brought to its knees. Like all families after a funeral, it's getting on with life. Sadder, inevitably, and with indelible memories of the tragedy, but nonetheless moving ahead. New York and America will survive. (Malachowski, 2001, p. 19)

## THE BROADER NARRATIVE AND THE YEAR-END ISSUES

During the month following the September 11 attacks, the three major American newsweekly magazines provided a chronicle of the tragedy and its aftermath, a story with a beginning, middle, and end. In the last week of the regular coverage discussed here, *Newsweek* reprinted its previous three covers (of dated weekly issues)—showing, respectively, the firefighters raising the flag at the World Trade Center site, the red-tinged face of Osama bin Laden, and a cover story on preparing for chemical warfare—with the caption: "Chronicling terror and recovery: From the attacks to the probe to the road ahead" (Letters, *Newsweek*, 2001c, p. 16).

All of the *Time* cover stories discussed here were by the same writer, Nancy Gibbs. Although the reporting for those stories was done by a team of journalists (a practice common to newsweekly journalism), the use of one writer provided stylistic continuity and a perspective that allowed her, and *Time*, to see the bigger "story" of the attacks and their aftermath. Nancy Gibbs also wrote the cover story for *Time*'s year-end issue summarizing the lasting meaning of the September 11 story. By then, she placed the attack within a broader narrative of war and generational heroism:

> We did not expect much from a generation that had spent its middle age examining all the ways it failed to measure up to the one that had come before—all fat, no muscle, less a beacon to the world than a bully, drunk on blessings taken for granted. ... The terrorists were counting on our cowardice. They've learned a lot about us since then. And so have we. (Gibbs, 2001/2002, p. 36)

This characterization drew on turn-of-the-century collective memory (which had been constructed largely through American journalism and film) of the generation that fought World War II. Strangely, it excluded from the story of September 11 anyone younger than "middle age," including most firefighters and many World Trade Center victims. Yet this characterization described the issue's cover subject, *Time*'s "Person of the year," New York City Mayor Rudolph Giuliani, who (along with runner-up President George W. Bush) presumably stood for redeemed American Baby Boomers with their own new war against foreign evil.

*Time*'s year-end issue (2001/2002) discussed the attack in a documentary but primarily memorial way, with black-and-white photographs, printed on black-bordered pages, of visitors looking at the site weeks after the attacks and of the lower Manhattan skyline without the World Trade Center towers. The issue also included a full-color picture taken from ground level, looking upward at the towers, whole, against a deep blue sky. *U.S. News & World Report*'s cover (2001/2002) combined memorial and optimism with a black background for its coverline, "A nation reborn: How America is moving ahead." *Newsweek* (2001/2002) used the burning Trade Center towers to form the "11", with "SEPT" above them, against the black background of its cover, but its skyline promoted an article titled "Who's next: People for the future."

*Newsweek* devoted the most attention to revisiting the early horror of the events. Its cover story, titled "The day that changed America" (Thomas, 2001/2002) focused particularly on firefighters, the group who had by year's end emerged as the primary heroes of the broader American story of the tragedy. The article opened alongside not a photograph but an illustration of a firefighter, reaching out (toward the reader) as smoke billowed behind him. One New York City firefighter, Bill Feehan, was prominent among the characters through whom it told "The story of September 11." The article included photographs of Feehan's son and son-in-law wearing fire gear and his two grandsons, little boys shown wearing firemen's helmets, and concluded with these passages:

> "Your grandfather was a hero, and he was killed by this," Brian told his son. "You must never forget him." ... Connor tells almost anyone he sees that when he grows up, he is going to be a fireman, too. ...

> Some firefighters are recalling the words of Tennyson's "Charge of the Light Brigade." "Was there a man dismay'd? / Not tho' the soldier knew / Someone had blundered: / Theirs not to make reply, / Theirs not to reason why, / Theirs but to do and die." (Thomas, 2001/2002, p. 71)

## DISCUSSION: THE HEALING POWER
## OF "EVERY AMERICAN"

This was an especially grand gesture, and it would be echoed in February 2002, when CBS aired the documentary film *9-11*, the first of many media texts to tell the story of September 11 as a story of the blue-collar bravery of firemen. As dramatic as *Newsweek*'s use of Tennyson may seem, it dovetails with the central themes of the *New York Times* series. For those remembered in the "Portraits of Grief," the larger qualities were the simplest ones—love of family, a work ethic, generosity, humor, good health. These victims became icons of familiarity, of the egalitarian virtues of the "everyAmerican."

Indeed, it was in this way that the Portraits differed most from obituaries, which highlight what the deceased did to distinguish themselves[7]; instead, they celebrated typical qualities. In his study of the mythological categories of editorial coverage of September 11, Jack Lule also notes this emphasis: "These were, after all, the paper stressed, ordinary people like us" (Lule, 2002, p. 282). Similarly, "real people"—victims, heroes, and mourners (who stood in for the reader)—were highlighted by the newsmagazines, especially during the middle stage of their coverage, the "liminal" period marked by anger and shock more than resolution. In news, writes Lule, the character of the common man helps to "give meaning to incredible events, to explain that which cannot be explained and to reaffirm values and beliefs, especially when those values and beliefs are challenged" (2001, p. 276).

*Newsweek*'s portrait of Bill Feehan would have fit well into the *Times*'s memorial Portraits. Like those who died in the towers above him, he was an ordinary person just doing his job. He did it selflessly and bravely for his family, just as the others cherished family and lived life to the fullest. He was portrayed as a common man who was nevertheless ideal.

Journalists' idealization of the victims of September 11 may call into question the accuracy of their reporting. Yet the accuracy of these stories is not as important as their cultural function. Narratives about death contribute to society by strengthening it collectively and by highlighting the importance of its individual members. They also provide an occasion to assess shared values and to construct future collective memory. Michael Kammen notes that national memories are more likely to be "activated and strengthened by conflict and the desire for reconciliation" (1991, p. 13), which certainly was the mood of New York and the nation in the uncertain weeks following September 11, 2001.

Moreover, sacrificial death stories in journalism ultimately are optimistic, looking toward the future. The newsmagazine coverage and the "Portraits of Grief" left Americans with an overall story bearing remarkable resemblance to what Edward Linenthal calls the "progressive narrative" that emerged in cultural responses to the 1995 Oklahoma City bombing. This story included the courage of victims and survivors but focused more on moving anecdotes about rescue volunteers:

> If the bombing was an event that would be remembered as a terrorist act of mass murder, the response would be recalled as a heroic saga, a moral lesson to be told and sung and celebrated for generations to come. ... Its most powerful theme, expressed in the language of civic renewal ... [was:] New life springs from death. (Linenthal, 2001, pp. 46, 49, 53)

It is through the major news media that this final message is constructed and conveyed after a national crisis, and that audiences feel that they, too, are a part of the story, able to participate in the ceremony of memorial coverage. They can witness the scenes of disaster, hear survivors' testimony and leaders' consolation, and see their own representation as mourners. And they can mourn the dead because they come to "know" them through the stories news media tell about the meanings of their lives. Although a crisis event initially happens in one place to particular people, when those people are explained as being "just like us," a narrative transformation takes place through which the event itself becomes a shared American experience—and larger, lasting lessons emerge in journalism.

# 9

## REPORTING ON "A GRIEVING ARMY OF AMERICANS"

*Citizen Testimony in the Misremembering of Ronald Reagan*

In a 1983 speech, Ronald Reagan paid tribute to the heroism of "ordinary Americans who never make the headlines and will never be interviewed" (Reagan, 1983). Yet this former actor, who as President liked to spotlight altruistic citizens in his State of the Union addresses, knew full well the symbolic power of the common man in heroic narratives. Indeed, interviews with ordinary Americans—and in a broader sense, the *idea* of a shared commonness that explained national values—were what ultimately validated the extraordinary amount of news coverage of Reagan's final scene.

"This week Americans mourned the passing and celebrated the life of a fellow citizen who, for all the pageantry of office, often seemed like the neighbor next door or just down the street," *CBS News* anchor Dan Rather said on the day of Ronald Reagan's burial (*48 Hours Investigates*, 2004). That service was the last of five official rituals that dominated journalism for more than a week after his death from Alzheimer's disease at age 93, on Saturday, June 5, 2004.

Media critics shook their heads in dismay at the amount and nature of this coverage. Thomas Kunkel, the dean of the University of Maryland's College of Journalism, wrote as editor of *American Journalism Review*: "Television, as has become typical in the big stories, was the worst offender, turning Reagan's life and death into visual wallpaper. But the torrent of worshipful, uncritical newspaper coverage—open page after open page—was scarcely better." Yet his conclusion echoed the very tone of the journalists he chided, as well as their own rhetorical conflation with "America" by the end of the week:

> I think many of those thousands of people who waited hours to pay their respects didn't so much agree with Ronald Reagan's views as they were thanking someone who rose above the pettiness of it all, who was the last of the gentlemen politicians. ... We were transfixed by the Reagan funeral and pageantry, so laden with symbolism and reminding us of the possibilities of America. (Kunkel, 2004, p. 4)

This chapter is based on nearly 1,000 news reports published or aired during the week following Reagan's death in four types of journalism: the ten top-circulation newspapers; the news programs of the three national broadcast television networks, ABC, NBC, and CBS; National Public Radio; and the three major newsweekly magazines, *Time*, *Newsweek*, and *U.S. News & World Report*.[1] The goal of this study is to explore not only how the coverage escalated as it did, but also how it took a final narrative turn common to other kinds of nationally significant death stories—becoming a story that, in the end, focused not on the dead former President but rather on "those thousands of people" and "the possibilities of America."

The "man on the street" has a particular authority in news, with "a uniform common sense attributed to him consonant with the conventional wisdom on public affairs," wrote John Westergaard (1977, p. 108). This character enables reporters to turn the spotlight away from themselves while also, if paradoxically, gaining authority to speak on behalf of the audience. In coverage of commemorative events, all of the participants—the newsmakers, the news reporters, and the news witnesses (ordinary people who also are the audience)—become actors in what Victor Turner (1982) called "social drama," "an interpretive reenactment of [a society's] experience" (pp. 69, 104).

Thanks in part to mass media, Americans are increasingly well prepared to participate in social dramas. Most of the Reagan mourners "remembered" (thanks to their repetition on television and in magazines) the iconic images and the specific rituals of the funeral of the slain President John F. Kennedy more than four decades earlier. And in a post-September 11 culture, Americans were quick to respond to any event perceived as a national tragedy by showing up in public space with candles and flags, knowing that their vigils and makeshift shrines would be well covered by media. Just two days after Reagan's death, National Public Radio interviewed Californian Casey Kiola, who had planted 40 American flags at the bottom of the hill below the Reagan Library, forming a border for "flowers and cowboy hats and jellybeans and letters and cards" left by other mourners. Kiola explained: "I work for Home Depot and I went to my boss yesterday when I heard the news and he gave me 10 flags. ... It's been very nice to be part of the history" (*Morning Edition*, 2004).

## "THOUSANDS OF PEOPLE ARE LINING THE STREETS": EARLY COVERAGE AND ITS FIRST SHIFT

The initial reports of Reagan's death contained the nostalgic themes that would characterize the tenor of coverage later in the week. *Good Morning America* anchor Charles Gibson began his report the day after the former President's death:

> Ronald Reagan was once asked what the American people saw in him, and he responded, "Would you laugh if I told you that I think maybe they see themselves, and that I'm one of them?" Of course no one would laugh. He was one of us, and so now just a quick look at his life (*Good Morning America*, 2004b).

This quotation illustrates two aspects of early coverage. First, it provided thematic cues for a seemingly original, grassroots public "response," evident in news coverage of California mourners a day later. Second, this passage suggests that journalists had expected coverage to be comprehensive but brief, dominating the news but only for a couple of days.

Much of the early reporting, in its comprehensiveness, was negative as well as positive, revisiting the scandals and failures of the Reagan Presidency as well as its perceived successes.[2] Broadcast news programs included commentary from political reporters, historians, and former Reagan advisers on the Iran-Contra scandal, Reagan's remarks about "welfare queens," his firing of air traffic controllers, his cutting of funding for social programs, his lack of attention to the AIDS crisis, his increases in military spending, and the likelihood that the Soviet Union was crumbling even before he took office. The African American *Philadelphia Inquirer* columnist Acel Moore (2004) noted that "the Reagan years were 'Morning in America' to some, but far from all. Too few of his great words included the poor, the urban, the less fortunate" (p. A19). *The New York Times* contained this qualification in its first coverage the day after Reagan's death:

> Gliding gracefully across the national stage with his boy-next-door good looks and his lopsided grin, he managed to escape blame for

political disasters for which any other president would have been excoriated. If the federal deficit almost tripled in his presidency, if 241 marines he sent to Beirut were killed in a terrorist bombing, if he seemed to equate Nazi storm troopers with the victims of the Holocaust, he was always able to rekindle public support. He became known early on as the Teflon president. (Berger, 2004, p. 28)

The following evening, ABC's *Nightline* host Ted Koppel pointed out: "He fares much better in our memories than he did in the polls. John Kennedy got a much higher job approval rating. … So did Eisenhower. So did the elder George Bush. And so, for that matter, does his son, President George W. Bush." (*Nightline: Portrait*, 2004)

Erasing such political realities surely was one objective of "Operation Serenade," the series of tributary rituals that Reagan aides had spent a decade preparing for, described by one of its planners in *The Wall Street Journal* as "a legacy-building event" (Schlesinger, 2004, p. A1). In its own right, this public pageant qualified as what Daniel Boorstin (1987) called a "pseudo-event," something that seems like news but in fact was planned "for the immediate purpose of being reported" (p. 11); it also fits Daniel Dayan and Elihu Katz's (1992) definition of a "media event," an occasion that prompts journalists to engage in "performance of symbolic acts that have relevance for one or more of the core values of society" and that "enthralls very large audiences" (p. 12). Those audiences are not merely the recipient of mediated communication about a public ritual; they are an integral *part* of the ritual. "Watching television means being part of a 'reverse-angle shot' consisting of everyone watching the same image at the same time, or … the imaginary community of those who are also believed to be watching," explains Dayan (2001), who adds that "[s]pectators who stay at home congregate into small celebratory communities whose members are perfectly aware of the millions of other similar communities all equally engrossed in the unfurling of the live broadcast" (pp. 743, 744, 752).

In between the official Reagan ceremonies were opportunities for more active public participation, and these too became part of the "media event" while transforming the nature and tone of its coverage. The result was a continuous week of rituals that seemed to combine official and vernacular culture (Bodnar, 1992) with the formal ceremonies linked together by what appeared to be a spontaneous outpouring of grief from more than 350,000[3] citizens who viewed the casket or lined the streets to watch the funeral procession pass by. Because the vernacular grief occurred in public places and the ordinary people participated in what were essentially vigils or parades, news media claimed that they could not avoid providing continuous coverage (Carter, 2004). Former Republican Senator Bob Dole suggested that the media had underestimated Americans' respect for Reagan, telling *NBC News* anchor Tom Brokaw: "I mean, thousands and thousands of people are lining the streets" (*NBC News Special Report: State Ceremony*, 2004). By the third day after Reagan's death, journalists had made the same rhetorical shift *AJR*'s Thomas Kunkel did: while self-reflexively fretting over all the fuss, they turned over authorship of the story to "regular Americans," whom presidential historian Douglas Brinkley described on *NBC News* as "the men … wearing baseball caps … and women with the Kodak Instamatics" (*NBC News Special Report: Ronald Wilson Reagan*, 2004).

By midweek, these people, whom the New York *Daily News* called "a grieving army of Americans" (Siemaszko, 2004, p. 5), had *become* the news of Ronald Reagan's death, the central characters whose presence in public space and time placed him in historic context. A *Washington Post* reporter compared the scene outside the Capitol Building to citizens' responses to national calamities of the past:

> … near the security checkpoint, people had deposited their small children to sleep, … their parents off somewhere in the snaking line, trusting their offspring to their fellow Americans, in the middle of the night, in the middle of the city, like it was 1942 again, like it was wartime, like we were all in this together. As night crept toward morning, and the thousands moved closer to the reality that they were too late for a viewing, the crowd grew quiet, and the shuffling sounded like it had at Ground Zero in New York in those weeks after the attack—a sweet sound of feet moving gently along, voices soft as if trying not to wake a child. (M. Fisher, 2004, p. B1)

Mourners' sentiments were reported in almost identical terms and images across media. While at the start of the week, the "man-on-the-street" sort of comments had been varied, most quickly took on one of three related themes: Reagan's sincerity that made him "real" and "a good man"; his optimism despite reality; and the need for children to witness and understand this great "historic moment." Together, these themes not only would make sense of the former President's life and death; they also would make use of the past (or a nostalgic vision of it) in making sense of American life and values in 2004. Also by midweek, the negative memories were gone from most[4] news media, replaced by the summaries of ordinary people crediting Reagan with the fall of communism and the nation's recovery from the "dark days" of the

1970s. This anecdote in *The Chicago Tribune* was a typical such comment that also contained the main themes:

> Tom Michel brought his son T.J., 3, with him to place an American flag on the front lawn of the Kingsley & Gates Moeller Murphy funeral home. He paused with his son in his arms and bowed his head. "I just think he was a man who embodied the American spirit," Michel said, his voice breaking with emotion. "He made us feel good about America again." (Schodolski & Martinez, 2004, June 7)

## "HE BELONGED TO US": THE ILLUSION OF REALITY AND THE REALITY OF ILLUSION

Earlier in the week, journalists had described Reagan as a President who never came to work without a coat and tie, who restored "grandeur" and ceremony to the White House, and who, while affable, seemed distant (for instance, *Dateline NBC*, 2004). "Politically and personally, he was extraordinarily complicated," said Tom Brokaw on the day he announced Reagan's death, adding that "almost no one felt that they knew him very well. And of course, he could be very controversial as a politician" (*NBC Nightly News*, 2004d). Reagan biographer Lou Cannon echoed this comment, speaking the same day on an *ABC News Special Report: Farewell* (2004): "He was a very smart guy and a very masterful politician. ... This 'aw, shucks' style of his ... concealed a very, very smart political brain."

Yet by midweek, ordinary mourners were saying just the opposite to reporters, with certainty and consistency, and the rhetoric of journalism shifted quickly. On Tuesday, June 8, *The New York Times* wrote that, at the Presidential Library in California, "thousands of ordinary Americans walked past Mr. Reagan's coffin in mournful tribute to a leader who proudly shared their humble roots" (Leduff & Broder, 2004, p. A19). In the nation's capital, an unidentified woman told *CBS Morning News* (2004), "He really was one us, down to earth, as we say here in Texas." During that network's "special report" on Wednesday, June 9, Dan Rather reported of a woman interviewed along the Washington parade route: "From her perspective, all the fanfare was for what she called a common man. She said, speaking of the Reagans, 'They didn't live in Camelot. They lived in reality with the rest of us'" (*CBS News Special Report*, 2004b). On his regular broadcast the same evening, Rather confided, "Well, he really did seem like one of us, a neighbor" (*CBS Evening News*, 2004e).

News reports were indeed full of Americans' testimony that they had felt a personal connection with Reagan, a transparency and accessibility that had earned their trust and that was rare in politics. "I never felt a bond like that with any other leader, before or since," a 40-year-old man told *The Dallas Morning News*. "He wasn't motivated by money or greed or power. He was really a kind man, and his motives were pure" (Gillman, 2004). Here are two other midweek examples, the second of which refers to Reagan's media persona as evidence of his "realness":

He was an honorable man. Yes, I realize he was a movie star, and sometimes that transition, in our minds seems impossible. But I found that with him and during his presidency and even afterwards, he was always an honorable man. (*Day to Day*, 2004)

He was the first one we knew that way, on our TVs all the time. It was a safe feeling, like you felt if you ever ran into him he'd pat you on the back and tell you everything was all right. Like he belonged to us. (Fisher, 2004, p. B1)

The New York *Daily News* said of the "multitude" who came to Washington, "It was as if they had lost not just a President, but a friend, the sort of friend who helped them see the best in themselves" (Thanks, 2004, p. 20). In turn, Reagan's goodness was certified by the mourners' own typicality, as in this anecdote:

Don Coles, [a] tattooed construction worker from Philadelphia, descended the Capitol steps just past 6 in the morning. The sun was coming up quickly, casting a faint pink glow over the building. Mr. Coles said he was awestruck and humbled by what he had seen during the night. "This," he said, "is the way a good man should be buried." (Stolberg, 2004, p. A20)

Journalists picked up this theme as their own, while attributing it to "people." NBC's Tom Brokaw hedged his analysis, noting the wishfulness inherent in these statements: "I think there's a real longing for authenticity in this country, and he was an authentic hero in the eyes of a lot of people" (*The Today Show*, 2004, June 10). When Reagan's body was flown back to California, *ABC News* anchor Peter Jennings remembered that, during his travels while President, "he would look out the window and look down and begin to talk earnestly and avidly about the people down there. The nation's capital … has recognized and celebrated a President today who ultimately was probably most at home with the common man." On the same network that evening, Judy Muller described the thousands of people lining the California freeway as Reagan's motorcade returned to the Presidential Library for his burial:

The atmosphere here feels like a local Fourth of July parade, with families and flags and coolers and strollers. Perhaps it is more like a homecoming parade, Peter. Because one person said, this man is a local hero to us. ... One man said, you know, he's a real cowboy. And I said, well, you know, he played a cowboy. And he goes, well, that's what all Americans do, don't they? And it was true (*ABC News Special Report: Farewell*, 2004).

This exchange captured the essence of Ronald Reagan's appeal when he was alive. On one hand, his actions as President seemed like movie scenes, as NBC's Chris Matthews recalled of Reagan's political speeches at the Statue of Liberty and his trip to the beaches of Normandy, concluding: "He reminded America [of] that cinematic America, that lost love of America we had through the newsreels in World War II" (*The Today Show*, 2004d). At the same time, as both an actor and the President, he seemed ordinary and sincere. "Because he acts himself, we know he is authentic," wrote the historian Garry Wills (1987) during Reagan's second term. "A professional, he is always the amateur" (p. 1). *U.S. News & World Report* acknowledged Reagan's own conflation of fiction and fact:

Reagan knew the movies were fantasy, but he knew that Americans loved fantasy, and it was a world in which he liked to dwell, a world where America was always right, where good always triumphed over evil, and where a sunny, can-do attitude and a bright smile were better than a pocketful of gold. ... Things would work out because they always did, they always had. All Americans needed was a leader who could give them a sense of confidence, inspiration, and hope—just as he had done in the movies. (Simon, 2004, p. 53)

## "A SIMPLER TIME OF PURE LOVE FOR AMERICA": NOSTALGIA FOR NOSTALGIA ITSELF

The day after Reagan's death, the *Los Angeles Times* included a similar, if more negatively phrased, assessment, calling him

the ultimate television president, a man schooled not in gritty precinct politics but in Hollywood movie acting. ... As president, Reagan was genial, ever-smiling—ignoring unpleasant facts, idealizing hopeful fantasies. He was supremely suited to take advantage of the electronic media that now dominate and shape modern political dialogue, placing image over substance. (A presidency, 2004, n.p.)

Historians have devoted considerable attention to Reagan's use of media to create an illusion of progress and good will in 1980s America, a rhetorical campaign in which, they note, he willfully misused the past. At the end of his second term, Susan Davis wrote that

> both historical commemoration and televised spectacles suited the years 1980-88 especially well, and the age of Reagan can be viewed as government by more or less permanent festival. ... As [ABC producer] David Wolper wrote of Liberty Weekend, "we set out to make America feel good about itself." All the created-to-be-viewed events have proved enormously useful at creating, if not consensus, good feelings, popularity and legitimacy. (1988, pp. 128-29)[5]

If, as such scholars contend, Reagan's own sunny presentation of the realities of the 1980s was a misrepresentation, then public memory of that era in 2004 news was a second layer of amnesia, a retrieved fantasy once more "renarrativized" for present-day purposes (Sturken, 1997, p. 42).

There was some acknowledgment of this twist in news coverage of the 2004 funeral ceremonies. Criticizing Reagan's "vicious policies" on civil rights and poverty during an interview with National Public Radio, the Princeton University professor Cornel West gave this explanation: "In the language of the great F. Scott Fitzgerald in ... *The Great Gatsby*, he believed in the green light. America would be better. Tomorrow it would be grander, tomorrow it would be more noble and so forth and so on" (*The Tavis Smiley Show*, 2004a).

The mourners who spoke to journalists recalled this quality but, unlike West, happily and uncritically embraced it, praising Reagan's optimism as a trait sadly missing from current American life and politics. They didn't care whether or not his positive assessment of the country's fortunes had been based on reality; instead, as suggested by the headline "Crowds Honor a President Who Believed in the Good," they admired him for having envisioned a bright future for the country (Leduff & Broder, 2004, p. A19).

Such a conscious preference for fantasy over reality constituted a double act of nostalgia in making public sense of Reagan's death. According to this logic, the 1980s were a better time for two seemingly contradictory reasons, both rooted in Reagan's "sunny optimism." First was his assurance of the country's future greatness, the theme of *Time* magazine's cover story:

> Hope is an infectious disease, and Reagan was a carrier. The country he courted and finally won over in 1980 was a dispirited

place, humiliated abroad, uncertain at home, with a hunger for heroes. ... "Let us renew our faith and our hope," he declared in his first Inaugural Address. "We have every right to dream heroic dreams." And he would serve as Dreamer in Chief. ... Somehow it took America's oldest President to make the country feel young again, its mission not yet completed, its glory days ahead. (Gibbs, 2004, pp. 5, 32, 34)

In Washington, a Pennsylvania man reiterated this tribute in an interview with National Public Radio: "He restored optimism, and he has restored the importance and the value of this great country to the American people. ... The truth is he believed in the greatness of this country ... he made all of us stand a little bit taller" (*Day to Day*, 2004). Here again, the word "truth" transformed this statement from a personal observation to citizen testimony correcting the media record. As the cultural critic Lawrence Grossberg has noted, the truth for Reagan was a matter of faith rather than facts, and "reality could not interfere" with his professed beliefs: "Both Reagan's politics and his popularity depended upon his sheer faith in visions" (1992, p. 315).

The rhetorician Ernest Borman identified that aspect of Reagan's "vision" as a "restoration fantasy" theme, tied to Puritan religious rhetoric, in which America's "problems stemmed from a falling away from the authentic and true basis of society as established by the founders" (1982b, p. 136). While this longing for the country's better nature imaginatively invoked the Colonial era, it also offered Reagan's own lifespan as evidence of what had been lost more recently. This subtheme came partly from official commentators, who noted that his life had spanned most of the twentieth century, and it came in a more general way from ordinary mourners:

Reagan Wilson, 28, of Los Angeles, who said he was named for the former president, said it had been an emotional several days for him. ... "The story of Reagan is the story of America, one of manifest destiny," Mr. Wilson said. "He knew the world was destined for peace." (Broder & Leduff, 2004, p. A18)

Christopher Simone and his children traveled nearly 300 miles to be here. Simone says Mr. Reagan was the same age as his dad. "The words that he spoke all the time as president reminded me of the great things my father told me about America growing up. My father told me this was the greatest country on the face of the world." (*World News Tonight*, 2004e)

When *The New York Times* reported that mourners "were moved by nostalgia for an era that seems, with the passing of time, to have been simpler and less mean," it was referring not to the 1980s, but to an earlier era of "lost innocence" in the imagined American past that Reagan was seen to embody, what NBC's Chris Matthews referred to as "a simpler time of pure love for America" (*The Today Show*, 2004d). As the scholar Paul Grainge notes, Reagan's "Rockwellian nostalgia ... invoked a vision of America unaffected by the social ruptures of the 1960s and the political and economic humiliations of the 1970s" (2002, p. 45). Yet in news eulogy, Reagan's strategic forgetting of those mid-century decades came across as just part of his age, his era, and his essential, personal character. Reagan's biographer told Peter Jennings, "Some of that innocence of that simpler time clung to him, I think, throughout his life. ... He had a vision of the future that was drawn from the past from a happier time" (*ABC News Special Report: Farewell*, 2004). On NBC's *Today* show, Anne Edwards, author of a book about the Reagans, remarked, "It's not the same America as I grew up with, in terms of the world. ... We look at him and we say, 'Yes, that is what America stood for'" (2004c).

Such comments—which seemed to travel back and forth between "real" Americans and "experts" (historians and biographers) in news media throughout the week—were less a matter of nostalgia for the past than nostalgia for nostalgia itself, a desire in the present to ignore present realities in favor of a better past time when "we" ignored present realities in favor of a better past time. Such memory required a streamlining of the former President's record, as nostalgia replaced historical summary in news. As Garry Wills wrote during Reagan's presidency:

> If one settles, instead, for a substitute past, an illusion of it, then that fragile construct must be protected from the challenge of complex or contradictory evidence, from any test of evidence at all. That explains Americans' extraordinary tacit bargain with each other not to challenge Reagan's version of the past. ... Because of that, we *will* a belief in all his stories. (1987, p. 386)

The same could be said of American news narrative two decades later.

## "I WANT THEM TO BE PART OF HISTORY": THE RITUAL SYMBOLISM OF CHILDREN

As ordinary citizens talked to reporters, they stressed that they were doing so in order to "pay tribute" to the former President's "legacy," something that would be appreciated by future Americans. Chief among the future Americans of concern to these mourners were their own children, who were described and pictured in recurring symbolic ways in this coverage. Inscribed in the figures of children were both the future of the nation and the weight of history:

> Marie Feddo, cradling her 9-month-old daughter, Kaye, in her arms, wiped a single tear as she saw Nancy Reagan wave from the window of the limousine. ... "I wanted the children to be part of something very special. They may not remember it, but I want them to be a part of history." (Shogren, Neuman, & Braun, 2004, n. p.)

> ... 85-year-old Boydson Baird ... flew in Wednesday from Knoxville to Atlanta, picked up his son and 14-year-old grandson, then flew to Washington. It was nearly 4 a.m., and the three of them had been waiting since 11:30 p.m. "I told him," Mr. Baird said, gently touching the arm of his grandson, Henry, "when he has children, to tell his children about this." ... "It's so majestic," said Kristin Bruhn, of Winchester, Va. She had arrived at 2:30 in the morning with her husband and four young children, the littlest of them, a 19-month-old girl adopted from China, cradled in a fabric sling on her back. "It just brings you back to the core of the country." (Stolberg, 2004, p. A20)

The latter quotation echoes the reactionary tone of the nostalgia theme, the notion of *returning* to something lost and better. Moreover, these vignettes constructed patriotism as a family value, a collective activity enacted by a father, a mother, and more than one child. A shared history as well as national identity was invoked in this scene from *USA Today*:

> Parents bent down to whisper to their children and point out the scenes from U.S. history painted on the walls. ... Each visitor was handed a card to mark the occasion, "the final tribute from a grateful nation." They got something else: a look at history, the kind they'd read about, the kind they'd seen in grainy newsreels from 1945 and black and white TV footage from 1963. Now they could tell their grandchildren, "when Ronald Reagan died, I stood in the line." (Memmott, Leinwand, & Watson, 2004, p. 16A)[6]

*The Washington Post* reported that "Aaron and Amy Godeaux of Manassas and their four children, ages 4 to 10, watched the procession pass with their hands over their hearts. 'We wanted the kids to be able to experience it'" (Ruane, 2004, p. A22). The newspaper also showed two little boys along the route, with this caption: "Grant Johnson, 7, holding flag, and brother Zachary, 3, watch the funeral procession on

Constitution Avenue. 'I wanted them to get a chance to experience history,' said father Daniel Johnson of Indianapolis" (Pressley, 2004, p. A28). The dominant photograph on *U.S. News & World Report*'s table of contents (Table, 2004, p. 1) featured a young girl with long blonde hair and a white dress, saluting the coffin in the Capitol Rotunda.

This theme persisted as Reagan's body was returned to California for burial. *The Los Angeles Times* reported that "the 40th President's entourage rolled past cabbage fields and condominiums, peering out at crowds who saluted, waved flags and held their small children up to see a slice of history" (Chawkins, 2004, n.p.).

In his study of images of Abraham Lincoln—whose funeral was the blueprint for Reagan's, as well as John F. Kennedy's, Washington ceremony—Barry Schwartz calls these kinds of images "adoration portraits," which are "pictorial rituals: portraits of the people looking at symbols of themselves." When reproduced in paintings (or, for the purpose of this study, photojournalism), the viewers of the images obtain "a second order of identification: viewers taking the place of people admiring Lincoln in pictures" (Schwartz, 1998, pp. 17–18). This insight offers an instructive perspective on news coverage not only of the "spontaneous" behavior of ordinary Americans, but also of the more official rhetoric that used symbolic children in order to anchor Ronald Reagan in "history." Capitalizing on the vernacular mourning, his former communications director, David Gergen, told this story to Peter Jennings:

> When Lincoln was in (*sic*) his funeral, there was a cortege that went through New York City bearing his body and there's a famous picture of a little child looking out a window and it's a young Teddy Roosevelt with his brother Elliott, watching and saying farewell to a President. And I kept thinking today, surely there's a young 5- or 6-year-old boy and a 5- or 6-year-old girl watching this today, not knowing who all these people are but being stirred by it. And somehow this is going to have the effect, over time, of inspiring the young to believe that politics can be noble, that leaders can do great things. (*ABC News Special Report: Farewell*, 2004)

## "LET US ALSO PRAY FOR ALL WHO MOURN": THE CONCLUDING COVERAGE AND FINAL STORY

Thus "regular Americans," so widely covered in news media during the week of "national mourning," became the presumed inspiration for the extent of official ceremony. Reporting from the National Cathedral on Friday, June 11, ABC's Robin Roberts said:

I couldn't help but notice a quote from a certain prayer that I thought was very appropriate. ... "Let us also pray for all who mourn, that they may cast their care on God, and know the consolation of his love." And I thought that was very appropriate given all the hundreds of thousands of people we have seen streaming past the president's casket in both Southern California and here in Washington. (*Good Morning America*, 2004c)

The day of Reagan's burial, the news focus was again on the formal pageantry—the dignitary-filled service at the National Cathedral in Washington and the star-studded family burial service in California, both covered live on television. Yet by then reporters had been narratively enfolded into the grieving nation, part of the nostalgically patriotic citizenry who—to journalists' "surprise"—seemed to have risen up from the heartland and stolen the show with what NBC anchor Tom Brokaw called "this outpouring of affection" (*The Today Show*, 2004f). In similar language, *Good Morning America* co-anchor Charles Gibson said, "One of the things we've asked ourselves, why this tremendous outpouring of support? I think it has surprised a lot of people how heartfelt and widespread it has been" (2004c).

What began as coverage of a ceremony sprung from political public relations became, over a week of journalism, seemingly a read on the pulse of America, a portrait of the character of the country's common folk and an assessment of their place in history. Reporting on the day of Reagan's funeral, Dan Rather embraced its main narrative theme:

We Americans have never gone in much for pomp and circumstance.... But once every long while, this country does accord a few leaders honors of the sort we witnessed this week, not because we're a nation ruled by anything close to a king, no, but because we are a nation led by fellow citizens. (*48 Hours Investigates*, 2004)

Gibson summed up the week in similar terms: "It was Americans in short-sleeved shirts and shorts ... it was really the common man who was coming through to pay their (*sic*) final respects. ... You felt the majesty of the city yesterday" (*Good Morning America*, 2004c).

The royalty who justified this otherwise un-American "pomp and circumstance" were the populace, the folks who made remarks such as "Ronald Reagan brought our country together, and our country came together again to say goodbye" (Ruane, 2004, p. A22). *The New York Times* declared: "The famous and powerful also came to pay their respects. ... But it was the ordinary Americans—the people who Mr. Reagan once said thought of him as 'one of them'—who infused the scene with raw emotion" (Stolberg, 2004, p. A20). This seeming reversal of power and influence was not an exception to the political status quo; it was a confirmation of it, as anthropologists explain about such rituals over centuries:

> Royal death rites are special because they are part of a political drama in which many people have a stake. Especially in kingdoms in which the state was personified by the monarch, the king's funeral was an event that reverberated with far-reaching political and cosmological implications. … Moreover, for the citizens, the king-as-hero encounters a death that is the archetype of the end of Everyman. (Metcalf & Huntington, 1991, p. 134)

## DISCUSSION

After his death, Reagan's wishful thinking, while not a description of reality, was echoed by "real people" through media, and then by journalists themselves. Such a phenomenon illustrates sociologists Scott Lash and John Urry's definition of nostalgia as "the belief … that in important ways the past was preferable to the present" and "the need nevertheless for a certain re-presentation of the past—to construct a cleaned-up heritage" (1994, p. 247). David Lowenthal calls the resulting recollection "memory with the pain taken out" (1985, p. 8).

This coverage also serves as an illuminating study in the role of the character of the common man in news media narratives, as well as the implied importance of the typical reader or viewer in public ritual and definitions of national identity. In doing so, it further provides a lens through which we may view journalism as a dialogic process: reporters quickly turned their focus from authoritative summary (provided by official sources such as historians and politicians) to coverage of "regular Americans" whose emotional responses were portrayed as authentic. The increasing uniformity of ordinary people's comments, however, suggested that they actually were taking their cues from each other through media coverage. In turn, journalists modified the content and tone of their own memories of Reagan based on the "spontaneous" and "surprising" behavior of Americans.

Because of their prominence in news coverage of national grief events, ordinary people are not only entitled to a role in national rituals; they are central to them, more central, perhaps, than even the dead. When their actions and words are covered by national news media, particularly television, those reading or watching become a part of the ritual as well. In Marita Sturken's words, such coverage is a "national text" in which "one participates as part of an imagined audience specifically coded as American" (1997, p. 25). In Reagan's case, of course, the public pageantry occurred within the choreography of a long-planned series of official ceremonies, and after decades of similarly nostalgic coverage emphasizing Reagan's special connection with the public, whether or not it ever really existed (see King & Schudson, 1987).

The result was a body of journalism that—on first critical impression—may have seemed contrived and reactionary (certainly that was the accusation of media criticism afterward) and yet that was in fact a more complicated public phenomenon, one that suggests journalists' susceptibility to the wishes of the public (or at the very least, to political-theatrical constructions of "public" events), in contrast to the more common charge of journalism's disregard of the public. Moreover, in the current political climate, it would have been difficult for journalists to challenge the legitimacy of a vernacular storyline. Following the pattern of coverage of the ongoing war in Iraq—in which journalists were critical of the war itself (and the political administration and military leadership behind it) while patriotically celebrating the courage of the American soldier and venerating "The Fallen"—the one unassailable character in the national story of Reagan's death was the typical citizen. Finally, given the number of citizen-mourners who turned out, and the fact that they turned out at more than one geographic location and traveled far in order to represent a variety of regions, their role in the story would have been hard for journalists to explain in terms of a stereotype or to characterize as a planned event.

The nostalgic and tributary themes of the official pageant that seemed overblown in early press coverage were legitimized when echoed by "real people" and re-reported as their beliefs. In their emphasis on the themes of Reagan's ordinariness and his historic importance (and their attribution of the truth of these themes to citizen-mourners), news media elevated the status of the ordinary American in the unfolding pageant: Reagan was the common man; Reagan was a historic leader; the common man turned out to pay tribute to him; the common man was historically important as well. The symbolic device of children became the ultimate rhetorical gesture through which Reagan's life and death—as celebrated by the typical citizen—was understood in news as a grand statement about America's past, present, and future, and about the country's "real" character and values. Ordinary people became, over the week of funeral coverage, the narrative device through which Ronald Reagan was publicly understood to be a mythic figure who nevertheless symbolized the best in all of us.

# 10

## "ALL THE FELLOWS THAT WENT ON BEFORE ME"

### Tribute, Memory, and Counter-Memory
### Among Veterans of "the Good War"

Frank Janse was laid to rest here on Thursday. He won two Soldier's Medals for Valor in North Africa and in France in the big
war … the only mourners at his funeral were two old buddies
from the American Legion Post 107 in Hoboken. Tom Kennedy,
78, a Korean War veteran and the post commander, received the
folded coffin flag from the honor guard. … Jack O'Brien, who lied
about his age and shipped out for the Mediterranean when he was
still 16, then took out his flute and gave a quavering, heartbreaking rendition of "Amazing Grace" over the coffin. The entire ceremony took about 10 minutes.

*—The New York Times* **(Peterson, 2004, p. A1)**

Such a sad description of a lonely old man's death, the lead of a story
about a veterans' cemetery in New Jersey, seems unlikely content for
the front page of *The New York Times*. But Frank Janse was buried just
two days before the dedication of the National World War II Memorial
in Washington, DC in May 2004. The article's point was that his end
was increasingly typical for "the greatest generation," an uncomfortable
truth for which the long-delayed Memorial was meant finally to atone.

Seventeen years in the making, the Memorial is imposing, situated
on the National Mall between the Lincoln Memorial and Washington
Monument, with pillars representing the U.S. states, arches symbolizing

the Atlantic and Pacific theaters of battle, and a wall of 4,000 gold stars, each star representing 1,000 casualties. While criticized for its size, the Memorial also was lamented as being built too late for a generation that was rapidly dying. The focus of its dedication thus became, in public ceremony as well as in news media, the thousands of elderly men and women who came for a "a bittersweet reunion" (*The Early Show*, 2004b). Facing their own mortality, these "old soldiers" shared their memories of—as one unidentified veteran said to a CBS reporter—"all the fellows that went on before me" (*CBS Evening News*, 2004c).

In an article titled "Memory Illuminated," *The Washington Post* defined "the overriding goal of the weekend's full schedule of World War II-themed events: to spark the memories of veterans, get them talking and allow others to listen, celebrate and learn" (Reel, 2004a, p. B1). The article noted that volunteers were recording veterans' testimonies for the Library of Congress's Veterans History Project, and that organizers had a bulletin board in a "Reunion Hall" tent where visitors could place notices that they were looking for certain old friends or for others who had shared a particular experience. Veterans spoke not only to the official oral history interviewers, but also to reporters, who sought them out as the most desirable and authoritative sources. "Though offspring of familiar names from the war era—Roosevelt, Churchill, Eisenhower—could be found in the crowd," the *Post* reported, "the focus of the attention throughout the day remained squarely on the veterans, who had served with little fanfare" (Reel, 2004b, p. A1).

As it was initially promoted in the months leading up to Memorial Day 2004, this kickoff of a summer-long "America Celebrates the Greatest Generation" Washington tourism event was to be a nostalgic return to the 1940s, with screenings of *Casablanca* and dancing to Big Band era music (see, for instance, Capital swings, 2004). The Oral History Project, however, created the theme that most interested the press: that these men, a group famously reluctant to talk about their war experiences for six decades, would now, finally, tell their stories. This Memorial Day weekend would be, according to ABC reporter Geoff Morrell, "their final mission" (*World News Tonight*, 2004d). CBS reporter Wyatt Andrews called this "last grand reunion of Americans who served" in World War II "the most aggressive attempt ever to collect unfiltered tales of war," concluding, "Sixty years ago, these heroes were asked to give everything. Now almost as a parting gift, they're giving their memory" (*CBS Evening News*, 2004b).

These stories were newsworthy precisely because their tellers were themselves near death, and because they were perceived as a social group with historical significance, referred to in broadcast news reports as "the disappearing generation" and "a dwindling band of brothers" (*World News Tonight*, 2004b; *ABC Special Report*, 2004). "In a few years, they'll all be gone," announced ABC reporter Jim Wooten (*World News Tonight*, 2004b). Especially when told in retrospect by survivors of traumatic experiences, such stories become a way of "bearing witness," which Barbie Zelizer defines (in her study of the role of news media in Holocaust memory) as "a specific form of collective remembering that interprets an event [or, in this case, people] as significant and deserving of critical attention" (1998, p. 11).

These were not, of course, "unfiltered tales of war"; they were tales of war filtered through memory and through the overt purpose of tribute, stories told "as a parting gift." "Through 'telling their lives,'" notes the anthropologist Janet Hoskins, "people not only provide information about themselves but also fashion their identities in a particular way, constructing a 'self' for public consumption" (1998, p. 1). The "self" constructed for public consumption in news coverage of the National World War II Memorial dedication was both a series of individual selves and a collective self. In representing a collective identity, the veterans spoke on behalf not only of themselves and other survivors, but also (indeed, especially) of the dead. These tensions—between the individual and the group and between the living and the dead—created the potential for counter-memory as well as consensus in news coverage of this national event.

Drawing on the theories of the philosopher Michel Foucault, George Lipsitz explains that counter-memory "starts with the particular and the specific and then builds outward toward a total story," and that it uses "localized experiences … to reframe and refocus dominant narratives purporting to represent universal experience" (1990, pp. 213). In the government's oral history project and, more publicly and immediately, in news media, the ways these veterans chose to tell their stories could shape current understanding and, perhaps, lasting memory of World War II. They could confirm the conventional wisdom that it had been "the good war" and could shore up American patriotism in the same month when news media showed photographs of American military abuses at Abu Ghraib prison in Iraq and when public criticism grew over America's continuing military presence there. Yet the sad and potentially graphic details of what the men had experienced also had the potential to remind news audiences of the horror of war, to issue a warning while a new generation of young Americans was dying on foreign soil.

Public narratives about death have, simultaneously, this affirming and disruptive power, especially when "real people" are invited to become the storytellers. Writing on the commemorations of the 50th anniversary of D-Day in 1994, Jean Pickering contended that

> The official narrative was interrogated by many of the veterans interviewed live through the extensive broadcasts who, in contrast to those giving prepared speeches as part of the commemoration service, frequently voiced latter day reevaluations of the enterprise they had survived. ... Television added to vernacular recollection: footage of the dead on Omaha Beach, never before shown to a U.S. audience. ... [the veterans] contributed their recollections to the public memory, as though they had traveled there to testify. Their voices contest the official narrative of heroism and glory, a narrative that has depended on their years of silence. The dead, it seems, have served their country more usefully than the living veterans. ... Whether the public memory will accommodate the resistant testimony of the veterans when they are no longer able to speak remains to be seen. (1997, pp. 205–207)

A decade later, as thousands of elderly veterans converged on Washington to "testify" again, Pickering's question remained unanswered. This chapter analyzes a month's worth of coverage—a total of 177 reports—between the opening (April 29, 2004) and the dedication (May 29, 2004) of the new Memorial, airing on the three major television broadcast networks (CBS, NBC, and ABC) and the cable news network CNN, and published in three newspapers, for two of which this was a story of great local interest: *The New York Times*, *The Washington Post*, and *USA Today* (which, while a "national" paper, is based in Washington). The following sections consider the ways in which the content and presentation of this coverage both confirmed and contested an official, patriotic memory of World War II.

## THE POLITICAL AND CULTURAL CONTEXT: A DECADE OF TRIBUTES TO THE COMMON SOLDIER OF WORLD WAR II

As part of its week-long special coverage leading up to the World War II Memorial dedication, *The Washington Post* printed "memories" it had solicited from readers in an article titled "An Unforgettable Experience" (2004). The published anecdotes were stories from current residents of the greater Washington, DC area who had had a variety of experiences during the war: several people who were then citizens of other countries (Russia, Austria, Poland, France, England, Belgium) and had been saved by the kindness of strangers or by U.S. soldiers; an American woman who had left her small-town home to come to Washington to work in the federal government; a French-born Jew whose father was taken by the Nazis but who escaped with his mother to the United States; and an American airman recalling a dogfight with a Japanese airplane so close he could see the pilot's face just before the other plane burst into flames. The latter correspondent wrote:

> I was a 19-year-old country boy when I joined the Army Air Corps in 1942. A year later, I was flying combat where our pilot losses were nearly 30 percent. It required that you grow up in a hurry. But neither I nor any of my squadron mates ever doubted the reason we were there. (p. W11)

While this roundup feature "remembered" the war through many types of people involved in it, it was the final kind of reminiscence that was most typical in news media during May 2004. This story's protagonist, an innocent "country boy" for whom the war was a rite of passage into manhood, confirmed the integrity of his "mates" and their certainty of purpose. His emergence as the central character of the story of the Memorial dedication was a natural extension of the commemorative tributes to World War II veterans that had begun in earnest during the 1990s and that remained in memorial culture in May 2004.

The issue of *Time* magazine then on the newsstands, for instance, bore the label "Anniversary Special," a reference to the 60th anniversary of the D-Day landing on June 6, 2004. Over a blurry, black-and-white Robert Capa photograph, a coverline promised "An Oral History by the Men Who Were There." This article, with the title "What They Saw When They Landed" and the running head "D-Day First Person," offered first-person testimony from veterans (eight American, one British, and one German) who had contributed to an oral history project at the Eisenhower Center for American Studies in New Orleans (What they saw, 2004, pp. 51-61).

As news media covered the arrival of veterans in Washington for the Memorial dedication, they simultaneously promoted their own upcoming coverage of the D-Day 60th anniversary one week later. CNN advertised "A People in the News Special: D-Day: A Call to Courage" (A people, 2004, sec. 1, p. 7), a program that "brings you stories of ordinary citizens who became extraordinary heroes." Meanwhile, the MSNBC cable television network (partly affiliated with NBC) called its "Celebration of Heroes" program a "Living History Event," urging readers to "hear first-hand accounts from a real-life Band of Brothers who fought for freedom against all odds" (A celebration, 2004, p. A5). The reference was to the HBO series *Band of Brothers*, rebroadcast throughout April 2004 on the History Channel, which owed its own popularity to the

1998 film *Saving Private Ryan* (whose star, Tom Hanks, spoke at both the World War II Memorial dedication in Washington and the D-Day anniversary commemoration in Normandy on consecutive weekends in May and June 2004).

The enormous popularity of those fictional television and movie texts, along with NBC anchor Tom Brokaw's bestselling book *The Greatest Generation*, had in fact laid the groundwork for news coverage of the eventual Memorial dedication—and for reporters' commentary on the meanings of veterans, and the meanings of death and sacrifice in national memory. It was the "band of brothers" who came to Washington for the May 2004 Memorial dedication who were the focus of news media coverage of that event.

## NARRATIVE EVASIONS: VETERANS' REFUSAL TO TELL THE EXPECTED STORY

Some of what they told reporters fit into the patriotic, reverential narrative about "the good war" that had been constructed over the previous decade. Yet much of what they had to say seemed disconnected from the news frames already set in place to receive their memories that weekend. Veterans spoke reverentially of the dead, but in ways that were extremely personal, that did not conjure up images of any war as "good," and that confirmed *why* "the silent generation" had remained that way for so long.

The Memorial itself was not uniformly popular with the veterans who went to Washington to see it. "I feel like I'm looking at my gravestone," 79-year-old George Idelson told *USA Today*. "This is a memorial a general would love" (Hampson, 2004, p. 2A). CNN reporter Jamie McIntyre noted that, despite the Memorial's symbolic representation of veterans as a single, united group (including its designer's decision not to list the names of the dead), "nevertheless, one of the traditions at the Vietnam Wall has apparently been brought here ... people leaving mementos ... faded photographs, in some cases, a tattered cap, leaving them here at the memorial as a reminder of those folks who didn't come back" (*CNN Live Saturday*, 2004).

Veterans' comments to journalists focused on the meaning of death and loss occurring among their generation not just during the war itself, but also in the years since. Repeatedly, news media reported the statistic that this cohort was dying at a rate of between 1,100 and 1,200 every day. "Our [VFW] post is losing eight to nine members a month," 81-year-old veteran Victor Fuentealba of Baltimore told *The New York Times*. "I'm happy I'm still around, particularly for the dedication, but

I feel so sorry for the people who won't be there" (Janofsky, 2004b, p. A18). Fuentealba's comment was typical. Although they were asked to tell their own stories, almost without fail veterans instead spoke to media about others who were not there for the celebration, those whom veteran and former Senator Bob Dole called "the millions of ghosts in navy blue and olive drab who we honor with this memorial" (*CBS Sunday Morning*, 2004). ABC's Diane Sawyer blended the living and the dead in promising, the day before the dedication, that viewers would "hear the voices of those whose spirits are honored by this memorial" (*Good Morning America*, 2004a).

This theme of absence—of the "dead comrades" honored by the gold stars on the Memorial wall, and of the "disappearing generation" of men who had died more recently—had been anticipated (*World News Tonight*, 2004c and 2004d). Even so, reporters seemed surprised by the extent to which the interviewed veterans talked about the dead instead of the war itself. When CBS reporter Joie Chen asked veteran Kenny Johnson, who had come to the dedication ceremony in his old uniform, for his memories of the war, the veteran replied: "No—no particular time. Buddies, yeah. Wish they were here. Yeah, sure wish they were here" (*The Early Show*, 2004a). NBC reporter Bob Faw set the stage for another veteran to talk about his combat experience with this introduction: "Memories overwhelm 82-year-old Frank Hayden, a callow, 22-year-old merchant seaman [on] D-Day, later nearly killed when a 120-pound Nazi bomb ripped through his supply ship," to which Hayden replied:

> We was just punching young kids. We didn't know what was going to happen… Best thing about the memorial would be remembering the fellows who lost their lives. It's hard to believe. … the ones who didn't come back. And we're here—and we're here representing them now. (*NBC Nightly News*, 2004b)

A similar non sequitur occurred when NBC News anchor Brian Williams closed his evening broadcast, on the day of the Memorial dedication, with "Purple Heart recipient Stanley Stepnitz [who] was an Air Force lieutenant colonel shot down over occupied France who lived to tell about it." With no reference to his own deeds, Stepnitz said: "You see all of these fellows that—wearing Purple Heart uniforms, crippled up, rolling around in wheelchairs, and they are friends of yours whether you know it or not" (*NBC Nightly News*, 2004c).

Other news reports simply contained isolated quotes from veterans, like these two unidentified men shown on NBC's *Today* show, the first one crying as he was interviewed: "We saw a lot of death, and we were

18 years old"; and "What hurts me is that so many of my buddies never lived to see this" (2004a). Reporting from Washington on the day the Memorial opened, a month before its dedication, *The New York Times* painted this picture:

> Carl Orjala, 83, of Aitkin, Minn., sat quietly in a wheelchair, tears welling up. He served in a medical corps in the Pacific, tending to wounded soldiers at the front. "I can't describe it," Mr. Orjala said. "I'm happy because this is done even this long after the war. But it doesn't do it justice—the loss was just so great. I wish people could understand what it was like." (Janofsky, 2004a, p. A14)

*CNN* began one of its programs with a sound bite from veteran Al Simpson: "I had to come because of my buddies that are not here." In the report itself, the anchor's narration was an astonishing evasion of what Simpson actually had to say:

> [CNN anchor Aaron Brown:] Schoolchildren will come flocking to the Memorial. They will hear history from their teachers. And if they are lucky, they will hear history, too, from men like Al Simpson.
> [Simpson:] There is not much good about war. I myself have never talked to my children about the war, because it is—I put it way back here those things I want to forget.
> [Brown:] But forgetting is not on the agenda just now. Now is about remembering. (*CNN Newsnight*, 2004).

Some veterans, of course, did respond directly to the narrative cues provided by reporters, reiterating the historical themes expected to be part of this public tribute. A month before the dedication of the Memorial, ABC's *World News Tonight* profiled soldiers who planned to attend. "Eighty-three-year-old Sergeant Walter Ehlers ... and his brother Roland ... were in the first wave to hit Omaha Beach on D-Day. Walter survived. His brother did not. Walter was awarded the Medal of Honor for taking enemy fire, giving his platoon cover to withdraw." The report quoted the survivor: "We wanted to be sure that somebody got back, anyway, and that was my job" (*World News Tonight*, 2004a). A month later, *NBC Nightly News* reporter Fred Francis interviewed Ehlers at the Memorial dedication: "Walter Ehlers, the last man standing from D-Day to wear the Medal of Honor, came, proud of what his band of brothers did." And Ehlers said into the camera, "From fascism to democracy, that's just fantastic. It's unbelievable. People can't realize what a big change in the world that made" (2004c).

Other veterans also, when cued by questions, did recount logistical and graphic specifics of particular places and events of the war. Interestingly, however, details were especially plentiful when "eyewitness" veterans were called upon to recount "forgotten" episodes of the war, subthemes that were not (yet) in the national memory.

## THE POTENTIAL FOR COUNTER-MEMORIES: SECRETS REVEALED AND ATYPICAL SOLDIERS HONORED

This subtheme of "secret" stories finally revealed—an example of how the standard news value of novelty (Gans, 1979) plays out even in the most non-breaking of stories—helped to fulfill reporters' promises that in coverage of this special event, the old soldiers finally would tell us what really had happened.

One example was the account of Bob Grimes, an American pilot who had been shot down but was saved by "the Comet Line, an underground railroad that secretly shuttled 800 British and American pilots, including Grimes, from Belgium, through France, over the Pyrenees Mountains, into Spain and back to England"; because of an Army Intelligence statement he had signed, Grimes had not told his family this story until "recently," a CBS reporter explained (*The Early Show*, 2004a). An episode of *Nightline* airing on Memorial Day revealed the saga of "Exercise Tiger," a practice for the D-Day invasion that went horribly wrong off the coast of Cornwall, resulting in the deaths of hundreds of Americans. *ABC News* reporter Chris Bury noted the double burden the survivors carried, the pain of the memory itself and their inability to tell anyone, having been sworn to secrecy; thus, "the U.S. troops involved never got the public recognition that is so much a part of this holiday." The program quoted veteran Al Sickley: "I see … a phantom of death. Comrades perished without gaining recognition for their actions and for their sacrifices. I see tragedy, fault, guilt and despair." The report noted that a lingering "bitterness among survivors" had to do not with the losses they and their fellow soldiers had suffered, but "with their place in history. They feel they don't really have one. … 'These boys didn't get the credit they deserved'" (*Nightline*, 2004).

The "story" in this report, in other words, was America's failure to pay tribute to the soldiers of Exercise Tiger, not the revelation of the disaster itself. Therefore, *Nightline*'s telling of this war memory changed the story, transforming a demoralizing mistake into a historic episode of sacrifice.

Though they were not told in such dramatic ways, a similar phenomenon could be seen and heard in stories about the involvement of women and American minorities in World War II. This had been a conflict in which women came under fire even though they were never given combatant status, and when the armed forces remained racially segregated and Japanese Americans were imprisoned in internment camps within the United States. If women and minorities were living witnesses to injustice, their recollections had the potential to disrupt the memory of a "good" war. Yet their inclusion in this memorial coverage also (like the revealing of "secret" stories) could serve as a long-awaited apology and acknowledgment.

Primarily, their stories functioned in the second way, and, as with other subplots outside the mainstream memory narrative, their stories were peppered with the kinds of details that the "regular" veterans were hesitant to provide. In these reports, the specifics of testimony confirmed that the interviewed person really had been involved in the war in some significant way (never a question in the case of white male veterans who were interviewed). Sometimes these counter-memories emerged unexpectedly in the midst of the mainstream storytelling, as in this anecdote in *The New York Times* (which also contained the more common loss-of-comrades theme):

> Gale Cornwell, 78, a marine from Kingman, Ariz., who landed on Normandy Beach on D-Day and served for 38 years in the military, stared ahead and wiped tears from his eyes. "I'm here primarily to honor my mother," Mr. Cornwell said, recalling Mabel Cornwell, an Army nurse. "She landed on Omaha Beach on D-Day plus four with Patton's Army." He could not stop the tears. "So many old friends who aren't here," he said haltingly. "They're all gone now." (Janofsky, 2004c, sec. 1, p. 22)

On the *CBS Evening News*, a woman, Lauren Balkam, was identified as a "Marine veteran" (2004a), while CNN showcased three women: Charlotte Merritt, who was in the Women's Army Medical Corps; Frances Tunnell-Carter, who worked as a "Rosie the Riveter" in an airplane-manufacturing plant in Alabama; and Martha Putney, an African American member of the Women's Army Corps, who later became a history professor and wrote a book about this experience. All three explained the nature of their war work. When asked, "What was it like for … you to have your service honored in such a beautiful way here this afternoon?" Putney replied, "Well, I think it's a bit late" (*CNN Live Saturday*, 2004).

A smiling woman identified as Donna Kluckman of Fredericksburg, Texas was pictured on front page of *The Washington Post* with a general reference to "her World War II Marine service" (Countdown, 2004, p. A1). That newspaper also included mentions of women's contributions to homefront efforts and government work in its five-part series, leading up to the dedication weekend, on how the war had transformed Washington. One of those articles recounted the experiences of local soldiers who had faced racism upon their return, and who were angry that the military remained segregated despite their service. Still, the piece ended on a happy note:

> … for many black veterans, time and the nation's growing recognition of their sacrifice has helped salve the wounds. When he learned that some of the events surrounding the memorial's dedication will honor African Americans, [one man] gave a smile free of rancor. "It does my heart good that they are giving us credit," he said (Aizenman, 2004, p. B4).

An even greater potential narrative challenge came from the experiences of Japanese Americans who had fought as American soldiers abroad while their families were interned in the United States, but news media portrayed them as similarly conciliatory. ABC's *World News Tonight* interviewed Virgil Westdale, who had been part of the Japanese American 442nd Army artillery and who said that the memorial "represents, I guess, the greatest generation. I just happen to be one of them, one among many" (2004d). *The New York Times* contained this vignette about three veterans who spoke inside the Veterans Services tent during the weekend of the dedication:

> Mr. Hirabayashi talked about how he was inducted into the war four days before Pearl Harbor and how he was taken into protective custody in his Army barracks after the attack. After what he politely termed "a difficult time," he went on to become one of only 14 Japanese-American soldiers in a 3,000-member unit called Merrill's Marauders, destroying Japanese supply and communications lines in and around Burma.
>
> Mr. Ichikawa shared his story of helping to negotiate the surrender of 200 Japanese soldiers near Manila. "There were only about 12 of us," he said. …
>
> Mr. Ichiuji told of being among the first of the Allied forces to liberate Jews from the camps of Dachau in April 1945. "When I saw the barbed wire it reminded me of the camp my family was in." (Clemetson, 2004, sec. 1, p. 22)

The first two of these stories surely represented complicated experiences and painful memories for their tellers, yet the article did not pursue the implied subtheme of the tension between national loyalty and racial identity. Instead, the article concluded with Mr. Ichiuji speaking directly with the reporter: "In 1942 we had very few friends. But just this, so many people so appreciative just to listen to us. Now we know that as a nation we have learned" (Clemetson, 2004, sec. 1, p. 22).

Coverage of female and minority veterans thus honored (or "celebrated") them by confirming that they really had done something important, and then by enfolding them within the larger patriotic narrative of World War II memory. This process of inclusion both added to the historic nature of the journalistic reports and enabled reporters to make sweeping summary statements about a single group of patriots. CNN's Paula Zahn said of the honorees, "They were children of the Depression who struggled through hardship, who proudly fought for freedom, fought for their nation, fought for the world" (*Paula Zahn Now*, 2004). CBS reporter Joie Chen called the ceremonial events "reminders of a time when America stood united in purpose, both at home and far away from it, a chance to relive that shared experience and that shining moment" (*CBS Sunday Morning*, 2004).

## CONNECTIONS TO THE WAR IN IRAQ: MILITARY SACRIFICE AS ONE CONTINUING STORY

Though understandable as tributes to senior citizens, such generalizations ultimately explained "the good war" as any war, and any war—when seen through the eyes of the typical soldier—as potentially good, or as fought by good Americans. And, while this was a predictable sentiment on any Memorial Day, such a news theme was especially useful on Memorial Day 2004, against the backdrop of the Abu Ghraib scandal and the escalating controversy over America's ongoing involvement in Iraq a year after that "operation" had been pronounced over.

The World War II veterans themselves did not make this connection; in their testimony, they rarely referred to other wars. When directly asked what they thought of the ongoing war in Iraq, most veterans contrasted their own experience with the current situation. Some expressed nostalgia, like veteran Jack Senor, who said on *Good Morning America*, "I wish it was like it was in the old days. I just don't feel that they have the appreciation that we had. I know when I was in uniform, you know, everybody respected you" (2004a). Others suggested that the political and military circumstances were not comparable: as U.S. Army Air Corps veteran Ted Taubert told CNN, "It was such a different war. Everybody knew what the mission was. There was an enemy that was known and they were right out there and you knew what had to be done" (*CNN Capital Gang*, 2004).

It was the narrative nature of news coverage—as well as, in some cases, very targeted prompting by reporters—that blended wars together into one memory narrative. As part of its coverage of Memorial Day ceremonies (two days after the dedication of the World War II Memorial), *NBC Nightly News* included a quote specifically about the Memorial from World War II veteran Norman Locksley, who said, "This means everything. I'm here because of the men in my battalion who did not come home." This was followed by a shot of then presidential candidate John Kerry visiting the Vietnam Memorial, and by coverage of a ceremony held in Baghdad, in memory of American soldiers killed in Iraq, where Lieutenant General Ricardo Sanchez said, "They must not have died in vain. We must not walk away from this mission" (2004d).

A connection between old and new wars was made with a heavier hand by CNN reporter Catherine Callaway in an interview with two men who had been prisoners of war, Ron Young in Iraq and Ernest Waymon in Germany. After Waymon explained the circumstances of his capture, the following extraordinary exchange occurred:

*Callaway:* [speaking to Young:] Do you have anything you would like to say to Mr. Waymon?

*Young:* I beg your pardon?

*Callaway:* I said, Ron, do you have anything you would like to say to Mr. Waymon?

*Young:* I'd like to say we appreciate your service to the nation and I know there's a lot of guys beside you and you hold them up just as much as do you yourself. I'd like to ask you, there's a new group of people called the next generation. They're fighting over in Iraq right now. What would you say to them to quell their fears and what they're going through?

*Waymon:* I think right now, they're doing the best they can. It's a shame that the people do not know what good they are doing. I have heard from various military over there about the building of schools and roads and all of the utilities and facilities that they are building. And I think it's an excellent job they're doing.

*Callaway:* Right, so we remember the good work that they're doing. You know, I just want to say that it is an honor to have you both with us. Ron, maybe one day there will be a dedication there for your generation as well.

*Young:* Well, we've got a long war to fight. So hopefully ... (*CNN Live Saturday*, 2004)

Yet other stories in which reporters drew parallels between World War II and the Iraq war could be understood as critical of war. Visiting the Armed Forces Retirement Home, CNN reporter Brian Todd interviewed Charles

Yoder, who had been in the Battle of the Bulge, and whose responses did not really fit into the narrative template that Todd pursued anyway:

Yoder:   I'm telling you, if you're ever hit or you're near a shell that explodes, it can be something. ... I don't like to be reminded of these things. I have forgotten all about them. ...

Todd:   Charles Yoder's story is compelling in so many different ways. His heroism and sacrifice clearly stand out. But ... you start to understand just how relevant his story is right now. When you hear about a mortar attack in Iraq, imagine a day in Germany March 1945. Yoder and his mates thought they were out of danger. At a farm, they lined up for a rare hot meal. They heard a whistling sound, then explosions ...

Yoder:   ... I went and got this guy out and led him back. I didn't know it was a lieutenant. ... And I had to go back and pick up the other guy. ...

Todd:   From that day, in a span of two weeks, Charles Yoder earned a Silver Star, two Purple Hearts and a Bronze Star. He doesn't consider himself highly decorated.

Yoder:   I don't know. A lot of the highly decorated guys and the guys that would be highly decorated are dead. (*Wolf Blitzer Reports*, 2004)

## "ON THIS NIGHT OF FINAL VICTORY": FROM MEMORY TO HISTORY

Even this attempt to pre-memorialize (and valorize) the war in Iraq contained the disconnect so common in interviews with the "old soldiers," survivors who represented a collective experience and a very public national memory, but whose "ghosts" were individual and, often, still indescribable. Across news coverage, journalists introduced themes that veterans' words or behaviors then dodged or damned—even as the subjects seemed to genuinely try to respond helpfully, to say the right thing. Under a heartbreaking photograph of a downcast elderly man in *USA Today*, an article began:

> Tomorrow comes the pomp and circumstance, the benedictions of presidents and generals for an honor long overdue.
> But today, an 82-year-old in a leather bomber jacket the color of pipe tobacco sits alone on a granite step. Gazing toward a wall of gold stars at the soon-to-be-dedicated National World War II Memorial, he tunnels into his past—and looks gratefully to the future.

"The nightmares stopped years and years ago, but the memories of involvement get starker with age," says Frank Capone, his neatly trimmed white beard glistening with tears. "This memorial will go on for eternity ..." (Bly, 2004, p. 1D)

Such a vignette makes it hard to believe that this veteran's memories have served him well, yet there he was, in uniform, speaking with a reporter and posing for a photograph, having traveled from Florida for the Memorial dedication. He was just one of many veterans who appeared in news reports both as individuals still horrified by the death they had seen and as members of a generation proud of having "saved the world." One after another, they revealed personal pain, even bewilderment, in being asked to recall, for the media, what had "really" happened six decades ago. This response suggests that the disruptive counter-narrative Jean Pickering detected in 1994 D-Day anniversary celebrations was still very much in evidence in 2004, and it confirms her contention that, even as they are "celebrated," the survivors of "the good war" indeed fail to serve the cohesive national memory narrative that the dead have served for more than half a century. Yet one must wonder, as she does, what will become of all this testimony, and whether or not the veterans' narrative contradictions will survive in future media memory of World War II soldiers after they all truly are gone.

Then the story will be solely in the hands of reporters and of memory-event organizers. One clue as to the eventual outcome might be seen in the reaction of NBC reporter Lester Holt when confronted with weeping elderly veterans at the Memorial dedication. Like other reporters, he attributed the veterans' "emotion" to their long-held silence, the stoic patriotism that had for so long compelled them to keep their memories to themselves, and then he explained away the veterans' open sorrow by providing summary testimony of his own. On *The Today Show*, Holt divulged, "I saw the veterans, some in their uniforms, some clearly emotionally taken by this. ... I turned from snapping pictures of the memorial to snapping pictures of those veterans ... these guys and their stories are a living testament, living memorial, to that incredible war" (2004b). As implied in the snapping of pictures, though, the "testament" would soon be a matter of documentation and not "living" memory, and, seen through the eyes of Americans in the present, it would best be understood as a group shot, a reunion picture of a national group of patriots.

News media were central to the crafting and the telling of this broader, official narrative on Memorial Day weekend of 2004 when the National World War II Memorial was dedicated, and they will continue to be the primary keepers and tellers of this tale. The use of veterans' memories—and of their presence to testify to heroic absence at a national ceremonial event—was not a creation of reporters in 2004, however. The pictures and comments and pomp and honor of news reports featuring "old soldiers" in May 2004 echoed newsreel footage of the many reunions (including Memorial Day events in Washington DC) of Civil War veterans, beginning with the 50th anniversary of the Battle of Gettysburg in 1913 (attended by 55,000 men, with the average age of 72) and extending even into the 1950s, when a few Union and Confederate veterans were still alive to be paraded in automobiles (*Echoes*, 2003).

As those veterans finally faded away, government officials were planning a series of Civil War centennial observations to begin in 1961. Much as reporters and generals blended the current Iraq war into the 2004 memorialization of "the good war," at midcentury these planners sought to create a final memory of the Civil War that would resonate during the Cold War. Historian John Bodnar explains:

> Their goal was to reinforce loyalty to the nation in an era when it was ostensibly threatened internally and externally by foreign ideologies. They, therefore, needed symbolic language that would allow both the North and South to find common ground in the centennial, and they found it in the idiom of the heroic ideal. ... The complexity of all combatants and of the past itself was reduced to one symbol that would best serve the interests of those who promoted the power of the state in the present. (1992, pp. 208–209)

Just as Civil War veterans became the most honored participants in patriotic parades of the 1940s and 1950s captured in newsreels, the Americans who were young men then are now the "old soldiers" who are most revered and are seated in chairs in the front row of nationally televised Memorial Day ceremonies. The evening after the dedication of the National World War II Memorial, many of the same men who had spoken to news media were seated on the White House lawn as the guests of honor at the annual National Memorial Day concert. Hosted by the actor Ossie Davis, an African American World War II veteran (who died the following year), the program also featured another veteran-turned-actor, Charles Durning, who provided a long and dramatically emotional account of the D-Day landing in which he had taken part. His five-minute monologue contained precisely the kinds of detail that the ordinary veterans had not been willing or able to deliver in neatly patriotic media tales. Yet those veterans shakily arose from their front-row seats at the request of actor Tom Hanks, who said to them:

> You and your generation changed the course of history. You did nothing less than preserve our freedom and help save the world from tyranny. I'm sure the events of this weekend have brought back many, many common memories. One of the most powerful must have been at the end of the war … that night when President Harry Truman spoke to you all by radio and said, "This is a time for great rejoicing and a time for solemn contemplation."
>
> He said, "I think I know the American soldier and sailor. He does not want gratitude or sympathy. He had a job to do. He did not like it, but he did it. And how he did it. On this night of total victory, we salute you of the armed forces of the United States. What a job you have done!" (*National Memorial Day Concert*, 2004)

This was a final tribute, an absolute affirmation of the goodness of the combatants of "the good war," whether or not they themselves would have used these words. So was the summary provided by *NBC Nightly News*, which saluted "reluctant warriors who left home as kids and returned to build history's most powerful nation" and concluded: "On the nation's Mall today, the soldiers who never said no, who never thought of losing, who never asked for thanks, got the memorial that now sanctifies those qualities for all time" (*NBC Nightly News*, 2004c). As NBC anchor Tom Brokaw—the journalist most responsible for beginning the decade-long series of tributes to the group he named "the greatest generation"—more succinctly proclaimed, "They fought, lived and died saving the world" (*The Today Show*, 2004a). With such benedictions, the old men seated on the White House lawn were lifted out of their own complicated, painful memories, and were placed into history.

# CONCLUSION

The studies in this book illustrate the many meanings of death in modern American life, as they are conveyed through journalism. These discussions and displays of "mourning" both increase and diminish the importance of the particular deaths that seem to be their focus. Although the dead get a lot of attention, they're not really the main subject of these tales. Regardless of their specific topic and circumstances—natural disaster, workplace accident, murder, or the natural passing of the elderly—the stories told about death in journalism are, ultimately, about "grief"; they are about the living far more so than they are about the dead.

Writing about the Columbine school shootings, Erika Doss acknowledges that the media's attention to the "visual and performative dimensions of mourning suggests new understandings of death in the public sphere." Yet she argues that

> a superficial focus on psychic closure—on healing and surviving—skirts the causal, historical dimensions of these visibly public deaths. It further fails to provide a shared set of rituals and commemorative forms that might allow citizens to critically consider how to change the conditions that contribute to the culture of violence in America. (2002, p. 71)

When a student at Virginia Tech shot and killed 32 other students and faculty in April 2007, news media emphasized themes of "healing and surviving" from the very start of coverage, displaying images of campus memorial ceremonies, candlelight vigils, and floral shrines, publishing photographs of the victims in the same format as media tributes to dead soldiers, and telling stories of "heroes." As with the Amish school shootings, "the story" was one of a strong, rural community united in grief, not of the country's growing problem of gun violence or the rage of mentally disturbed men. That story briefly took an unexpected turn when NBC aired part of the killer's video diatribe, including a segment in which he pointed a gun directly at the camera (and by implication, everyone in the viewing audience), an image then reprinted in newspapers. The network was immediately criticized, not only for giving the gunman the public forum he had wanted and for conveying such disturbing messages, but also for reopening wounds. One student told *The New York Times*: "At the convocation and vigil, it was very sad, and then there was this sense of happiness because we were becoming united as one. But now with the videos, people are angry" (Banerjee, 2007, p. A16).

In the journalism surveyed in the preceding chapters, the move toward healing predominates. It can be seen not only in the more unexpected cases, such as the Amish tragedy and the natural disasters, but also in the mining accident in West Virginia and the various celebrity deaths. This narrative urge for closure and consolation demands that some nuances (and in some cases, many significant details) of lives and deaths must be minimized, and eventually forgotten, in order for the story to provide a lasting lesson that is a positive one.

The news coverage examined here also collectively serves as a strong confirmation that the "enduring values in the news" that the sociologist Herbert Gans (1979, pp. 42–52) discovered three decades ago are still very much in place in American journalism. Among the values he enumerated were

- ethnocentrism ("American news values its own nation above all … the clearest expression … appears in war news");
- altruistic democracy ("politics should follow a course based on the public interest … [symbolized by] the rural town meeting—or rather … a romanticized version of it");
- responsible capitalism (the belief that business functions "to create increased prosperity for all … refrain[ing] from unreasonable profits and gross exploitation of workers");
- small-town pastoralism ("Today's small towns are reported nostalgically" with a focus on their "cohesiveness, friendliness, and slow pace");
- individualism ("The ideal individual struggles successfully against adversity and overcomes more powerful forces. The news looks for people who act heroically during disasters … the news pays homage to the individual"); and
- moderatism ("an enduring value that discourages excess or extremism").

Altruistic democracy and responsible capitalism are related ideals, rooted in the political and economic structure of the country; so is ethnocentrism, in the sense that it is a dimension of the philosophy of American exceptionalism. Because journalism defines the lessons of death primarily in terms of national ideals and capitalistic democracy (the idea of an "American character," even an "American dream"), these values seem inevitable in this kind of news coverage. One consequence is the ignoring or comparative diminishment of otherwise parallel death events occurring in foreign countries, explaining them away as happenings in, to use Jack Lule's term, "the Other World" (2001, pp. 24–25), an exotic and inexplicable place full of "primitive" people with "strange beliefs," people who are by definition not "us." While this is truest of news coverage of faraway countries, it also plays out closer to home. For instance, one month after the Sago mine explosion, a similar explosion at the Pasta de Conchos coal mine in Mexico killed 65 miners, but it received relatively little attention in American news (and the attention it did receive tended to be a contextual backdrop for the recent, additional deaths of miners in West Virginia and Kentucky).

Even the culture of West Virginia—whose story of dead miners, hailed as heroes, nevertheless called into question the ideal of "responsible capitalism"—was reported as unusual, a nostalgically exoticized life "in the hollows and hills" of rural America. Indeed, news subjects may be symbolically placed into "the other world" when they are inside America, especially if their stories do not have full narrative closure or if their subjects behave differently than most of us would in a difficult situation. Lule's "Other World" provides a useful mythic template for understanding news portrayal not only of rural miners, but also of the desperate, angry poor of New Orleans, and of the Amish, intentionally living apart from "the world" in southeastern Pennsylvania.

At the same time, however, the portrayal of those three particular groups also comfortingly illustrates the value of small-town pastoralism, and, by extent, the altruistic democracy embedded within a romanticized notion of the rural town meeting. The use of the Amish and the West Virginia miners to convey an idyllic vision of rural life is not surprising. Yet Gans's definition of the symbolic meaning of the small town in news—a cohesive community where "neighbors" stick together—also emerged in characterizations of the flood- and earthquake-stricken residents of New Orleans, San Francisco, and Los Angeles. What was discovered in coverage of these various death events was not literally rural America, but rather, as Gans noted, a nostalgic *ideal* about small-town American values. Thus, the simple life was celebrated in Guntersville, Alabama, an actual small town whose residents are blue-collar Americans who love place and family. Yet it equally was celebrated in New York City, by a major newspaper and leading news magazines that typically report on elites; at arguably that city's greatest moment of crisis and grief, they wrote about basic values and the heroic spirit.

Heroism may be the most pervasive theme within the journalism examined in this book. Its definition springs from the news values of individualism (tempered by moderatism) and altruistic democracy, an ideal in which we are a nation of equals who take care of each other. The most famous individuals discussed in this book, a former U.S. President and four celebrities, were approvingly remembered in news eulogy only to the extent that their lives—their challenges, fears, and dreams—could be explained as typical. Conversely, news coverage of all sorts of events perceived as disastrous told stories of heroes, of ordinary individuals who did extraordinary things when circumstances called for them to take action and when other people needed their help. One of the most disturbing lessons of news about violent death, from a tornado or from terrorism, is its randomness, the realization that death can come at any time for any of us. Yet this troubling theme yields the most comforting theme in this coverage as well: just as anyone can be a victim, anyone can be a hero. The potential, as the story goes, is there in all of us. This egalitarian belief was conveyed in news coverage of the heroism of individuals during crisis events such as September 11 and Hurricane Katrina. It was perhaps most powerfully advanced by the tales told by the elderly World War II veterans—stories not about their own exploits, but about the comradeship, loyalty, and quiet heroism of their dead buddies. This look back to "all the fellows that went on before" created a narrative bridge to all the fellows coming along in the future, as World War II memories were blended together with tributes to American soldiers currently fighting in Iraq.

Those fellows are indeed the subjects of American news coverage most likely today to explain death as heroism. As illustrated by coverage of the Memorial Day dedication of the World War II Memorial, national media salute fallen soldiers on patriotic national holidays and at the end of a calendar year. Today, such tributes are made almost daily on local television news broadcasts and in local newspapers all across the country. Although an ongoing war may seem like a different kind of death event from those discussed in this book, news coverage of the casualties of the Iraq war is strikingly similar in its themes and lasting lessons. One of the most common elements in such coverage is anecdotal testimony to the dead soldier's typicality and his altruistic commitment to helping others within his community—not just in the military, but also (especially) in his ordinary life. As they are pronounced heroic, they also are remembered (like the residents of Guntersville) for their idiosyncrasies and their simple good nature.

The following examples appeared recently in the Harrisburg *Patriot-News*, published in the Pennsylvania state capital and typical of midsized daily newspapers. All of these were front-page tributes to individual "local heroes" who died in Iraq, and they were full of quotes from family and friends testifying to the soldiers' typicality. One described the family photographs displayed next to the casket of John Fralish of New Kingstown, Pennsylvania: "a boy diving into his birthday cake; Fralish and his sister, Lea Anne, poring over their Halloween trick-or-treat haul; a youth swinging a baseball bat ..." (Gibson, 2006, p. A20). Articles offered anecdotes that were comically touching, such as this remembrance of Gettysburg native Eric McColley:

> Before Scout swimming competitions, the avid swimmer would don toddler water wings or a big, yellow duck life preserver. While training to be a Marine, he sometimes wore Groucho Marx glasses, making even his drill instructor smile. "He loved to eat crabs, tacos and doughnuts," [a friend] said. "He loved Jimmy Buffett concerts." (Klaus, 2006, p. A10)

Another story began this way:

> To his fellow firefighters at the New Bloomfield Fire Company, Army Sgt. Brent Dunkleberger will be remembered as Baby New Year 2000. Dunkleberger played the role for the borough's New Year's Eve huckleberry drop at the Perry County Courthouse—complete with sash, cloth diaper and bottle of champagne. (Elias, 2006, p. A1)

New Bloomfield also was the hometown of Lance Corporal Jason Frye, a Marine whose death in Iraq in late 2005 was noted by the newspaper. The reporter conveyed a message from Frye's family and friends asking residents to "bring yourself and an American flag" and to stand along the route between the church and the cemetery "in tribute to [this] fallen soldier" (Kiner, 2005, p. A1). A year later, precisely this kind of scene dominated the front page of the *Patriot-News* when Dunkleberger was buried (in coverage that dwarfed a smaller notice of the death of former U.S. President Gerald Ford). Under the title "Honoring a 'hero'" was a large, color photograph of American flags held by 100 members of the Patriot Guard Riders, a motorcycle group that travels to soldiers' funerals (Honoring, 2006, p. A1). Reporting on the 600 people who attended the service at the local middle school, the paper painted this verbal picture:

> Yellow school buses scooped the mourners from the far corners of the [parking] lots ... inside, mourners ... climbed into the

bleachers. ... Asked to applaud Sgt. Brent Dunkleberger, a hero who died during his second tour of Iraq, the crowd responded, then stood spontaneously and as one. ... Near the entrance to the school, comrades, many from an earlier unpopular war, lined the sidewalk, holding flags. (Eshelman, 2006, p. A16)

As these examples suggest, this kind of ongoing news coverage focuses less on the war deaths than on the domestic rituals that have sprung up around them. The Patriot Guard Riders, many of them Vietnam veterans, are increasingly common characters in such stories, and their presence inserts the Vietnam War into the new, patriotic narrative connecting World War II and the Iraq war. This group also appears in news coverage of ceremonies on Memorial Day, Veterans Day, and September 11. In late August 2006, for example, a reverent article about the funeral of a 25-year-old soldier from nearby Martinsburg, West Virginia appeared on the front page of the Hagerstown, Maryland *Herald Mail* next to an article about a local visit made by 600 of the motorcyclists in the "America's 9/11 Ride," bound for Somerset, Pennsylvania, and then for New York City (Ballard, 2006; Umstead, 2006). Their attendance at soldiers' funerals is meant to pay respect, but also to minimize the damage done by frequent picketers representing the Kansas-based Westboro Baptist Church, who believe that God is punishing America for its tolerance of homosexuality. This group also picketed at the funerals of the Sago miners and threatened to do so at the funerals of the Amish schoolgirls.

While it has received some news coverage, the Westboro group is a good example of the kind of detail that must be minimized in journalism (as well as in public ritual culture) in order for death stories to provide closure, let alone affirmations of "the American character." Other examples of problematic narrative elements in the stories told in this book might include ignored predictions that the Sago mine was unsafe and that New Orleans would flood with a major storm; reports on the Abu Ghraib prison scandal appearing amid veneration of the veterans of "the good war"; and the fact that teenagers will continue to take risks no matter what lessons adults circulate in the form of slogans. The Westboro protesters were, however, particularly troubling news characters in these stories because they come from "the heartland" (the symbolic location of "small-town pastoralism") and because death coverage is one of the few kinds of journalistic storytelling that emphasizes, validates, and even embraces religiosity.

Journalists have a hard time writing about the spiritual, though death forces them—along with audiences—to confront mortality and to raise and attempt to answer questions about faith, the consequences of sin, and possibilities of redemption. God enters into the coverage in interesting ways. For instance, in disaster coverage, people give God credit for their survival but do not blame God for the destruction. The same was true of the Amish and the rural West Virginians, both stories in which the professed religiosity of the news subjects provided an opportunity for journalists to discuss faith openly. Stewart Hoover contends that "the underlying religiosity of the American public" (1998, p. 184) is part of the cultural context that shapes news narrative today. We should consider the equal possibility that media content shapes religion and politics as much as religion and politics shape media content. We also should acknowledge that popular journalism has acquired a major role in articulating some of our most important cultural ideals, and that at times journalism itself takes on the qualities of religious ritual.

Certainly news about death is more than merely a reporting process. It is a dialogic process in which audience members are, if only rhetorically, included in the various forms of tribute that play out on television and in the pages of newspapers and magazines. It also is a form of professional practice in which journalists have an unusually close relationship with newsmakers and the public, as well as an unusual level of awareness of (or, at any rate, reflexive commentary about) their own presence in the story.

The symbiotic relationship between reporters and the public can be seen in the evolution of coverage during the 10 days following Ronald Reagan's death: as journalists focused on "ordinary mourners," more and more people turned up at the public ceremonies to speak to reporters, thus confirming that their "spontaneous" public tribute was in fact the story, and thus greatly changing the tone of the coverage. Sometimes journalists are cast in the role of villains in death stories, as insensitive intruders who only make the horror worse. This was true to some extent in public discussion (ironically, through journalism itself) of the Amish murders and of coverage of victims of various kinds of disasters—what some critics have called "disaster porn." More often, though, such circumstances elevate the status and authority of reporters, on whom citizens depend for crucial information amid chaos and rumor. In these situations, news media are not only witnesses and interpreters with cameras, but also vehicles for statements from public officials and forums for the exchange of information within the community. In these and other kinds of upsetting events, journalists serve as healers, consolers, and mourners themselves, overtly sympathetic to their subjects.

Journalists' deference to their sources and subjects was evident in their open admiration of the Amish community and in their outrage over the plight of Katrina victims. Similarly, many news subjects sought out journalists, either to get help (disaster victims) or to send the general public a cautionary message (teen deaths) or a declaration of tribute (family remembrances of the dead of September 11). When they spoke about their friends "for the record," the World War II veterans were acknowledging not just journalism's status as the first draft of history, but also their own impending deaths—and journalists were there because of their own respect for that inevitability.

For the general audience, coverage of death is instructive in a number of ways. It is prescriptive, in that it shows us what not to do (drive drunk) and how to behave should we ever find ourselves in a crisis. Sometimes the news contains useful information about survival in particular circumstances, though more often it offers broader lessons: stick together, help your neighbors, trust in God, repent your sins, believe in miracles. Coverage also teaches us how to mourn. We know to show up with teddy bears, candles, and pictures at memorial sites, just as we know to show up with a casserole at the family home of someone who died. The difference is that the newer traditions are transmitted via mass media.

The studies in this book shed light on the cultural functions of journalism—informational and instructive, communal and ritual. Together, they create a model for understanding journalists not only as purveyors of timeless narratives, but also as central participants in the culture they "cover," especially at times when tragedy or remembrance prompts a shared, public assessment of American values. This coverage also teaches us about death itself, or, at any rate, cultural ideals about death, raising the question: What do we owe the dead?

The most common news themes tell us that we owe their bodies respect, recovery, dignified treatment, and burial at home. Those ideals were in place in American society before mass media were a factor in public life, let alone the central forum for social expressions of public grief. Since they have taken over that function, though, journalistic coverage of death stresses one theme above all others: that what we owe the dead is ritual that promises that we will remember them. Tribute enacted in public space (which includes journalism) is what mediated death stories allow audiences to be a part of, and what we collectively owe the dead.

In coverage of culturally important death, news becomes a moral fable. It provides closure by reinforcing what are presented as timeless values: the American spirit of hard work, the importance of family and community solidarity, the pride of patriotism, the power of religious faith, and the satisfaction of a "simple" life lived according to "traditional" values. Encoded in these themes are national ideals and nationalist sentiments, and their appearance in news (in coverage of many topics, not just death) is always an occasion for criticism of the political conservatism of the American press. Yet these values are not entirely, or even primarily, the wishful construction of journalists; they come from, and continuously circulate within, the broader culture, as do journalists themselves.

Our modern "hunger for heroism" didn't begin with Ronald Reagan; indeed, it is not even modern. The "enduring values" that Gans identified in news, and that this study confirms, are just that—enduring. They come from the past and will survive into the future. The death coverage itself contains specific references to the past, as well as warnings or promises for the future. Coverage of Hurricane Katrina contained the same kind of shocking brutality, and moralizing about death, that David Copeland and other historians found in the Colonial-era press. To understand the 1989 California earthquake, people looked back to 1906; when Oklahoma was hit by tornadoes in 1999, observers recalled the trauma of the bombing of the Murrah Federal Building four years earlier. Certainly tributes to World War II veterans recall the past, just as those veterans' faithful recounting of their friends' lives is a form of revisiting the past. Obituaries of ordinary, small-town residents of Alabama recalled their links to great moments in American history.

Yet death coverage also is about the future. It offers warnings and prescriptions, and it promises that "enduring" values will indeed continue. As it tells us stories about our fellow Americans who experience some crisis, this kind of news story invites audiences to speculate: How will I, or my neighbors or my countrymen, react in a crisis? Will we be selflessly heroic, or might we not be?

On the whole, news stories about death reassure us about both the past and the present. While their affirming, mythic themes may be conservative, they also are preservative. These kinds of stories do function to reassure local communities after a traumatic event. And nationally, they create at least the illusion of public participation in a ritual of respect, a discussion about what really matters. That discussion rarely lasts, of course; people (journalists and audiences alike) forget "lessons learned," and even the most traumatic events fade in public memory over time. Yet news is a matter of "eternal recurrence," as Paul Rock put it (1973, p. 226). And so are death stories. The examples surveyed in this book are those that happen to be among us now. They contain the echoes of the moral fables of the past and the likely lessons of the future, as our human condition is assessed in American journalism. Ultimately, these are stories that teach us how to live as well as how to die.

# NOTES

## CHAPTER 3

1. This statement is based on an extensive search of American national broadcast transcripts (of CBS, NBC, ABC, CNN, Fox, and other networks) conducted via the LexisNexis electronic database. While these news media all covered the Nickel Mines shootings, their transcripts contained almost no evidence of reflexive discussion of the role of the media in intruding upon the local community, except to point out that the Amish are not used to media attention. Some reports included expressions of concern that media exposure may prompt "copycat" killings (see, for instance, *The O'Reilly Factor*, 2006). One news program on the Fox network did ask: "Did the media behave responsibly bringing themselves into this Old World community?" The conclusion was partly that "The media don't cover religion very well," but beyond this, the consensus was that media had been respectful of the Amish (*Fox News Watch*, 2006).

2. The daily newspapers in the first two categories are the Lancaster *Intelligencer Journal* (16 miles away from Nickel Mines, the site of the crime); the Lancaster *New Era* (16 miles); the *Reading Eagle* (39 miles); the Wilmington (DE) *News-Journal* (40 miles); the *York Daily Record* (41 miles); the Harrisburg *Patriot-News* (50 miles); *The Philadelphia Inquirer* (59 miles); *The Philadelphia Daily News* (59 miles); the Allentown *Morning Call* (74 miles); and *The Baltimore Sun* (76 miles). For the categories within 50 and 100 miles of Nickel Mines, all daily newspapers with circulations above 50,000 have been included. This group includes all cities in this geographic area and excludes only a few daily papers in the lowest circulation category as defined by the Newspapers Association of America, under 50,000 (see <www.naa.org>, accessed October 21, 2006). Distances (to city center) are from <mapquest.com>, accessed October 21, 2006.

3. According to the Audit Bureau of Circulations (accessed online at <www.accessabc.com> on October 21, 2006), these were the top-10-circulation

daily newspapers in the U.S., beginning with highest circulation; in parentheses is their distance from Nickel Mines: *USA Today* (112 miles); *The Wall Street Journal* (145 miles); *The New York Times* (145 miles); *The Los Angeles Times* (2,662 miles); *The Washington Post* (112 miles); *The Chicago Tribune* (708 miles); the New York *Daily News* (145 miles); *The Philadelphia Inquirer* (59 miles); *The Denver Post* (1,699 miles); and *The Houston Chronicle* (1,516 miles).

4. Of the rest, only *The Denver Post* and *The Los Angeles Times* sent their own reporters to Nickel Mines.

5. The only other major American newspapers to send their own reporters to Nickel Mines were *The New York Post* (five photo spreads with brief text), *The Boston Globe* (one on-site report), and *The St. Petersburg* (FL) *Times* (three on-site reports).

6. Several newspapers from Canada, England, Ireland, and Australia also assigned their own reporters (already based in the U.S.) to cover this story, according to a LexisNexis "general news/major papers" search conducted October 25, 2006.

7. The LexisNexis database was used to make sure that, with regard to the 20 newspapers studied, all coverage was identified, even if hard copy was available. In some cases this electronic database was the source of the text. In other cases, coverage was accessed via the respective newspapers' own Web site. Yet whenever possible, printed versions of these newspapers were consulted, owing to the importance of understanding headline placement and use of photographs in the context of these newspapers' discussions of the propriety of the coverage. Hard-copy coverage was obtained for seven of the 10 "local/regional" papers (not those from Wilmington, Reading, or Allentown, though with regard to the last, the *Morning Call*'s own print coverage discussed its use of photographs) and for six of the 10 "national" papers (not those from Chicago, Houston, Denver, or Los Angeles).

## CHAPTER 4

1. In a deviation from the citation style of this book, obituaries in this chapter will be listed alphabetically in the reference section, using full names. For example, the headline for this particular article was "Porter Harvey, 91," but is cited as "Harvey, Porter, 91." This was done to make finding individual references easier. Following the standard citation style, authors of other types of articles will be listed by last name and first initial.

2. These issues were found at the Guntersville Public Library, 1240 O'Brig Avenue, Guntersville, AL 35976. They are included under call number MIC 976.194 in the microfilm collection, reels 70991 (January–June 1965), 70992 (July–December 1965), 71059 (January–June 1995), and 71060 (July–December 1995).

3. This personal letter was written by Sam Harvey to Janice Hume, dated January 4, 2006, after he had read an earlier published version of this study in *Grassroots Editor*, 46:4 (Winter 2005), 1–8.

## CHAPTER 5

1. Examples of subsequent coverage would include promotion and reviews of the biopic films *Ray*, starring Jamie Foxx, later in 2004, or *Walk the Line*, about Johnny Cash, in 2005. The plots of these films—featuring actors approved by the celebrities themselves prior to their deaths, and full of "authentic" details meant to create the feeling of documentary rather than fictional texts—strengthen and advance the stories that were told in journalism just after Charles's and Cash's death, and they are relevant to the broader cultural phenomenon examined in this paper. They are not analyzed here, however, since study of the conventions of film versus those of journalism may call for expanded theory and method not within the purview of this study.
2. I owe this insight to Patricia Bradley, Professor Emeritus at Temple University, in correspondence about the death of Richard Pryor (December 12, 2005). She commented on the forgiving nature of news coverage of his passing, noting, "bad boys are allowed to be bad boys when their badness apparently only hurts themselves. The truth is that badness always impacts negatively on the world around them. But since these negative aspects of bad boyhood primarily hurt women, they are brushed aside (how many interviews have we seen with any of the exes, even the many that bear celebrity children)?"
3. For this insight, I thank an anonymous reviewer of an earlier version of this work, who rightly noted that "celebrity journalism is full of the tribulations of stars who work hard against the threat of fat, and their struggle is documented approvingly, making them more human and sympathetic. Brando's indifference to this is reproval to the code of celebrity, and I think it is an important element in his failure to be redeemed."

## CHAPTER 6

1. This estimate is for 2003. See the Web site of the National Center for Health Statistics, http://www.cdc.gov/nchs/fastats/lifexpec.htm (2006, 10 March).

## CHAPTER 7

1. *The Charleston Gazette* is West Virginia's largest newspaper, and it devoted the most attention to the accident than any other news organization in this study. *The Pittsburgh Post-Gazette* is geographically the

closest major paper to both the Sago mine and the Quecreek mine, and it provided extensive coverage of both accidents.

2. *The Charleston Gazette* accounts for 383 articles, more than half of the total sample, in this study. Of those, 149 were about mine safety, the United Mine Workers, the public hearings on Sago, and the Mine Safety and Health Administration. Most were written by Ken Ward, Jr.

3. Though its attention to Sago was tiny compared to the other news media (just 11 articles over eight months), *The Wall Street Journal* covered it as a business story about the International Coal Group and Wilbur Ross, the bankruptcy specialist who had purchased the mine in late 2005; about the "losses" of mine accidents and deaths; and about the likelihood of stiffer fines. (Not surprisingly, the *Journal's* focus was on the fate of the corporation and the industry as a whole, not of labor.)

## CHAPTER 8

1. The hour-long documentary, "Portraits of Grief," was co-produced by The Discovery Channel and New York Times Television.

2. All of the Portraits, as well as the great majority of the magazine coverage discussed in this chapter's second study, were published in 2001. Subsequent parenthetical citations will not repeat this date unless doing so is necessary to distinguish among citations with the same leading word.

3. The regular weekly issues were dated September 24, October 1, October 8, and October 15. In addition, *Time* published one special issue, while *Newsweek* and *U.S. News & World Report* each published two. All of the newsweeklies are published on Mondays and carry the issue's *off*-sale date, so issues dated September 24 were on sale on September 17, six days after the attack. Although two of them were undated, the "special editions" issued by all three magazines were on sale on Friday, September 14, three days after the attack. The analysis includes all text and photographs in these issues, including reader letters, which played an important role in the story's closure. *Newsweek* noted that it received 2,000 letters per week during the time period covered by this study (Letters, 2001b, p. 14, and 2001c, p. 15).

4. These words are used by Nico H. Frijda in his discussion of the funeral service (1997, p. 114), though Frijda and other scholars have based their arguments on the theoretical foundation laid by anthropologist Arnold van Gennep in his seminal work, *The Rites of Passage* (1960/1908).

5. The Tennyson quote actually came from literary critic Harold Bloom, as his recommendation of what Americans should read in order to gain perspective and consolation.

6. By the following week, the main story was terrorists' mailing of letters containing anthrax.

7. For an essay on *The New York Times* obituaries, see Baker (1996).

## CHAPTER 9

1. The top-circulation newspapers were (according to the Audit Bureau of Circulations, retrieved June 6, 2004, from http://www.accessabc.com), in order: *USA Today, The Wall Street Journal, The New York Times, The Los Angeles Times, The Washington Post, The Chicago Tribune,* the New York *Daily News, The Denver Post/Rocky Mountain News, The Philadelphia Inquirer,* and *The Dallas Morning News.* These papers include the three geographic areas most important in Reagan's life: Washington, Los Angeles, and Chicago (his home state of Illinois). Some newspapers were purchased in print while others were accessed online; in the latter case, care was taken to access online content on the same day it was posted, in order to be sure of the date of content origination. CNN was omitted primarily because its 24-hour coverage cycle (over 10 days) yielded content that would have exceeded coverage of all the rest of the journalistic media put together. Although the public grieving process played out over a seven-day period (Saturday, June 5 to Friday, June 11, 2004), a 10-day period of news coverage was chosen because it allowed for inclusion of (1) reports on the Friday-evening (June 11) burial service published in the Monday (June 14) issues of the two newspapers included in this study that do not publish regular editions on weekends (*USA Today* and *The Wall Street Journal*), and (2) the second week of coverage by the newsmagazines (which carry their off-sale date, so the latest of those included in the study, though dated June 21, 2004, were on sale on June 14, 2004).

2. See, for instance (all 2004): A presidency; *All Things Considered*, June 7; Berger; *CBS Evening News*, June 7; *CBS News Special Report*, June 5; *Face the Nation*; *NPR News Special Report*; Ronald Reagan, 1911–2004; *Talk of the Nation*; *The Tavis Smiley Show*, June 10; *This Week with George Stephanopoulos*; Toner & Pear; Fausset.

3. This figure is based on news estimates of the number of people present at three sites: approximately 100,000 who went to see Reagan's casket earlier in the week when it was at the Presidential Library in California; 104,684 who went through the Capitol Rotunda while he lay in state; and approximately 150,000 who lined the route of the motorcade in California the day of his burial (*Good Morning America*, June 11; *NBC News Special Report: Ronald Wilson Reagan, 1911–2004*; *The Today Show*, June 9; all 2004).

4. National Public Radio was the only one of the journalistic organizations included in this study that continued to provide coverage of the political nuances of Reagan's "legacy," bad as well as good, throughout the week, and to include several reports specifically on his "culture of hostility toward the poor," including African Americans (*The Tavis Smiley Show*, 2004b).

5. It is interesting, within this quote, that a television producer gave the credit for "mak[ing] America feel good about itself" to television itself, not to Reagan. Davis further points out that Reagan's two terms were the era of "the defunding of public memory," the cutting of federal monies for the National Park Service, libraries, and museums. She accuses Reagan of ignoring history while promoting "historical mythologizing" (S. Davis, 1988, p. 138). For additional discussion of Reagan's rhetoric, see: Combs, 1993; Erickson, 1985; C. Smith, 1987; and Wills, 1987.

6. Like the *Washington Post* article that compared the nighttime scene outside the Capitol to public congregations during World War II and just after September 11, this passage made heavy-handed references to other historical events, linking public mourning for Reagan to the public mourning for two earlier U.S. Presidents who had died *while in office* (one by assassination)—as though Reagan's death were an unexpected tragedy.

# REFERENCES

1 teen in crash out of hospital. (2004, May 27). *The Seattle Times*, p. B3.

111 unidentified corpses at crematory perplex investigators. (2003, April 9). *The New York Times,* p. A12.

*48 hours investigates.* (2004, June 11). Columbia Broadcasting System (CBS).

60 second symposium. (2001, October 1). *Time*, 13.

*ABC news special report.* (2004, May 29). American Broadcasting Company (ABC).

*ABC news special report: Farewell to a President.* (2004, June 11). ABC.

Abdoul Karim Traor—success in America. (2001, December 19). *The New York Times*, p. B7.

Adams, H. C. (2006, October 15). "Speaking the same language." *Sunday News* (Lancaster, PA), pp. A1, A6.

Adams, N. (2001, October 4). Wendell Jamieson discusses how *The New York Times* is handling obituaries for those killed in the terrorist attacks. *All Things Considered*. National Public Radio (NPR).

Adams, W. C. (1986). Whose lives count?: TV coverage of natural disasters. *Journal of Communication, 36*, 113–122.

Aizenman, N. C. (2004, May 26). Black soldiers battled fascism and racism. *The Washington Post*, pp. B1, B4.

Alaniz, V. (1995, May 9). A death in the family. *Dallas Morning News*, p. A21.

Allan, S. (1999). *News culture.* Buckingham: Open University Press.

*All things considered.* (2004, June 7). National Public Radio (NPR).

*All things considered.* (2006, January 4). NPR.

Alter, J. (2001, n.d. [fall]). Patriotism. *Newsweek: Commemorative issue*, 80–83.

Altheide, D. L. (2002). *Creating fear: News and the construction of crisis.* New York: Aldine de Gruyter.

Always in demand. (2001, October 18). *The New York Times*, p. B13.

Always making plans. (2001, September 27). *The New York Times*, p. B11.

Amato, J. A. (1993). Death and the stories we don't have. *Monist, 76*, 252–269.

Anderson, E. (2005a, September 2). Teams to sweep stricken area to find those killed. *New Orleans Times-Picayune*, p. A1.

Anderson, E. (2005b, September 29). Katrina tragedy becomes personal. *New Orleans Times-Picayune*, p. A1.

Anthony, S. (2004, February 2). Teen killed in accident "had really matured." *St. Louis Post-Dispatch*, St. Charles County Post, p. 1.

Apartment complex is the focus for death. (1994, January 18). *St. Petersburg Times*, p. A6.

Arey, N. (2002a, February 20). Crematory probe: A shock as home searched. *Atlanta Journal-Constitution*, p. B1.

Arey, N. (2002b, February 21). Efforts to drain pond under way. *Atlanta Journal-Constitution*, p. B1.

Arey, N. (2002c, February 27). Charges against Marsh mount. *Atlanta Journal-Constitution*, p. A1.

Arey, N. (2002d, March 1). Crematory probe: State urges judge to end gag order. *Atlanta Journal-Constitution*, p. D3.

Arey N. (2002e, March 5). Tri-State puzzle: Crematorium isn't broken. *Atlanta Journal-Constitution*, p. C1.

Arey, N. (2002f, March 23). Tri-State Crematory probe: Ruling delayed on Marsh bond. *Atlanta Journal-Constitution*, p. E3.

Arey, N. (2002g, April 19). Marshes may go home today. *Atlanta Journal-Constitution*, p. C6.

Arey, N. (2002h, July 26). Crematory suspect is allowed to make bail. *Atlanta Journal-Constitution*, p. D1.

Arey, N. (2002i, July 31). Marsh safety issues surface. *Atlanta Journal-Constitution*, p. B1.

Arey, N. (2002j, August 9). Tri-State defendant denied protection. *Atlanta Journal-Constitution*, p. D1.

Arey, N. (2002k, August 28). Marsh leaves jail to jeers, sees family. *Atlanta Journal-Constitution*, p. B1.

Arey, N. (2002l, September 8). Marsh attorney can take the heat. *Atlanta Journal-Constitution*, p. C1.

Arey, N. (2003a, February 8). Marsh allowed more liberty. *Atlanta Journal-Constitution*, p. C3.

Arey, N. (2003b, February 9). Shock has dissipated, but anger runs high. *Atlanta Journal-Constitution*, p. E1.

Arey, N. (2003c, June 20). Tri-State findings grimmer. *Atlanta Journal-Constitution*, p. B1.

Arey, N. (2003d, September 24). Crematory trial costs escalate. *Atlanta Journal-Constitution*, p. C1.

Arey, N. (2003e, November 17). Marsh wants taxpayers to pick up legal tab. *Atlanta Journal-Constitution*, p. B1.

Arey, N. (2003f, November 18). Hearings begin in crematory case. *Atlanta Journal-Constitution*, p. B1.

Arey, N. (2004a, March 2). Suit costs millions for funeral homes. *Atlanta Journal-Constitution*, p. D1.

Arey, N. (2004b, March 12). Tri-State civil settlement gives families $39.5 million. *Atlanta Journal-Constitution*, p. D3.

Arey, N. (2004c, August 26). Lawyer describes crematory trouble. *Atlanta Journal-Constitution,* p. C2.

Arey, N. (2004d, October 13). Crematory owner wins appeal. *Atlanta Journal-Constitution,* p. B5.

Arey, N. (2004e, October 14). Crematory deal may avert trial. *Atlanta Journal-Constitution,* p. A1.

Arey, N. (2004f, November 20). Guilty plea in huge crematory scandal. *Atlanta Journal-Constitution,* p. A1.

Arey, N. (2005a, January 8). Ex-crematorium operator faces families of deceased. *Atlanta Journal-Constitution,* p. E3.

Arey, N. (2005b, February 1). Marsh sentenced as emotions flow. *Atlanta Journal-Constitution,* p. B1.

Argento, M. (2006, October 8). Fatal attraction. *York Sunday News,* pp. B1, B6.

Ariès, P. (1974). *Western attitudes toward death: From the Middle Ages to the present.* Baltimore: Johns Hopkins University Press.

Armstrong, Royce, 92. (1995, September 20). *Guntersville Advertiser-Gleam,* p.18.

Arthur Warren Scullin: A schmoozer extraordinaire. (2001, November 25). *The New York Times,* p. B8.

Associated Press. (2004, August 23). Civil trial to open over bodies found untended at crematory. In *The New York Times,* p. A3.

Associated Press. (2006, March 1). Mine survivor returns home. In *The Washington Post,* p. A3.

Auchincloss, K. (2001a, September 24). We shall overcome. *Newsweek,* 18–25.

Auchincloss, K. (2001b, n.d. [fall]). Back on our feet. *Newsweek: Commemorative issue,* 14–18.

Audit Bureau of Circulations. (2006). Top 200 newspapers by largest reported circulation www.accessabc.com).

Austin, J. P. (2001, October 15). Letters. *Time,* 11.

Avila, J., Brokaw, T., Cummins, J., & Williams, B. (1999, May 5). Oklahoma/tornadoes. *NBC Evening News,* National Broadcasting Company (NBC).

Ayers, Floyd. (1995, July 26). *Guntersville Advertiser-Gleam,* p. 16.

Ayres, B. D. Jr. (1994, January 25). The earthquake: In city of motorcycle-cop mystique, an officer, and quake victim, is laid to rest. *The New York Times,* p. A16.

Back at work, as a captain. (2001, September 22). *The New York Times,* p. B13.

Baker, R. (1996). Foreword. In M. Siegel (Ed.), *The last word* (pp. v–xii). New York: William Morrow.

Baldasty, G. J. (1992). *The commercialization of news in the nineteenth century.* Madison: University of Wisconsin Press.

Ballard, P. (2006, August 19). Motorcycle ride is rolling memorial to 9/11. *The Herald Mail* (Hagerstown, MD), pp. A1, A2.

Banerjee, N. (2007, April 20). In shadow of a tragedy, longing for normalcy but enveloped by grief. *The New York Times,* p. A16.

Barkin, S. M. (1984). The journalist as storyteller: An interdisciplinary perspective. *American Journalism, 1*(2), 27–33.

Barnett, Crawford. (1995, April 19). *Guntersville Advertiser-Gleam,* p. 8.

Barringer, F., & Goodman, B. (2006, January 6). Coal miners' notes of goodbye, and questions on a blast's cause. *The New York Times,* pp. A1, A18.

Barry, D. (2005, September 8). Macabre reminder: The corpse on Union Street. *The New York Times,* p. A1.

Barry, E. (2006, October 4). Gunman planned sex assault on Amish girls, police say. *Los Angeles Times,* p. A9.

Barry J. McKeon: Leading by example. (2001, December 28). *The New York Times,* p. B8.

Barthes, R. (1972). *Mythologies.* A. Lavers (Trans.). New York: Hill and Wang.

Barthes, R. (1977). *Image – music – text.* S. Heath (Trans.). New York: Hill and Wang.

Battaglio, S. (2005, December 19). Tribute: Richard Pryor, 1940–2005. *TV Guide,* 13.

Baughman, J. L. (1998). The transformation of *Time* magazine. *Media Studies Journal, 12*(3), 120–127.

Bazar, E. (2006a, January 6–8). Despite tragedy, miners' way of life will live on. *USA Today,* pp. 1A, 2A.

Bazar, E. (2006b, January 9). Goodbyes begin for W.Va. miners. *USA Today,* p. 1A.

Bazar, E. (2006c, February 9). For miner, fog is lifting. *USA Today,* pp. 1A, 4A.

Bazar, E. (2006d, April 28). Survivor tells of Sago Mine ordeal. *USA Today,* p. 1A.

Bazar, E., & Vanden Brook, T. (2006, January 13–15). "I never caught up with them." *USA Today,* pp. 1A, 4A.

Becker, E. (1973). *The denial of death.* New York: Free Press.

Beckerman, G. (2004, May/June). Across the great divide—faith. *Columbia Journalism Review, 43,* 26–30.

Bennett, A. (2006, October 8). Reporting a tragedy, with compassion. *The Philadelphia Inquirer,* p. C7.

Bennett, W. L., Gressett, L. A., & Haltom, W. (1985, Spring). Repairing the news: A case study of the news paradigm. *Journal of Communication, 35*(2), 50–68.

Bentley, Mac. (1999, May 6). Profiles of life. *The Oklahoman,* p. 20.

Berger, M. (2004, June 6). Ronald Reagan dies at 93. *The New York Times,* pp. 1, 28–31.

Berry, D. (2006, February 9). Domestic violence increases with rising unemployment rates. *The Charleston Gazette,* p. 5A.

Bird, F. (1980). The contemporary ritual milieu. In R. B. Browne (Ed.), *Rituals and ceremonies in popular culture* (pp. 19–35). Bowling Green, OH: Bowling Green University Popular Press.

Bird, S. E. (1992). *For enquiring minds: A cultural study of supermarket tabloids.* Knoxville: University of Tennessee Press.

Bird, S. E. (2003). *The audience in everyday life: Living in a media world.* Routledge: New York and London.

Bird, S. E., & Dardenne, R. W. (1997). Myth, chronicle, and story: Exploring the narrative qualities of news. In D. Berkowitz (Ed.), *Social meanings of news* (pp. 333–350). Thousand Oaks, CA: Sage.

Bishop, Minnie, 103. (1995, April 8). *Guntersville Advertiser-Gleam*, p. 18.

Bishop, Mrs. R. V. (1965, August 4). *Guntersville Advertiser-Gleam*, p. 1.

Bizjak, T. & Sandalow, M. (1989, October 20). I-880 death estimate is falling. *The San Francisco Chronicle*, p. A1.

Blackstone, J., Bowen, J., & Rather, D. (1989, October 19). North California/earthquake/Oakland. *CBS Evening News.*

Block, M. (2006, March 23). Bodies still being discovered in New Orleans cleanup. *All Things Considered*, NPR.

Blue eyes and red cars. (2001, October 26). *The New York Times*, p. B 11.

Bly, L. (2004, May 28). WWII memorial: The D.C. salute. *USA Today*, pp. 1D, 2D.

Bodnar, J. (1992). *Remaking America: Public memory, commemoration, and patriotism in the twentieth century.* Princeton, NJ: Princeton University Press.

Bodnar, J. (2003). *Blue-collar Hollywood: Liberalism, democracy, and working people in American film.* Baltimore: Johns Hopkins University Press.

Bonds: Financial and family. (2001, October 31). *The New York Times*, p. B12.

Boorstin, D. J. (1987). *The image: A guide to pseudo-events in America.* 25th anniv. ed. New York: Random House.

Borman, E. G. (1982a). Colloquy: Fantasy and rhetorical vision: Ten years later. *Quarterly Journal of Speech, 68,* 288–305.

Borman, E. G. (1982b). A fantasy theme analysis of the television coverage of the hostage release and the Reagan inaugural. *Quarterly Journal of Speech, 68,* 133–145.

Borman, E. G. (1985). Symbolic convergence theory: A communication formulation. *Journal of Communication, 35*(4), 128–138.

Bowen, J., Chung, C., Hughes, S., Rather, D., Threlkeld, R., & Whitaker, B. (1994, January 17). California/earthquake. *CBS Evening News.*

Bowen, J., & Rather, D. (1989, October 18). North California/earthquake. *CBS Evening News*, CBS.

Bowers, C., Pitts, B., & Rather, D. (1999, May 6). Oklahoma/tornadoes. *CBS Evening News*, CBS.

Braudy, L. (1986). *The frenzy of renown: Fame and its history.* New York: Oxford University Press.

Breakdown at Sago. (2006, January 15). *Pittsburgh Post-Gazette*, p. A1.

Breed, A. G. (2006, January 7). Families plan funerals. Associated Press, in *The Patriot-News* [Harrisburg, PA], p. A3.

Bridges, Joy, 50. (1995, May 13). *Guntersville Advertiser-Gleam*, p. 13.

Briggs, B., & Dunn, J. (2004, November 28). Wasted lessons. *The Denver Post*, p. A1.

Broder, J. M., & Leduff, C. (2004, June 9). 100,000, one by one, pay tribute to a president. *The New York Times*, pp. A1, A18.

Brothers, Ervin. (1995, June 10). *Guntersville Advertiser-Gleam*, p. 16.

Brown, M. (2005, September 11). Guard's mission: Morbid "recovery." *New Orleans Times-Picayune*, p. A2.

Brown, R. (2006, October 6). Help Amish by leaving them alone, expert says. *The News Journal* (Wilmington, DE), n.p. Accessed online at <delaware-online.com> on October 22, 2006.

Brown, S. (2005, December 23). Richard Pryor, 1940–2005. *Entertainment Weekly*, 14–18.

Brubaker, J. (2006a, October 5). First Amish girl's funeral begins two-day process of burying five schoolhouse murder victims in same cemetery. *The New Era* (Lancaster, PA), p. A1.

Brubaker, J. (2006b, October 20). Rainbow poetry calms community after Amish tragedy. *The Lancaster New Era*, p. A8.

Bryant, Alvatine Biddle. (1995, January 14). *Guntersville Advertiser-Gleam*, p. 14.

Buckelew funeral. (1995, October 4). *Guntersville Advertiser-Gleam*, p. 12.

Buffet, E. P. (1870, March). Is death painful? *Putnam's Monthly Magazine of American Literature, Science and Art, 15*(27), 11–319.

A bundle of energy. (2001, November 7). *The New York Times*, p. B8.

Burdette, Tiny. (1995, January 14). *Guntersville Advertiser-Gleam*, p. 14.

Burnette II, D. (2005, May 26). 2 killed, 3 hurt in two northern Colo. wrecks. *The Denver Post*, p. B3.

Business and Buddhism. (2001, September 30). *The New York Times*, p. B11.

Byerly, K. R. (1961). *Community journalism*. Philadelphia: Chilton.

Caldwell, Vera. (1995, August 2). *Guntersville Advertiser-Gleam*, p. 14.

Capital swings and jitterbugs to honor the vets. (2004, May 28). *USA Today*, p. 1D.

Carey, J. (1987). "Why and how?": The dark continent of American journalism. In R. K. Manoff & M. Schudson (Eds.), *Reading the news* (pp. 146–196). Newbury Park, CA: Sage.

Carey, J. (1989). *Communication as culture*. Boston: Unwin Hyman.

Carlsen, W. (1989, October 27). How estimates of the quake dead grew in the media. *The San Francisco Chronicle*, p. A17.

Carpe diem, to music. (2001, September 26). *The New York Times*, p. B11.

Carpenter, P. (2006, October 13). A clash of views on Amish photos hits a newsroom. *The Morning Call* (Allentown, PA), p. B1.

Carter, B. (2004, June 12). Day after day, funeral filled the small screen. *The New York Times*, p. A10.

Carter, Seburn. (1995, February 15). *Guntersville Advertiser-Gleam*, p. 14.

Catching up with friends. (2001, October 19). *The New York Times*, p. B11.

Caughey, J. L. (1984). *Imaginary social worlds: A cultural approach*. Lincoln: University of Nebraska Press.

*CBS evening news.* (2004a, April 29). CBS.

*CBS evening news.* (2004b, May 27). CBS.

*CBS evening news.* (2004c, May 29). CBS.

*CBS evening news.* (2004d, June 7). CBS.

*CBS evening news.* (2004e, June 9). CBS.

*CBS evening news.* (2004f, June 11). CBS.

*CBS evening news.* (2006, January 4). CBS.

*CBS morning news.* (2004, June 10). CBS.

*CBS news special report.* (2004a, June 5). CBS.

*CBS news special report.* (2004b, June 9). CBS.

*CBS Sunday morning.* (2004, May 30). CBS.

A celebration of heroes: D-Day at 60: An MSNBC living history event. (2004, June 4). Advertisement in *The New York Times*, p. A5.

Chawkins, S. (2004, June 12). Lasting memories gleaned along the final leg. *The Los Angeles Times*. Retrieved June 12, 2004, from http://www.latimes.com.

Childress, R. V. (1995, July 5). *Guntersville Advertiser-Gleam*, p. 2.

Chung, C., Hughes, S., & Rather, D. (1994, January 24). California/earthquake. *CBS Evening News.*

Claiborne, R., Jennings, P., Muller, J. & Rose, J. (1994, January 17). California/earthquake, *NBC Evening News*, NBC.

Clark, J., & Franzmann, M. (2006). Authority from grief, presence and place in the making of roadside memorials. *Death Studies, 30,* 579–599.

Clark, R. P. (2002, February 4). Portraits of grief. The Poynter Institute. Retrieved February 4, 2002, from http://www.poynter.org.

Clemetson, L. (2004, May 30). Stories of World War II quietly told by those who won it. *The New York Times*, sec. 1, p. 22.

Cloud, D. L. (1998). *Control and consolation in American culture and politics: Rhetorics of therapy.* Thousand Oaks, CA: Sage.

*CNN capital gang.* (2004, May 29). Cable News Network (CNN).

*CNN live Saturday.* (2004, May 29). CNN.

*CNN newsnight.* (2004, May 27). CNN.

Combs, J. (1993). *The Reagan range: The nostalgic myth in American politics.* Bowling Green, OH: Bowling Green State University Popular Press.

Common tragedy and culprits [editorial]. (2006, October 3). *The Washington Post*, p. A16.

Congbalay, D. (1989, November 29). Friends mourn quake survivor Buck Helm. *The San Francisco Chronicle*, p. B6.

Conner, S. M., & Wesolowski, K. (2004). Newspaper framing of fatal motor vehicle crashes in four Midwestern cities in the United States, 1999–2000. *Injury Prevention, 10,* 149–153.

Cooper, Howard, 55. (1995, April 12). *Guntersville Advertiser-Gleam*, p. 8.

Copeland, D. (1997). *Colonial American newspapers: Character and content.* Newark: University of Delaware Press.

Copeland, L. (2002a, February 19). Crematory operator back in jail. *USA Today*, p. A3.

Copeland, L. (2002b, February 20). Body discoveries devastate town in Ga. *USA Today,* p. A10.

Copeland, L. (2002c, February 22). Crematory owners respected. *USA Today,* p. A3.

Corliss, R. (2003, September 22). The man in black. *Time,* 60–66.

Couldry, N. (2003). *Media rituals: A critical approach.* London: Routledge.

Councill, A. (2006, January 1). Quiet horsemen. *The New York Times,* p. 62.

Countdown to the ceremony. (2004, May 23). *The Washington Post,* p. A1.

Courogen, C. (2006, October 19). Heartbreaking. *The Patriot-News* (Harrisburg, PA), pp. A1, A16.

Cox, E. Wade. (1995, September 23). *Guntersville Advertiser-Gleam,* p. 16.

Craig Montano: Offbeat interests. (2001, December 31). *The New York Times,* p. B6.

Cramer, B. (1999a, May 7). Tornado victim showed integrity in life, death, loved ones say. *The Oklahoman,* p. A1.

Cramer, B. (1999b, May 9). Profiles of Life. *The Oklahoman,* p. A11.

Cramer, B. (1999c, May 12). Profiles of life. *The Oklahoman,* p. A6.

Cramer, B. (1999d, May 13). Life or death meeting. *The Oklahoman,* p. A1.

Cranford, Horace. (1995, November 18). *Guntersville Advertiser-Gleam,* p. 20.

Crawford, E. (1997, January 31). Winter death toll a grim reminder. *The Forum,* Metro & State, p. 1.

Crematory declared disaster area as hundreds of corpses found strewn about site. (2002, March 4). *Jet,* 12.

Crematory operator must give deposition. (2002, November 29). *Atlanta Journal-Constitution,* p. D8.

Cunningham, Edna. (1995, February 18). *Guntersville Advertiser-Gleam,* p. 12.

Dabbs, Bobby, 47. (1995, August 9). *Guntersville Advertiser-Gleam,* p. 12.

Dahlgren, P. (1999). Television news narrative. In M. S. Mander (Ed.), *Framing friction: Media and social conflict* (pp. 189–214). Champaign: University of Illinois Press.

Daly, C. (2001). Letters. *Newsweek,* October 1, p. 12.

Dao, J. (2006a, January 4). Miner's body found; search continues for others. *The New York Times,* pp. A1, A15.

Dao, J. (2006b, January 5). In miners' town, grief, anger and questions. *The New York Times,* pp. A1, A19.

Darden, Waymon. (1995, September 13). *Guntersville Advertiser-Gleam,* p. 4.

Darnton, R. (1975). Writing news and telling stories. *Daedalus, 104,* 175–194.

*Dateline NBC.* (2004, June 5). NBC.

*Dateline NBC.* (2006, March 30). NBC.

*Dateline NBC: Miracle in the mountain.* (2002, July 28). NBC.

David B. Brady: A soccer dad. (2001, December 8). *The New York Times,* p. B8.

David Kovalcin: Portraits in the mist. (2001, December 9). *The New York Times,* p. B8.

Davis, D. J. (1997). *Death ritual and belief: The rhetoric of funerary rites.* London: Cassell.

Davis, R., & DeBarros, A. (2006, January 25). First year in college is the riskiest. *USA Today,* p. A1.

Davis, S. (1988). "Set your mood to patriotic": History as televised special event. *Radical History Review, 42,* 122–43.

A day for laying wreaths at Arlington Cemetery [photo caption]. (2006, December 15). *The New York Times,* p. A1.

*Day to Day.* (2004, June 10). NPR.

Dayan, D. (2001) The peculiar public of television. *Media, Culture & Society, 23,* 743–65.

Dayan, D., & Katz, E. (1992). *Media events: The live broadcasting of history.* Cambridge, MA: Harvard University Press.

Deam, J. (2004, July 6). Driven to save teens. *The Denver Post,* p. F1.

Death, and a new life. (2001, October 24). *The New York Times,* p. B11.

DeCurtis, A. (2003, October 16). Johnny Cash, 1932–2003. *Rolling Stone,* 70–73.

DeCurtis, A. (2004, July 8–22). Ray Charles, 1930–2004. *Rolling Stone,* 97–98.

The democratization of death. (2002, February 1). *Chronicle of Higher Education,* p. 4.

Deneen, P. J. (2002, September/October). Desecration. *Society,* 48.

Denise Elizabeth Crant. (2001, December 6). *The New York Times,* p. B10.

Dennis L. Devlin: Her cheerleader. (2001, December 9). *The New York Times,* p. B8.

Deppa, J., with Russell, M., Hayes, D., & Flocke, E. L. (1993). *The media and disasters: Pan Am 103.* London: David Fulton.

Determined to do it all. (2001, November 4). *The New York Times,* p. B11.

Dewan, S. (2005a, September 21). With information on bodies hard to come by, relatives of victims wait in anguish. *The New York Times,* p. A18.

Dewan, S. (2005b, September 28). Returning home, a handful find bodies. *The New York Times,* p. A28.

Dewan, S. (2006, April 11). In attics and rubble, more bodies and questions. *The New York Times,* p A1.

Dietz, D. (1989, October 18). "Please God, let that freeway hold." *San Francisco Chronicle,* p. A4.

Dominick Pezzulo: The unusual was typical. (2001, December 15). *The New York Times,* p. B8.

Donaldson, J. O. (1995, May 6). *Guntersville Advertiser-Gleam,* p. 14.

Donna Marie Giordano: Family friends. (2001, December 16). *The New York Times,* p. B8.

Doss, E. (2002). Death, art and memory in the public sphere: The visual and material culture of grief in contemporary America. *Mortality, 7,* 63–82.

Doucette, B., & Sutter, E. (1999, May 14). Last missing victim identified. *The Oklahoman,* p.A1.

Dow, D., & Rather, D. (1989, October 24). North California/earthquake/aftermath. *CBS Evening News,* CBS.

Downes, L. (2006, December 11). Editorial. *The New York Times,* Sec. 4, p. 11.

A dream realized. (2001, October 23). *The New York Times*, p. B11.

Duke, D.C. (2002). *Writers and miners: Activism and imagery in America.* Lexington: University Press of Kentucky.

Dunn, Viola. (1995, October 21). *Guntersville Advertiser-Gleam*, p. 16.

Durkheim, E. (1973/1915). *The elementary forms of religious life.* K. E. Fields (Trans.). New York: Free Press.

Dyar, Billy. (1995, January 11). *Guntersville Advertiser-Gleam*, p. 14.

Dyer, R. (1986). *Heavenly bodies: Film stars and society.* London: BFI/Macmillan.

Dykstra, R. R. (2000). Imaginary Dodge City: A political statement. In: How the west got wild: American media and frontier violence, a roundtable. *Western Historical Quarterly, 31,* 277–295.

*The early show.* (2004a, May 29). CBS.

*The early show.* (2004b, May 31). CBS.

*The early show.* (2006a, January 3). CBS.

*The early show.* (2006b, January 9). CBS.

*The early show.* (2006c, March 31). CBS.

Eason, D. (1981). Telling stories and making sense. *Journal of Popular Culture, 15,* 125–129.

An easygoing best friend. (2001, October 20). *The New York Times*, p. B11.

*Echoes of the blue & gray: Civil War veterans on DVD.* (2003). Prod. and dir. W. B. Styple. Kearny, NJ: Belle Grove.

Edward R. Vanacore: A sunset hog in the rain. (2001, November 18). *The New York Times*, p. B10.

Edy, J. A. (1999). Journalistic uses of collective memory. *Journal of Communication, 49*(2), 71–85.

Eisler, B. (1983). *Class act: America's last dirty secret.* New York: Franklin Watts.

Elias, J. (2006, December 14). New Bloomfield man killed in Iraq. *The Patriot-News* (Harrisburg, PA), pp. A1, A22.

El-Ghobashy, T. (2005, September 8). FEMA begins to gather bodies. *New York Daily News*, Newspaper Source Database, Academic Search Premier.

Eller, Evelyn H. (1995, September 17). *Guntersville Advertiser-Gleam*, p. 16.

Ellis, R. (1999, May 4). Tornadoes shred state: At least 25 killed; 1,000 homes destroyed in city area. *The Oklahoman*, p. A1.

Endres, F. F. (1984). Frontier obituaries as cultural reflectors: Toward operationalizing Carey's thesis. *Journalism History, 11,* 54–60.

Ensure crematory owner's safety. (2002, August 2). *Atlanta Journal-Constitution*, p. A23.

Entman, R. M. (1993). Framing: Toward clarification of a fractured paradigm. *Journal of Communication, 43*(4), 51–58.

Erickson, P. D. (1985). *Reagan speaks: The making of an American myth.* New York: New York University Press.

Eshelman, N. (2006, December 28). Solemn day produces an array of emotions. *The Patriot-News* (Harrisburg, PA), pp. A1, A16.

Espinoza, G. (2005, December 26). Richard Pryor. *People*, 66–68.

Eugene Clark: From the terrace. (2001, November 18). *The New York Times*, p. B10.

Eugene Whelan: Guilty of serial hugging. (2001, December 23). *The New York Times*, p. B6.

Evan, N. (2002, June). Burial rights, know the facts about cremation. *Black Enterprise, 281.*

Exploring the word. (2001, October 2). *The New York Times*, p. B9.

Eyre, E. (2006, January 9). 6 miners laid to rest. *The Charleston Gazette*, p. A1.

*Face the nation.* (2004, June 6). CBS.

Fairclough, N. (1995). *Media discourse.* London: Arnold.

Families raise new concerns over operation of crematory. (2002, March 11). *The New York Times*, p. A19.

Family costume night. (2001, October 13). *The New York Times*, p. B12.

Family first and foremost. (2001, October 15). *The New York Times*, p. B12.

A family man's gifts. (2001, October 28). *The New York Times*, p. B11.

Farewell. (2001, October 1). *Time*, 114.

Farley, C. J. (2004, June 21). The genius of Brother Ray. *Time*, 90.

Farrell, J. J. (1980). *Inventing the American way of death, 1830–1920.* Philadelphia: Temple University Press.

Fast, J. D. (2003). After Columbine: How people mourn sudden death. *Social Work, 48,* 484–491.

Fausset, R. (2004, June 9). For some, unpleasant memories. *Los Angeles Times.* Retrieved June 10, 2004, from http://www.latimes.com.

Federal civil trial begins in crematory case. (2004, March 6). *Atlanta Journal-Constitution*, p. E2.

Feeling Maine's glow. (2001, October 17). *The New York Times*, p. B11.

Ferré, J. P. (2005). Last words: Death and public self-expression. In C. H. Badaracco (Ed.), *Quoting God: How media shape ideas about religion and culture* (pp. 129–142). Waco, TX: Baylor University Press.

Fields-Meyer, T., Helling, S., & Sider, D. (2002, March 11). Shroud of sadness. *People*, 141.

A fight for his beloved. (2001, September 16). *The New York Times*, p. B8.

Finn, S. (2006a, January 5). Mine families turn to faith, prayer. *The Charleston Gazette*, p. 1C.

Finn, S. (2006b, January 16). "They're West Virginians." *The Charleston Gazette*, p. 1A.

Firestone, D. (2002, February 28). Cremation case calls for creative prosecution. *New York Times*, p. A16.

Firth, R. (1973). *Symbols: Public and private.* Ithaca, NY: Cornell University Press.

Fisher, M. (2004, June 12). On the Mall, a full measure of devotion. *The Washington Post*, p. B1.

Fisher, W. R. (1985). The narrative paradigm: In the beginning. *Journal of Communication, 35,* 74–89.

Fiske, J., & Hartley, J. (1978). *Reading television.* London: Methuen.

Fitzgerald, A. (1991, April 28). Andover suffers as reality hits. *The Wichita Eagle*, p. A15.

Flynn, N. (1991, April 29). Those who died. *The Wichita Eagle*, p. A4.

Foote, K. E. (1997). *Shadowed ground: America's landscapes of violence and tragedy*. Austin: University of Texas Press.

Fox, B. (2006, October 4). This time, the big story hit close to home for local media. *The Patriot-News* (Harrisburg, PA), p. A4.

Fox, K., & McDonagh, M. (2004, July 25). The Brando factor. *TV Guide*, 6–7.

*Fox News Watch*. (2006, October 7). Fox News Network. Transcript retrieved October 23, 2006, from LexisNexis on October 23, 2006.

Frank, T. (2006, February 10). Fines may not bring compliance. *USA Today*, p. A3.

Frankel, T. C. (2003a, August 19). Autopsy offers no clues in teen's death. *St. Louis Post-Dispatch*, p. B1.

Frankel, T. C. (2003b, November 11). Organs given, pain assuaged. *St. Louis Post-Dispatch*, p. B1.

Frankie Serrano: Anything for his dog. (2001, December 14). *The New York Times*, p. B8.

Frates, C. (2005, July 1). Tougher rules of the road in force. *The Denver Post*, p. B1.

Fred Ill Jr.: Extra effort. (2001, November 24). *The New York Times*, p. B7.

Frederick Rimmele III: Doctor with a ponytail. (2001, December 26). *The New York Times*, p. B8.

Frijda, N. H. (1997). Commemorating. In J. W. Pennebaker, D. Paez, & B. Rimé (Eds.), *Collective memory and political events* (pp. 103–127). Mahwah, NJ: Erlbaum.

Fry, K. (2003). *Constructing the heartland: Television news and natural disaster*. Cresskill, NJ: Hampton Press.

Furedi, F. (1997). *Culture of fear: Risk-taking and the morality of low expectation*. London and New York: Continuum.

Furedi, F. (2004). *Therapy culture: Cultivating vulnerability in an uncertain age*. London and New York: Routledge.

Gammage, J. (2006, October 4). Toll rises as tale unfolds. *The Philadelphia Inquirer*, pp. A1, A14.

Gamson, J. (1994). *Claims to fame: Celebrity in contemporary America*. Berkeley: University of California Press.

Gans, H. J. (1979). *Deciding what's news: A study of CBS Evening News, NBC Nightly News, Newsweek, and Time*. New York: Pantheon.

Gary Shamay: Upward, ever upward. (2001, December 20). *The New York Times*, p. B8.

Gately, G. (2006a, January 9). Hundreds express grief and faith as 6 miners are buried. *The New York Times*, p. A14.

Gately, G. (2006b, January 16). Life, hope and healing are focus of service for miners. *The New York Times*, p. A9.

Gates, D. (2003, September 22). The man in black. *Newsweek*, 98–101.

Gates, D. (2004, June 21). We can't stop loving him. *Newsweek*, 75.

George C. Cain: Skiing like the wind. (2001, December 17). *The New York Times*, p. B7.

George Howard: Going to work on a day off. (2001, November 30). *The New York Times*, p. B10.

Gerard P. Dewan: Finding a home. (2001, December 21). *The New York Times*, p. B7.

Geringer, D. (2006, October 6). A day of mourning and forgiveness. *Philadelphia Daily News*, pp. 4–5.

Gibbs, N. (2001a, n.d. [fall]). If you want to humble an empire. *Time: Special report*, n.p. [no pagination at all in this special issue].

Gibbs, N. (2001b, September 24). Mourning in America. *Time*, 14–27.

Gibbs, N. (2001c, October 1). Life on the home front. *Time*, 14–17.

Gibbs, N. (2001d, October 8). What comes next? *Time*, 22–25.

Gibbs, N. (2001, December 31/2002, January 7). Person of the year. *Time*, 34–39.

Gibbs, N. (2004, June 14). The all-American president. *Time*, 5, 32–47.

Giblin, P. & Hug, A. (2006). The psychology of funeral rituals. *Liturgy, 21*, 11–19.

Gibson, E. (2006, February 19). "His loss leaves us with emptiness." *The Sunday Patriot-News* (Harrisburg, PA), pp. A1, A20.

Gillin, B. (2005, September 28). Katrina spawned rumors; media ran with them. *The Philadelphia Inquirer*, Newspaper Source Database, Academic Search Premier.

Gillman, T. J. (2004, June 7). He "gave hope to a generation." *The Dallas Morning News*. Retrieved June 7, 2004, from http://www.dallasnews.com.

Gimbel, S. (2006, October 6). After the shootings. *The Philadelphia Inquirer*, p. A21.

Gitlin, T. (1980). *The whole world is watching: Mass media in the making & unmaking of the new left*. Berkeley: University of California Press.

Gliatto, T. (2004, July 19). Wild one. *People*, 80–86.

"Go ahead. I'll follow." (2001, November 4). *The New York Times*, p. B11.

Goffman, E. (1974). *Frame analysis: An essay on the organization of experience*. New York: Harper and Row.

Golf, gadgets and gifts. (2001, September 28). *The New York Times*, p. B11.

*Good morning America*. (2004a, May 28). ABC.

*Good morning America*. (2004b, June 6). ABC.

*Good morning America*. (2004c, June 11). ABC.

*Good morning America*. (2006a, January 3). ABC.

*Good morning America*. (2006b, January 5). ABC.

*Good morning America*. (2006c, March 30). ABC.

Goodstein, L. (2006, October 4). Strong faith and community may help Amish cope with loss. *The New York Times*, p. A20.

Goody, J. (1975). Death and the interpretation of culture. In D. E. Stannard (Ed.), *Death in America* (pp. 1–8). Philadelphia: University of Pennsylvania Press.

Gordon, M. (2005, September 28). In St. Tammany, tragedy takes a human face. *New Orleans Times-Picayune*, p. A1.

Gostomski, C., & Micek, J. (2006, October 4). Tragedy compels collision of cultures. *The Morning Call* (Allentown, PA), p. A1.

Gottlieb, A., & Workman, D. (2006, October 8). The dirty little secret of "gun-free school zones." *York Sunday News*, p. B1.

Graber, D. (1980). *Crime news and the public.* New York: Praeger.

Grace, S. (2005, September 15). Katrina's dead deserve utmost respect. *New Orleans Times-Picayune*, p. A1.

Grady, D., & Dao, J. (2006, January 6). While lone survivor lies in coma, many speak of miracle. *The New York Times*, p. A18.

Grainge, P. (2002). *Monochrome memories: Nostalgia and style in retro America.* Westport, CT: Praeger.

Gray, Granny. (1995, March 8). *Guntersville Advertiser-Gleam*, p. 14.

Gray, K. L. (2003, October 7). Mom mourns for sweet, helpful son. *The Columbus Dispatch*, p. C3.

Green, S. J. (2005, April 20). South Seattle teen dies after shooting. *The Seattle Times*, p. B1.

Grogan, J. (2006, October 4). A gentle paradise, lost. *The Philadelphia Inquirer*, p. A15.

Gross, J. (2006, May 20). For the families of the dying, coaching as the hours wane. *The New York Times*, pp. A1, A10.

Grossberg, L. (1992). *We gotta get out of this place: Popular conservatism and postmodern culture.* Routledge: New York and London.

Ground zero. (2001, September 14). *U.S. News & World Report*, 44–49.

Gustin, G. (2004, November 23). Illinois Police will have no tolerance for seatbelt scofflaws. *St. Louis Post-Dispatch*, p. C1.

Guthrie, Rev. McCoy. (1995, May 13). *Guntersville Advertiser-Gleam*, p. 13.

Halbwachs, M. (1992) *On collective memory.* L.A. Coser (Ed., trans.). Chicago: University of Chicago Press.

Halverson, N. (2003, December 9). Teen found dead outside school; suicide suspected. *The Denver Post*, p. B5.

Hambright, B. (2006a, October 4). Slayer of Amish girls tortured by his past. *Intelligencer Journal* (Lancaster, PA), p. A1.

Hambright, B. (2006b, October 14). "Grace and mercy." *Intelligencer Journal* (Lancaster, PA), p. A1.

Hambright, B. (2006c, October 18). Father reflects on daughter's slaying. *Intelligencer Journal* (Lancaster, PA), p. A1.

Hampel, P. (2004, August 11). Teen is killed in jump from bluff into water. *St. Louis Post-Dispatch*, p. B1.

Hampson, R. (1999, May 5). 'Everything was gone' Sky's dark wall of death leaves nowhere to run. *USA Today*, p. A1.

Hampson, R. (2004, April 19). 17 years in the making, WWII shrine is a reality. *USA Today*, pp. 1A, 2A.

Hampson, R. (2006, October 5). Amish community unites to mourn slain schoolgirls. *USA Today*, p. 3A.

Handling travel and crafts. (2001, October 1). *The New York Times*, p. B11.

Hard work, danger all part of job. (2006, January 4). *Pittsburgh Post-Gazette*, pp. A1, A6.

Harper, Kathleen. (1995, January 11). *Guntersville Advertiser-Gleam*, p. 14.

Harris, Cull. (1995, March 11). *Guntersville Advertiser-Gleam*, p. 11.

Harris, G. (2006, January 10). Endemic problem of safety in coal mining. *The New York Times*, p. A13.

Harris, Grover. (1995, April 5). *Guntersville Advertiser-Gleam*, p. 8.

Harry, J. C. (2004). "Trailer park trash": News, ideology, and depictions of the American underclass. In D. Heider (Ed.), *Class and news* (pp. 213–229). Lanham, MD: Rowman and Littlefield.

Hart, A. (2004a, March 5). National briefing south: Georgia: Jury in crematory trial. *The New York Times*, p. A15.

Hart, A. (2004b, November 20). Guilty plea and apology from crematory manager. *The New York Times*, p. A16.

Hart, Lucille. (1995, March 11). *Guntersville Advertiser-Gleam*, p. 11.

Hartley, J. (1982). *Understanding news*. London and New York: Routledge.

Harvey, Porter, 91. (1995, March 11). *Guntersville Advertiser-Gleam*, p. 11.

Harvey, S. (1997). *High adventure: Porter Harvey and the Advertiser-Gleam*. Montgomery, AL: Black Belt Press.

Hawkes, J. (2006, October 5). To the Amish, there is only forgiveness. *The Intelligencer Journal* (Lancaster, PA), p. B1.

He always was my hero. (2001, September 17). *The New York Times*, p. A10.

He kept 15 captains happy. (2001, October 25). *The New York Times*, p. B11.

He traveled the world. (2001, October 6). *The New York Times*, p. B11.

"He would never give up." (2001, October 16). *The New York Times*, p. B11.

Hedges, M. (2005, September 12). Daunting task: Houston company collecting remains. *The Houston Chronicle*, p. 16A.

The heroes. (2001). *Newsweek: Commemorative edition*, n.d. [fall], pp. 46–60.

Hesman, T. (2005, December 14). Treating an illness, fighting a stigma. *St. Louis Post-Dispatch*, p. A1.

Hill, Walter. (1995, July 5). *Guntersville Advertiser-Gleam*, p. 2.

His bright Irish smile. (2001, November 3). *The New York Times*, p. B11.

His motto: "Let's do it!" (2001, October 12). *The New York Times*, p. B15.

Holloway, K. (2002). *Passed on: African American mourning stories*. Durham, NC: Duke University Press.

Honoring a "hero." (2006, December 28). *The Patriot-News* (Harrisburg, PA), pp. A1, A16.

Hood, Homer. (1995, December 13). *Guntersville Advertiser-Gleam*, p. 14.

Hoover, S. M. (1998). *Religion in the news: Faith and journalism in American public discourse*. Thousand Oaks, CA: Sage.

Hoskins, J. (1998). *Biographical objects: How things tell the stories of people's lives*. New York: Routledge.

Houlbrooke, R. (1989). Introduction. In R. Houlbrooke (Ed.), *Death, ritual, and bereavement* (pp. 1–24). London: Routledge.

Hoversten, Paul. (1999, May 10). Spirit of renewal amid wreckage, rubble, Okla. displays faith and hope. *USA Today*, p. A3.

Howell, D. (2006, October 15). Photographing the grief of the Amish. *The Washington Post*, p. B6.

Howlett, D., & Nichols, B. (1989, October 19). Road shook 'like God was coming down.' *USA Today*, p. A1.

Huffstutter, P. J., & Simon, S. (2006, January 5). Mines' call is deep within. *The Los Angeles Times*, p. A12.

Hughes, J. (2005, April 8). House OKs bill putting brakes on new teen drivers. *The Denver Post*, p. B2.

Hume, J. (2000). *Obituaries in American culture*. Jackson: University Press of Mississippi.

Hundley, Charlie. (1965, February 10). *Guntersville Advertiser-Gleam*, p. 1.

Huntington, R., & Metcalf, P. (1979). *Celebrations of death: The anthropology of mortuary ritual*. Cambridge: Cambridge University Press.

Hutchinson, B. (1994, January 19). Brockton man dies in L.A. quake, Brockton family loses son in Calif. devastation. *The Boston Herald*, p. A1.

Hutchison, M. A., & Jackson, R. (1999, May 8). Mother sacrifices life for son. *The Oklahoman*, p. 15.

Huy Vu, N. (2004, March 18). Warning signs of troubled teens. *The Seattle Times*, p. B3.

Hyde, I. B. (1965, April 14). *Guntersville Advertiser-Gleam*, p. 1.

"I saw things no one should ever see." (2001, n.d. [fall]). *Newsweek: Extra edition*, pp. 54–64.

Itkowitz, K. (2006, October 6). Laid to rest. *Intelligencer Journal* (Lancaster, PA), pp. A1, A7.

Jacobson, S. (1995, May 14). Service recalls flood victims' faith, spirit. *The Dallas Morning News*, p. A31.

Janofsky, M. (2004a, April 29). 59 years later, memorial to World War II veterans opens on Washington Mall. *The New York Times*, p. A14.

Janofsky, M. (2004b, May 19). War memorial provokes mixed emotions. *The New York Times*, p. A18.

Janofsky, M. (2004c, May 30). Veterans gather to dedicate World War II memorial. *The New York Times*, p. A22.

Jeannine M. Laverde: A soft spot for snow. (2001, December 10). *The New York Times*, p. 8.

Jensen, L. (2005, October 2). Living among the dead. *New Orleans Times-Picayune*, p. B1.

Jimmy Riches: A way with women. (2001, December 24). *The New York Times*, p. B7.

Joe Romagnolo: Family came first. (2001, December 26). *The New York Times*, p. B8.

John Patrick Gallagher: Making sense of life. (2001, December 31). *The New York Times*, p. B6.

Johnson, E. (2005, April 8). Car crashes are top teen killer. *Current Events*, 1–3.

Johnson, K., & Willing, R. (2005, November 15). Evacuees find dead in return to homes. *USA Today*, p. A1.

Johnson, M. (2006). *The dead beat*. New York: HarperCollins.

Johnson, S. (1999, May 12). Profiles of life. *The Oklahoman*, p. 6.

John Vigiano and Joseph Vigiano: Growing up right. (2001, December 29). *The New York Times*, p. B8.

Jones, Calvin L. (1995, July 7). *Guntersville Advertiser-Gleam*, p. 1.

Jones, Nannie B. (1995, June 21). *Guntersville Advertiser-Gleam*, p. 13.

Jones, T. (2006a, January 4). Community wears a shroud of silence. *The Washington Post*, p. A4.

Jones, T. (2006b, October 5). Side by side. *The Washington Post*, pp. C1, C5.

Jones, T., & Tyson, A. S. (2006, January 5). After 44 hours, hope showed its cruel side. *The Washington Post*, pp. A1, A8.

Jorgensen-Earp, C. R., & Lanzilotti, L. A. (1998). Public memory and private grief: The construction of shrines and the sites of public tragedy. *Quarterly Journal of Speech, 84,* 150–170.

Joseph Sacerdote: Sadness for a family man. (2001, December 13). *The New York Times*, p. B9.

Joseph V. Maggitti: Tickets to Paradise Island. (2001, December 1). *The New York Times*, p. B8.

Joshua Aron: Reveled in life's details. (2001, December 16). *The New York Times*, p. B8.

Kaminer, W. (2002, April 8). Ashes to concrete. *The American Prospect*, 9.

Kammen, M. (1991). *Mystic chords of memory: The transformation of tradition in American culture*. New York: Alfred A. Knopf.

Kaplan, T. (1994, January 22). Friends, family mourn victims. *The Los Angeles Times*, p. B1.

Kaplan, T., & Krikorian, G. (1994, January 18). 33 die, many hurt in 6.6 quake. *The Los Angeles Times*, pp. A1, A10.

Kastenbaum, R. (2000). The kingdom where nobody dies. In K. J. Doka (Ed.), *Living with grief: Children, adolescents, and loss* (pp. 5–20). New York: Taylor & Francis.

Kastenbaum, R., Peyton, S., & Kastenbaum, B. (1976–1977). Sex discrimination after death. *Omega, 7,* 351–359.

Kear, A., & Steinberg, D. L. (Eds.). (1999). *Mourning Diana: Nation, culture and the performance of grief*. London: Routledge.

Kearl, M. C., & Rinaldi, A. (1983). The political uses of the dead as symbols in contemporary civil religions. *Social Forces, 61,* 693–708.

Kee, L. (2005, June 5). When death comes too soon. *St. Louis Post-Dispatch*, p. E1.

Kelley, J., & Stauffer, C. (2006, October 5). Hundreds line roads to pay respects. *The New Era* (Lancaster, PA), p. A1.

Kelley, J., & Umble, C. (2006, October 9). We open our hearts & wallets. *The New Era* (Lancaster, PA). Retrieved October 21, 2006, from <lancasteronline.com>.

Kelly, R. (2004, July 20). Park Hills, Mo., teen may have died in heat after getting lost riding in Arizona desert. *St. Louis Post-Dispatch*, p. B8.

Kennamer, Bruce, 56. (1995, March 15). *Guntersville Advertiser-Gleam*, p. 16.

Kennedy, B. M. (1974). *Community journalism: A way of life*. Ames: Iowa State University Press.

Kennedy, H. (2006, October 8). Amazing grace. *Daily News* (New York, NY), pp. 24–25.

Killed in wreck at Swearengin store. (1995, July 15). *Guntersville Advertiser-Gleam*, p. 9.

Kiner, D. (2005, October 15). Communities plan tributes to dead Marine. *The Patriot-News* (Harrisburg, PA), pp. A1, A8.

King, E., & Schudson, M. (1987, November/December). The myth of the great communicator. *Columbia Journalism Review*, 37–39.

King, M. (2004, October 13). When grief knocks at an early age. *The Seattle Times*, p. F1.

Kinney, M. Y. (2006, October 5). Tough gun laws can make a difference. *The Philadelphia Inquirer*, pp. B1, B7.

Kirksey, J. (2003, October 6). Rollovers kill 3 teens, 1 adult. *The Denver Post*, p. B3.

Kirksey, J. (2005, July 29). Teen dies in car rollover. *The Denver Post*, p. B2.

Kitch, C. (2005). *Pages from the past: History and memory in American magazines*. Chapel Hill: University of North Carolina Press.

Klaus, M. (2006, February 27). "I was just doing my job." *The Patriot-News* (Harrisburg, PA), pp. A1, A10.

Klueger, Flora, 94. (1995, April 22). *Guntersville Advertiser-Gleam*, p. 8.

Koetting, T. (1991, April 29). Those who died. *The Wichita Eagle*, p. A 4.

Kohler, J. (2004, December 13). Teen's death is ruled accidental drowning. *St. Louis Post-Dispatch*, p. B2.

Kouwe, Z., & Frates, C. (2003, October 12). 3 teens hurt in drag race honored at ballgame. *The Denver Post*, p. B6.

Kovach, B., & Rosenstiel, T. (2001). *The elements of journalism: What newspeople should know and the public should expect*. New York: Three Rivers Press.

Kranz, D. (1997, January 26). Man who lost 2 friends: "God was good to me." *The Argus Leader*, p. A1.

Kraybill, D. B. (2006, October 8). Forgiveness is integral in Amish faith. *The Sunday Patriot-News* (Harrisburg, PA), pp. F1, F3.

Krupa, M. (2005, September 13). Bodies lie for days awaiting retrieval. *New Orleans Times-Picayune*, p. A1.

Kumar, D. (2004a). Media, class, and power: Debunking the myth of a classless society. In D. Heider (Ed.), *Class and news* (pp. 6–21). Lanham, MD: Rowman and Littlefield.

Kumar, D. (2004b). War propaganda and the (ab)uses of women: Media constructions of the Jessica Lynch story. *Feminist Media Studies, 4,* 297–313.

Kumar, D. (2005). "What's good for UPS is good for America": Nation and class in network television news coverage of the UPS strike. *Television & New Media, 6,* 131–152.

Kunkel, T. (2004, August/September). Above the fold: Fade-out. *American Journalism Review,* 4.

Laderman, G. (1996). *The sacred remains: American attitudes toward death, 1799–1883.* New Haven: Yale University Press.

Lambert, M. J. (1995, June 14). *Guntersville Advertiser-Gleam,* p. 11.

Lane, M. B. (2005, July 25). Pals pitch in to honor teen. *The Columbus Dispatch,* p. C1.

Larson, S. G., & Bailey, M. (1998). ABC's "Person of the Week": American values in television news. *Journalism & Mass Communication Quarterly, 75,* 487–499.

Lash, C. (2006, March 31). Miracle miner goes home. *The Pittsburgh Post-Gazette,* pp. A1, A14.

Lash, C., & Cleary, C. (2006, October 8). Bottom line is child safety. *The Pittsburgh Post-Gazette,* pp. B1, B2.

Lash, S., & and Urry, J. (1994). *Economies of signs and space.* London: Sage.

Lathan, Maudie, 99. (1995, May 3). *Guntersville Advertiser-Gleam,* p. 16.

Latson, J. (2005, October 12). More bodies found in New Orleans' Ninth Ward. *Knight-Ridder Tribune,* Newspaper Source Database, Academic Search Premier.

Lattin, D. (1989, October 21). Spiritual aid to the shaken, Quake victims turn to clergy for comfort. *The San Francisco Chronicle,* p. C9.

Lauterer, J. (2000). *Community journalism: The personal approach.* 2nd ed. Ames: Iowa State University Press.

Law and order. (2002, August 10). *Atlanta Journal-Constitution,* p. H3.

Lawrence, J. S., & Timberg, B. (1979). News and mythic selectivity: Mayaguez, Entebbe, Mogadishu. *Journal of American Culture, 2,* 321–330.

Lawrence, R. G., & Birkland, T. A. (2004). Guns, Hollywood, and school safety: Defining the school-shooting problem across public arenas. *Social Science Quarterly, 85,* 1193–1207.

Leach, S. L. (2005, January 19). How to tell story of the dead without offending the living. *The Christian Science Monitor,* p. 11.

Ledesma, I. (1994). Natural disasters and community survival in Texas and Louisiana in the Gilded Age. *Gulf Coast Historical Review, 10,* 72–84.

Leduff, C., & Broder, J. M. (2004, June 8). Crowds honor a president who believed in the good. *The New York Times,* p. A19.

Lemley, Annie, 97. (1995, December 27). *Guntersville Advertiser-Gleam,* p. 13.

Leonard W. Atton Jr.: Into the flames. (2001, December 1). *The New York Times*, p. B8.

Letter from the Ebersols. (2006, October 18). *Intelligencer Journal* (Lancaster, PA), p. A6.

Letters. (2001a, October 1). *Newsweek*, 12–15.

Letters. (2001b, October 8). *Newsweek*, 14–16.

Letters. (2001c, October 15). *Newsweek*, 15–19.

Letters. (2001a, October 1). *Time*, 8–12.

Letters. (2001b, October 8). *Time*, 12–18.

Letters. (2001c, October 15). *Time*, 11–22.

Levin, A. (2006, October 6). Grief travels through Amish country. *USA Today*, p. 4A.

Levin, A., & Bowles, S. (1999, May 6). Okla. Determined to overcome new tragedy, mammoth rebuilding task ahead. *USA Today*, p. A4.

Lewis, G., & Schneider, M. (1994, January 23). California/earthquake. *NBC Evening News*.

Lifton, R. J. (1992, August 23). Can images of Bosnia's victims change the world? *The New York Times*, sec. 2, p. 26.

Linda Rivera: A signature giggle. (2001, December 12). *The New York Times*, p. B12.

Linenthal, E. T. (2001). *The unfinished bombing: Oklahoma City in American memory*. New York: Oxford University Press.

Lipsitz, G. (1990). *Time passages: Collective memory and American popular culture*. Minneapolis: University of Minnesota Press.

Lives crushed by earthquake. (1994, January 24). *The Houston Chronicle*, p. A4.

Living large, playing hard. (2001, September 28). *The New York Times*, p. B11.

Living the life she wanted. (2001, October 5). *The New York Times*, p. B13.

Loftis, R. L., & Lopez, N. (1995, May 7). 16 deaths blamed on storm. *The Dallas Morning News*, p. A1.

Logan County teen killed in one-car crash. (2005, August 10). *The Columbus Dispatch*, p. B2.

A long drive home. (2001, October 1). *The New York Times*, p. B11.

Lonny Stone: Life is like a good burger. (2001, December 20). *The New York Times*, p. B8.

Lost lives. (2001, n.d. [fall]). *Newsweek: Commemorative issue*, 90–99.

Louis J. Minervino: A very quiet life. (2001, December 21). *The New York Times*, p. B7.

Love, Josie. (1995, March 11). *Guntersville Advertiser-Gleam*, p. 11.

Love and loss. (2001, September 24). *Newsweek*, 89–95.

Love at first sight. (2001, December 23). *The New York Times,* p. B6.

Love to fill a doorway. (2001, October 30). *The New York Times*, p. B11.

Loved wine, hated silence. (2001, October 3). *The New York Times*, p. B11.

Lovelady, Cobb. (1965, September 22). *Guntersville Advertiser-Gleam*, p. 1.

Lowenthal, D. (1985). *The past is a foreign country*. Cambridge: Cambridge University Press.

Lowenthal, D. (1989). The timeless past: Some Anglo-American historical pre-conceptions. *Journal of American History, 25,* 1263–1280.

Lule, J. (2001). *Daily news, eternal stories: The mythological role of journalism.* New York: Guilford Press.

Lule, J. (2002). Myth and terror on the editorial page: *The New York Times* responds to September 11, 2001. *Journalism & Mass Communication Quarterly, 79,* 275–293.

MacDonald, G. J. (2004, January 7). A devastating question: Does suicide discourse help or hurt teens? *The Seattle Times,* p. F1.

Malachowski, M. (2001, October 15). Letters. *Newsweek,* 19.

Mallon, T. (2002). The mourning paper. *American Scholar, 71*(2), 5–8.

Man dies of injuries suffered in tornado. (1999, May 24). *Topeka Capital-Journal.* Retrieved September 28, 2006, from www.cjonline.com.

The man in black. (2003, November 1). *TV Guide,* 43.

Mann, F. (1991, April 28). A bitter truth. *The Wichita Eagle,* p. A1.

Manners and a motorcycle. (2001, October 16). *The New York Times,* p. B11.

Manning, C. (1999, May 4). Tornado's pattern leaves some areas in ruin, others unscathed. *Topeka Capital Journal.* Retrieved September 28, 2006, from www.cjonline.com.

Marquez, M. (2005). Zero access adds up to prior restraint. *News Media and the Law, 29,* 8–9.

Martin, C.R. (2004). *Framed! Labor and the corporate media.* Ithaca, NY: ILR Press.

A maximum mom. (2001, October 24). *The New York Times,* p. B11.

Mazzarella, S. R., & Matyjewicz, T. M. (2002). "The day the music died"—again: Newspaper coverage of the deaths of popular musicians. In S. Jones (Ed.), *Pop music and the press* (pp. 219–232). Philadelphia: Temple University Press.

Mazzocco, D. W. (1994). *Networks of power: Corporate TV's threat to democracy.* Boston: South End Press.

McCaffrey, R., & Ruane, M. E. (2006, October 5). An Amish community grieves for its little ones. *The Washington Post,* p. A3.

McCloy's wife sues *National Enquirer* (2006, January 28). *The Charleston Gazette,* p. 11A.

McCombs, Annette. (1995, March 29). *Guntersville Advertiser-Gleam,* p. 8.

McDonald, M. (2001, September 24). Courage under terrible fire. *U.S. News & World Report,* 40–43.

McGinn, D. (2001, October 8). "We'll pull through." *Newsweek,* 50–53.

McGowan, J. (2002, Fall). What do the living owe the dead? *Southern Humanities Review,* 301–347.

McGuigan, C. (2001, October 8). Out of the rubble. *Newsweek,* 12.

McIlwain, C. D. (2004). *When death goes pop: Death, media, and the remaking of community.* New York: Peter Lang.

Mead, G. H. (1934). *Mind, self and society.* Chicago: University of Chicago Press.

*Meet the press.* (2002, July 28). NBC.

Memmott, M., Leinwand, D., & Watson, T. (2004, June 11). Thousands united by desire for last look. *USA Today*, pp. 15A–16A.

A message from the Nickel Mines community. (2006, October 15). *Sunday News* (Lancaster, PA), p. A7.

Metcalf, P., & Huntington, R. (1991). *Celebrations of death: The anthropology of mortuary ritual*. 2nd ed. Cambridge: Cambridge University Press.

Meyer, J. (2004, September 21). Earlier head injury eyed in teen's death. *The Denver Post*, p. B1.

Meyerhoff, B. G. (1977). We don't wrap herring in a printed page: Fusion, fictions and continuity in secular ritual. In S. F. Moore & B. G. Meyerhoff (Eds.), *Secular ritual* (pp. 199–224). Amsterdam: Van Gorcum.

Meyrowitz, J. (1994). The life and death of media friends: New genres of intimacy and mourning. In S. J. Drucker & R. S. Cathcart (Eds.), *American heroes in a media age* (pp. 62–81). Cresskill, NJ: Hampton Press.

Michael A. Marti: Chum to the underdog. (2001, December 10). *The New York Times*, p. B8.

Michael Paul Ragusa—what would Mikey do? (2001, December 25). *The New York Times*, p. B7.

Michelle L. Titolo: An angel between sisters. (2001, December 11). *The New York Times*, p. B7.

Minutaglio, B., & Garcia, E. (1995, May 7). Lives lost, families torn. *Dallas Morning News*, pp. A1, A30–31.

Mitchell, K. (2004, February 29). Drag race suspected in deadly I-25 crash. *The Denver Post*, p. B1.

Mitchell, K., & Depperschmidt, A. (2004, January 18). Teen killed, 5 hurt in Adams crash. *The Denver Post*, p. D2.

Mitchell, R., & Pitts, B. (1999, May 9). Plains States/tornadoes/Bridge Creek. *CBS Evening News*.

Montagne, R. (2005, September 28). Louisiana to release more details about Hurricane Katrina deaths. *Morning Edition*, NPR.

Moore, A. (2004, June 8). Left out of "morning in America." *The Philadelphia Inquirer*, p. A19.

Moore, Odell. (1995, July 15). *Guntersville Advertiser-Gleam*, p. 9.

Moore, S. F., & Meyerhoff, B. G. (1977). Introduction: Secular ritual. In S. F. Moore & B. G. Meyerhoff (Eds.), *Secular ritual* (pp. 3–24). Amsterdam: Van Gorcum.

Moore's, Shank, funeral (1995, September 23). *Guntersville Advertiser-Gleam*, p. 16.

*Morning Edition*. (2004, June 7). NPR.

Morone, J. A. (2003) *Hellfire nation: The politics of sin in America*. New Haven: Yale University Press.

Morrow, L. (2001, n.d. [fall]). The case for rage and retribution. *Time: Special report*, n.p.

Mungin, L. (2002, August 10). State security urged for Marsh. *Atlanta Journal-Constitution*, p. H3.

Nachtwey, J. (2001, October 1). Viewpoint: Red, white and blue. *Time*, 88–93.

*The National Memorial Day Concert*. (2004, May 30). Public Broadcasting System (PBS).

*NBC news special report: Ronald Wilson Reagan, 1911–2004*. (2004, June 11). NBC.

*NBC news special report: State ceremony for former President Reagan*. (2004, June 9). NBC.

*NBC nightly news*. (2002, July 26). NBC.

*NBC nightly news*. (2004a, May 28). NBC.

*NBC nightly news*. (2004b, May 29). NBC.

*NBC nightly news*. (2004c, May 31). NBC.

*NBC nightly news*. (2004d, June 5). NBC.

*NBC nightly news*. (2006a, January 3). NBC.

*NBC nightly news*. (2006b, January 4). NBC.

*NBC nightly news*. (2006c, January 5). NBC.

*NBC nightly news*. (2006d, January 7). NBC.

Never liked to sit around. (2001, November 13). *The New York Times*, p. B8.

Newhouse, D. (2006, October 5). About our coverage. *The Patriot-News* (Harrisburg, PA), p. A3.

*Newsweek*. (2001a, n.d. [fall]). *Extra edition*.

*Newsweek*. (2001b, September 24).

*Newsweek*. (2001c, n.d. [fall]). Commemorative issue.

*Newsweek*. (2001d, October 1).

*Newsweek*. (2001e, October 8).

*Newsweek*. (2001f, October 15).

*Newsweek*. (2001, December 31/2002January 7).

Nicholson, J. (2004, August 19). Remembering Marlon. *Rolling Stone*, 53–55.

Nicholson, K., Espinoza, A., & Duran, B. (2004, June 20). Douglas wreck leaves 4 dead. *The Denver Post*, p. C3.

*Nightline*. (2004, May 31). ABC.

*Nightline*. (2006, January 4). ABC.

*Nightline: Portrait of a President*. (2004, June 7). ABC.

Nimmo, D. L., & Combs, J. E. (1985). Nightly horrors: Crisis coverage by television network news. Knoxville: University of Tennessee Press.

Nix, J. E., dies while watching game on TV. (1965, September 22). *Guntersville Advertiser-Gleam*, p. 1.

Nolte, C. (1989, October 20). Days of disbelief, when the unbelievable converged with the unforgettable. *The San Francisco Chronicle*, p. B3.

Nord, D. P. (2001). *Communities of journalism: A history of American newspapers and their readers*. Urbana: University of Illinois Press.

Norris, M. (2006, February 13). New Orleans seeks final home for nameless victims. *All Things Considered*, NPR.

*NPR news special report*. (2004, June 5). NPR.

Oaks, Dovard. (1995, February 1). *Guntersville Advertiser-Gleam*, p. 14.

Olinger, D. (2004, February 8). Lakewood wreck kills 1, hurts 6. *The Denver Post*, p. B1.

On the death of an infant. (1850). *Harper's New Monthly Magazine, 1*(2), 183.

O'Neil, T. (2003, September 11). Teen hit on head with skateboard dies. *St. Louis Post-Dispatch*, p. B1.

O'Neill, A. W., & Chu, H. (1994, January 18). At least 15 die in collapsed apartments. *The Los Angeles Times*, p. A1.

One office, two families. (2001, October 11). *The New York Times*, p. B15.

*The O'Reilly factor.* (2006, October 2). Fox News Network. Transcript retrieved October 3, 2006, from LexisNexis.

Ott, D. (2005, October 19). New Orleans coroner at center of another storm. *Knight-Ridder Tribune*, Newspaper Source Database, Academic Search Premier.

Owen, P. (1999, May 23). Unofficial victim still a hero. *The Oklahoman*, p. 4.

Paletz, D.L., & Schmid, A.P. (Eds.) (1992). *Terrorism and the media*. Newbury Park, CA: Sage.

Parenti, M. (1978). *Power and the powerless*. New York: St. Martin's Press.

Parenti, M. (1986). *Inventing reality: The politics of the mass media*. New York: St. Martin's Press.

Parker, Bob. (1995, October 11). *Guntersville Advertiser-Gleam*, p. 16.

Parrett, A. (2004) Montana's worst natural disaster: The 1964 flood on the Blackfeet Indian reservation. *Montana, 5*(2), 20–31.

A past in the movies. (2001, October 23). *The New York Times*, p. B11.

Patrick J. Brown: The bravest and grumpiest. (2001, November 27). *The New York Times*, p. B9.

*Paula Zahn now.* (2004, May 28). CNN.

Pawlaczyk, G. (2005, November 11). Officials debunk one of the most disturbing Katrina stories. *Knight-Ridder Tribune*, Newspaper Source Database, Academic Search Premier.

Pawlaczyk, G., & Garcia, M. (2005, September 27). Loved ones grapple with confusion, red tape in search for missing. *Knight-Ridder Tribune*, Newspaper Source Database, Academic Search Premier.

*People.* (2005, December 26).

A people in the news special: D-Day: A call to courage. (2004, June 6). Advertisement in *The New York Times*, p. A7.

Perez, S. (1991, April 28). Woman searching ruins finds husband's body. *The Wichita Eagle*, p. A11.

Perez-Lugo, M. (2004). Media uses in disaster situations: A new focus on the impact phase. *Sociological Inquiry, 74,* 210–225.

The perfect daddy. (2001, November 9). *The New York Times*, p. B11.

Perlstein, M. (2005, October 10). 911 tapes guide team as victim search ebbs. *New Orleans Times-Picayune*, p. A1.

Peter F. Raimondi: Life in perspective. (2001, December 6). *The New York Times*, p. B10.

Peterson, I. (2004, May 29). Old soldiers, fading away at a grim pace. *The New York Times*, p. A1.

Peyser, M. (2004, July 12). Marlon Brando, 1924–2004. *Newsweek*, 73.

Peyser, M., & Samuels, A. (2005, December 19). Richard Pryor, 1940–2005. *Newsweek*, 61.

*The Philadelphia Inquirer* [front page]. (2006, October 4). p. A1.

Phillips, J. (2004). Constructing a televisual class: Newsmagazines and social class. In D. Heider (Ed.), *Class and news* (pp. 129–149). Lanham, MD: Rowman and Littlefield.

Pickering, J. (1997). Remembering D-Day: A case history in nostalgia. In J. Pickering & S. Kehde (Eds.), *Narratives of nostalgia, gender, and nationalism,* (pp. 182–210). New York: New York University Press.

Plumberg, D. (1999, May 12). Storms' death toll 42 as woman, 89, dies. *The Oklahoman*, p. A1.

Pompilio, N. (2006, October 8). When worlds collide. *The Philadelphia Inquirer*, pp. B1, B5.

Pope, J. (2005a, September 6). Makeshift morgue has grim task. *New Orleans Times- Picayune*, p. A9.

Pope, J. (2005b, September 18). Little peace found at funeral homes. *New Orleans Times-Picayune*, p. A6.

Porter, P. W., & Luxon, N. N. (1935). *The reporter and the news.* New York: Appleton-Century.

A presidency characterized by paradox [editorial]. (2004, June 6). *Los Angeles Times*. Retrieved June 6, 2004, from http://www.latimes.com.

Pressley, S. A. (2004, June 10). Thousands come to watch history, honor loved one. *The Washington Post*, pp. A1, A28.

Price, David, 36. (1995, February 22). *Guntersville Advertiser-Gleam*, p. 16.

*Primetime live: A tragedy in the mountain.* (2006, January 5). ABC.

Pro, J. A. (2002, July 29). "We have so much to be thankful for this morning." *The Pittsburgh Post-Gazette*, p. A4.

Profiles of life. (1999). *The Oklahoman*, May 6, p. 20; May 7, p. 15; May 8, p. 15, May 9, p. 11.

Prothero, S. (2002, March 13). Bodies in limbo. *Christian Century,* 6–7.

*Publick Occurrences: Both Forreign and Domestick.* (1690, September 25). Retrieved December 12, 2006, from www.masshist.org.

Puette, W. J. (1992). *Through jaundiced eyes: How the media view organized labor.* Ithaca, NY: ILR Press.

Quake victims—the people behind the statistics. (1989, October 30). *San Francisco Chronicle*, p. A10.

Quinn, K. (2004, March 15). Teen's death is a somber reminder of dangers associated with asthma. *St. Louis Post-Dispatch*, Health & Fitness p. 3.

Raffaele, M. (2006, October 8). "I hope this isn't right." *York Sunday News*, p. C5.

Ramsey, Azzie Cherry. (1995, September 16). *Guntersville Advertiser-Gleam*, p. 11.

Ranney, D. (1999, May 6). The lives lost. *The Wichita Eagle*, p. A1.

Raphael, B. (1986). *When disaster strikes: How individuals and communities cope with catastrophe.* New York: Basic Books.

Ratcliffe, H. (2003, February 12). Drag racing may have led to crash that killed teen. *St. Louis Post-Dispatch*, p. A1.

Ray Charles (2004, June 28). *People*, 58–59.

Reagan, R. (1983, January 25). Speech transcript from the U.S. Government Printing Office's *Weekly Compilation of Presidential Documents*. Quoted in: C. A. Smith (1987), Mister Reagan's neighborhood: Rhetoric and national unity. *Southern Speech Communication Journal, 52*, 210–239.

Reel, M. (2004a, May 28). Memory illuminated. *The Washington Post*, pp. B1, B7.

Reel, M. (2004b, May 30). Deferred but lasting gratitude. *The Washington Post*, p. A1.

Regan, Naomi, 91. (1995, January 18). *Guntersville Advertiser-Gleam*, p. 13.

Reilly, P. J. (2006, October 6). In tragic days, a calm voice. *Intelligencer Journal* (Lancaster, PA), pp. A1, A6.

Reinhold, R., Navaro, M., & Rabinovitz, J. (1989, October 29). The freeway dead: Portraits from Oakland—A special report. *The New York Times*, p. A1.

Remembering Johnny. (2003, October 16). *Rolling Stone*, 74–76.

Rice, P. (2005, March 3). Students say "enough" to road deaths. *St. Louis Post-Dispatch*, Jefferson County Post, p. 3.

Richardson, Henry P. (1995, February 12). *Guntersville Advertiser-Gleam,*, p. 1.

Ripley, A., Berestein, L., Berryman, A., DeQuine, J., Land, G., & van Dyke, D. (2002, March 4). Dead and forsaken. *Time*, 41–42.

Ritz, D. (2004, July 8–22). Last words of Brother Ray. *Rolling Stone*, 98–100.

Roane, K. R. (2006, January 16). Prayers for the brave men in the mine. *U.S. News & World Report*, 10–11.

Robert Regan: A real "Mr. Mom." (2001, December 6). *The New York Times*, p. B10.

Robertson, M. (1989, October 18). The quake's eerie selection of victims. *The San Francisco Chronicle*, p. A4.

Rock, P. (1973). News as eternal recurrence. In S. Cohen & J. Young (Eds.), *The manufacture of news* (pp. 226–243). London: Sage.

Rodell, S. (2006, January 13). Sacrifices of soldiers, miners alike. *The Charleston Gazette*, p. 4A.

Ronald Reagan, 1911–2004 [editorial]. (2004, June 6). *The Philadelphia Inquirer.* Retrieved June 6, 2004, from http://www.philly.com.

Rosenbaum, T. (2005, January 17). Stop muzzling wounded. *National Law Journal, 26*, 26.

Rosenblatt, R. (2000, May 29). How we remember. *Time*, 26–30.

Ruane, M. E. (2004, June 10). A somber procession of present and past. *The Washington Post*, pp. A21–A22.

Rubble tells a bitter truth. (1991, April 28). *The Wichita Eagle*, p. A1.

Sago survivor's wife sues his brother (2006, February 9). *The Charleston Gazette*, p. 1C.

Sallee, R. (1999, May 6). Terror on the plains; Minister killed in Oklahoma tornado was inspiration to Houston clergymen. *The Houston Chronicle*, p. A25.

Salvatore F. Pepe: For family, a tomatofest. (2001, November 25). *The New York Times*, p. B8.

Sandalow, M., & Congbalay, D. (1989, October 21). Workers may reach all I-880 cars today. *The San Francisco Chronicle*, p. A5.

Scelfo, J., & Springen, K. (2004, May 31). The high cost of summer cash. *Newsweek*, 61.

Schickel, R. (2004, July 12). A hostage of his own genius. *Time*, 73–74.

Schlesinger, J. M. (2004, June 10). Operation Serenade: Laying groundwork for Reagan's funeral. *The Wall Street Journal*, pp. A1, A4.

Schodolski, V. J., & Martinez, M. (2004, June 7). Nation mourns with gestures simple, grand. *The Chicago Tribune*. Retrieved June 7, 2004, from http://www.chicagotribune.com.

Schools caught short on safety. (2006, October 8). *The Philadelphia Inquirer*, pp. A1, A18–A19.

Schrader, A. (2004a, January 18). Crash that killed 3 nets teen probation. *The Denver Post*, p. B.3.

Schrader, A. (2004b, January 18). Teen avoids jail for Feb. wreck. *The Denver Post*, p. B5.

Schrader, A. (2004c, February 15). 2 Lakewood teens charged in wreck linked to racing. *The Denver Post*, p. B5.

Schrader, A. (2004d, June 23). Wrecked car will tour to warn teens. *The Denver Post*, p. B1.

Schrader, A., & Kirksey, J. (2003, October 3). Student killed in 1-car crash, 4 other teens survive. *The Denver Post*, p. B1.

Schrimsher, Herman. (1995, May 10) *Guntersville Advertiser-Gleam*, p. 15.

Schrimsher, Wiley (1995, August 16). *Guntersville Advertiser-Gleam*, p. 16.

Schudson, M. (1995). *The power of news*. Cambridge, MA: Harvard University Press.

Schuler, S. L. (2001, November 24). *The New York Times*, p. B7.

Schwartz, B. (1982). The social context of commemoration: A study in collective memory. *Social Forces, 6*, 374–402.

Schwartz, B. (1998). Frame images: Towards a semiotics of collective memory. *Semiotica, 121*, 1–40.

Schwarzbaum, L. (2004, July 16). Marlon Brando, 1924–2004. *Entertainment Weekly*, 26–28.

Scolforo, M. (2006a, October 3). Rural peace shattered. *York Daily Record*, pp. 1A, 5A.

Scolforo, M. (2006b, October 19). Amish papers tell of school "tragedy." *The New Era* (Lancaster, PA), pp. A1, A4.

Scott, J. (2001, December 31). Closing a scrapbook full of life and sorrow. *The New York Times*, p. B6.

Scott, R. T. (2005, October 17). Long wait for closure. *New Orleans Times-Picayune*, p. A1.

Season of loss in a small town, A. [Title with photograph.] (2006, October 6). *The Washington Post*, p. A1.

Secret Santa revealed, A. (2001, November 2). *The New York Times*, p. 11.

Securing school safety. (2006, October 8). *York Sunday News*, pp. A1, A11.

Segna, B. (2001, October 1). Letters. *Time*, 8.

Sharp, D. (1999, May 5). More tornadoes, but death toll lower than in '98. *USA Today*, p. A19.

Shearer, A. (1991). *Survivors and the media*. London: Broadcasting Standards Council.

Shephard, J. (1996, July–August). The strength of weeklies. *American Journalism Review, 18,* 32–36.

Shilts, R., & Sward, S. (1989a, October 18). Hundreds dead in huge quake. *San Francisco Chronicle*, p. A1.

Shilts, R., & Sward, S. (1989b, October 19). Devastating reports from big quake area. *San Francisco Chronicle*, p. A1.

Shinkle, P. (2003, April 27). Funeral for 3 teens will be in gym. *St. Louis Post-Dispatch*, p. C2.

Shogren, E., Neuman, J., & Braun, S. (2004, June 10). Ritual and pageantry usher Reagan's coffin to Capitol. *The Los Angeles Times*. Retrieved June 10, 2004, from http://www.latimes.com.

Siegel, M. (1997). *The last word:* The New York Times *book of obituaries and farewells*. R. Baker (Foreword). New York: William Morrow.

Siegel, R. (2005, November 21). Profile: Costs, complexity slow identification of Katrina dead. *All Things Considered*, NPR.

Siegel, R. (2006, May 11). Genetics IDs Katrina victims, some were long missing. *All Things Considered*, NPR.

Siemaszko, C. (2004, June 10). A nation's final salute. *The New York Daily News*, pp. 4–5.

Silk, M. (1995). *Unsecular media: Making news of religion in America*. Urbana: University of Illinois Press.

Simerman, J. (2005, October 15). Officials ask for patience as bodies await autopsies in morgue. *Knight-Ridder Tribune*, National Newspaper Database, Academic Search Premier.

Simon, R. (2004, June 21). Sunny side up, always. *U.S. News & World Report*, 53.

Simon V. Weiser: Medieval history buff. (2001, December 22). *The New York Times*, p. B11.

Simonich, M. (2006, October 5). "It's incredibly sad." *Pittsburgh Post-Gazette*, p. A4.

Sinclair, T. (2004, June 25/July 2). Ray Charles, 1930–2004. *Entertainment Weekly*, 42–47.

Singer, M. (2002, January 14). The talk of the town: The grief desk. *The New Yorker*, 30.

Site, The (2001, October 15). *Time*, 86–87.

Smart, G. (2006, October 15). Going "Amish" to get story. *Sunday News* (Lancaster, PA), pp. A1, A4.

Smith, C. A. (1987). Mister Reagan's neighborhood: Rhetoric and national unity. *Southern Speech Communication Journal, 52,* 210–339.

Smith, R. & Newman, E. (2005, October). Covering trauma and disaster: Impact on the journalist. Dart Center for Journalism and Trauma, retrieved 29 April 2007 from http://www.dartcenter.org/research/fact_sheets/fact_sheet1.html

Smith, R. R. (1997). Mythic elements in television news. In D. Berkowitz (Ed.), *Social meanings of news* (pp. 325–332). Thousand Oaks, CA: Sage.

Smolowe, J., & Dougherty, S. (2003, September 29). Fade to black. *People,* 79–94.

Sobolewski, M. (2006, January 8). [Letter to the editor] Mining tragedy prompts letters worldwide. *The Sunday Gazette-Mail* (Charleston, WV), p. 3C.

Some kind of moves. (2001, November 11). *The New York Times,* p. B8.

Sondheimer, J. M. (2005, April 17). Poor sacrifices of our enmity. *The Seattle Times,* p. D5.

Special advertising section: Fall health & fitness. (2001.) *Newsweek,* October 15, n. p. [between editorial pp. 40–41].

Special report: E-learning. (2001, October 15). *U.S. News & World Report,* 43–78.

Stacked like cordwood. (2002, February 23). *The Economist,* 38.

Stanford, D. D. (2002, February 22). Crematory probe: Regulators tried to close Tri-State. *Atlanta Journal-Constitution,* p. C1.

Stauffer, C., & Kelly, J. (2006, October 13). Gunman's family thanks Amish for "forgiveness, grace, mercy." *The Lancaster New Era,* p. A6.

Stein, J. (2001, September 24). Digging out. *Time,* 60–66.

Steinberg, T. (2000). *Acts of God: The unnatural history of natural disaster in America.* New York: Oxford University Press.

Stepping out. (2001, October 8). *Newsweek,* 18–19.

Stewart, B. (2002, January/February). Amid so much death, celebrations of life. *Columbia Journalism Review,* 66–67.

St. John, W. (2006, April 27). Web sites set up to celebrate life recall lives lost. *The New York Times,* pp. A1, A19.

Stolberg, S. G. (2004, June 11). After long distances and long waits, everyday admirers say their goodbyes. *The New York Times,* p. A20.

Strong determination, A. (2001, September 27). *The New York Times,* p. B11.

Sturken, M. (1997). *Tangled memories: The Vietnam war, the AIDS epidemic, and the politics of remembering.* Berkeley: University of California Press.

Sturken, M. (2007). *Tourists of history: Memory, mourning, and kitsch in American culture.* Durham, NC: Duke University Press.

Sunset Hills wants to put the brakes on hill-jumping. (2003, March 24). *St. Louis Post-Dispatch,* West Post, p. 7.

Table of contents (2004, June 21). *U.S. News & World Report,* 1.

*Talk of the nation.* (2004, June 8). NPR.

Talley, Jake. (1995, March 22). *Guntersville Advertiser-Gleam*, p. 14.

Talley, T. (1999, May 4). Killer tornadoes slice through Oklahoma, Kansas. *The Topeka Capital-Journal*. Retrieved September 28, 2006, from www.cjonline.com.

Tarel Coleman: Unbridled and unabashed. (2001, December 10). *The New York Times*, p.B8.

*The Tavis Smiley show.* (2004a, June 9). NPR.

*The Tavis Smiley show.* (2004b, June 10). NPR.

Taylor, Alice. (1995, August 12). *Guntersville Advertiser-Gleam,* p. 14.

Teen commits suicide with pistol at school. (2004, December 13). *The Seattle Times*, p. B3.

Teen sentenced in "car surfing" death. (2005, July 1). *The Denver Post*, p. B.2.

Thanks of a grateful nation [editorial]. (2004, June 11). *The New York Daily News*, p. 20.

Thevenot, B., & Russell, G. (2005, September 26). Never happened. *New Orleans Times-Picayune*, p. A1.

Thin but grateful, miner is sent home. (2006, March 31). *Los Angeles Times*, p. A11.

Things were going so well. (2001, September 26). *The New York Times*, p. B11.

*This week with George Stephanopoulos.* (2004, June 6). ABC.

Thomas, E. (2001, December 31/2002, January 7). The day that changed America. *Newsweek*, 40–71.

Thomas, Flop. (1965, January 27). *Guntersville Advertiser-Gleam,* p. 1.

Thomas Foley: Fame and firefighting. (2001, December 7). *The New York Times*, p. B11.

Thompson, C. (2006, October 8). State police leader walked a fine line. *The Sunday Patriot-News* (Harrisburg, PA), p. A4.

Those who died. (1991, April 29). *The Wichita Eagle*, p. A4.

*Time.* (2001a, n.d. [fall]). *Special report.*

*Time.* (2001b, September 24).

*Time.* (2001c, October 1).

*Time.* (2001d, October 8).

*Time.* (2001e, October 15).

*Time.* (2001, December 31/2002, January 7).

Time for her sons. (2001, October 9). *The New York Times*, p. B15.

*The today show.* (2004a, May 28). NBC.

*The today show.* (2004b, May 29). NBC.

*The today show.* (2004c, June 7). NBC.

*The today show.* (2004d, June 8). NBC.

*The today show.* (2004e, June 9). NBC.

*The today show.* (2004f, June 10). NBC.

*The today show.* (2006a, January 3). NBC.

*The today show* [*Saturday today*]. (2006b, January 7). NBC.

*The today show* [*Sunday today*]. (2006c, January 15). NBC.

*The today show.* (2006d, March 30). NBC.

Toner, R. & Pear, R. (2004, June 9). Critics see a Reagan legacy tainted by AIDS, civil rights and union policies. *The New York Times*, p. A18.

Tornado victims sift ruins of home; rain threatens. (1991, April 29). *The Oklahoman*, p. A1.

Tornadoes hit state. (1995, May 14). *The Oklahoman*, p. 12.

Tornadoes kill at least 30 in Oklahoma and Kansas; Entire neighborhoods are leveled, and hundreds of people suffer injuries. (1999, May 4). *St. Louis Post-Dispatch*, p. A3.

Tornadoes kill 3 in Love County. (1995, May 8). *The Oklahoman*, p. A1.

Torres, V., & Johnson, J. (1994, January 18). Death, fickle in the ruins, takes at least 33. *Los Angeles Times*, p. A4.

Trammell, R. (1991, April 28). Tornado "didn't miss a thing:" Walters sees "unbelievable" state damage. *The Oklahoman*, p. A1.

A tribute to the Sago miners. (2006, January 15). *The Sunday Gazette-Mail* (Charleston, WV), p. 1C.

Tri-State opinion causes debate. (2002, May 24). *Atlanta Journal-Constitution*, p. C5.

Tsai, J., & Fitzgerald, T. (2005, September 13). Louisiana governor blasts FEMA over recovery of bodies. *Knight-Ridder Tribune*, Newspaper Source Database, Academic Search Premier.

Tucher, A. (1994). *Froth and scum: Truth, beauty, goodness, and the ax murder in America's first mass medium.* Chapel Hill: University of North Carolina Press.

Tuchman, G. (1978). *Making news: A study in the construction of reality.* New York: Free Press.

Tucker, Dan. (1995, August 16). *Guntersville Advertiser-Gleam*, p. 16.

Tucker, D. D. (1997, January 18). 2 men found dead in car near Pukwana were lifelong friends. *The Argus Leader*, p. A1.

Tuckwiller, T. (2006a, January 7). Community hopes tragedy will spur mine safety. *The Charleston Gazette*, p. 1A.

Tuckwiller, T. (2006b, February 19). A recurring nightmare. *The Sunday Gazette-Mail* (Charleston, WV), p. 1A.

Tuckwiller, T. (2006c, April 30). Before there were Quecreek and Sago, there was Hominy Falls. *The Sunday Gazette-Mail* (Charleston, WV), p. 1E.

Turner, V. (1977/1969). *The ritual process: Structure and anti-structure.* Ithaca: Cornell University Press.

Turner, V. (1982). *From ritual to theater: The human seriousness of play.* New York: Performing Arts Journal Publications.

Twister death toll drops to 23, Residents in Kansas search mobile home wreckage for more victims. (1991, April 28). *St. Louis Post Dispatch*, p. A10.

Umble, C. (2006, October 3). News crews replace mourners at murder site. *The New Era* (Lancaster, PA), p. A8.

Umstead, M. (2006, August 19). With full honors. *The Herald Mail* (Hagerstown, MD), pp. A1, A3.

An unforgettable experience. (2004, May 28). *The Washington Post,* pp. W10–W13.

Urbina, I. (2006a, January 24). Senators have strong words for mine safety officials. *The New York Times,* p. A17.

Urbina, I. (2006b, February 6). As roadside memorials multiply, a second look. *The New York Times,* pp. A1, A19.

Urbina, I. (2006c, October 6). An old world close to a new world horror. *The New York Times,* p. A14.

*U.S. News & World Report.* (2001a, September 14).

*U.S. News & World Report.* (2001b, September 24).

*U.S. News & World Report.* (2001c, October 1).

*U.S. News & World Report.* (2001d, October 8).

*U.S. News & World Report.* (2001e, October 12). Special report.

*U.S. News & World Report.* (2001f, October 15).

*U.S. News & World Report.* (2001, December 31-2002, January 7).

Vanden Brook, T. (2006, February 15). Recruits hungry for good jobs head off to coal mines. *USA Today,* pp. 1B, 2B.

van Gennep, A. (1960/1908). *The rites of passage.* Chicago: University of Chicago Press.

Vanzandt, Lawayne, 55. (1995, September 27). *Guntersville Advertiser-Gleam,* p. 16.

Veazey, Janet. (1995, June 14). *Guntersville Advertiser-Gleam,* p. 11.

Venesha Richards: A dream of Paris. (2001, December 28). *The New York Times,* p. B8.

The victims. (2001, September 24). *Time,* 68–77.

Victor, D. (2006, October 3). Droves of reporters put Amish in spotlight they usually shun. *The Patriot-News* (Harrisburg, PA), p. A6.

Viets, J. (1989, October 27). They drove into gap, survivor recalls death of sister on Bay Bridge. *The San Francisco Chronicle,* p. A21.

Violation of a sacred trust. (2002, December 20). *People,* 122.

Vitez, M. (2006, October 14). Bedrock faith helps a close community endure. *The Philadelphia Inquirer,* p. A14.

Walsh, E. (1991, April 27). Spring terror in "tornado alley"; Twister leaves trail of death in trailer park on Kansas plains. *The Washington Post,* p. A3.

Walter, T. (1991). The mourning after Hillsborough. *Sociological Review, 39,* 599–625.

Walter, T. (1994). *The revival of death.* London: Routledge.

Walter, T. (1999a). *On bereavement: The culture of grief.* Buckingham: Open University Press.

Walter, T. (Ed.). (1999b). *The mourning for Diana.* Oxford: Berg.

Walter, T., Littlewood, J., & Pickering, M. (1995). Death in the news: The public invigilation of private emotion. *Sociology, 29,* 579–596.

Wanting to be together. (2001, December 3). *The New York Times,* p. B9.

Ward, Jr., K. (2006a, February 19). Mining for truth. *The Charleston Gazette,* p. 1A.

Ward, Jr., K. (2006b, May 3). Sago families describe losses, demand answers to disaster. *The Charleston Gazette*, p. 1A.

Warner, W. L. (1959). *The living and the dead: A study of the symbolic life of Americans*. New Haven: Yale University Press.

Watwood, Wint. (1995, January 25). *Guntersville Advertiser-Gleam*, p.14.

A way about him. (2001, September 24). *The New York Times*, p. B11.

Weatherly, Birdie. (1965, March 17). *Guntersville Advertiser-Gleam*, p. 1.

Weaver-Zercher, D. (2006, October 8). In God they trust. *The Pittsburgh Post-Gazette*, pp. H1, H4.

Weber, H. R. (2005, February 1). Former crematory operator sentenced to 12 years, but gives no answers for dumping. *The Associated Press BC Cycle*, retrieved from LexisNexis Academic Index.

*Weekend Edition Sunday*. (2006, January 8). NPR.

Weich, S. (2005a, March 8). Teens' deaths spark grief, memories. *St. Louis Post-Dispatch*, St. Charles County Post p. 1.

Weich, S. (2005b, April 29). Prom memories shouldn't be of drinking, death, says teen's mom. *St. Louis Post-Dispatch*, St. Charles County Post p. 1.

Weil, M. (1989, October 18). Violent earthquake strikes northern California, killing dozens, causing widespread damage; Sections of bridge, highway collapse in rush hour. *The Washington Post*, p. A1.

Wenzl, R., & Elliott, P. (1999, May 4). Tornadoes rip region. *The Wichita Eagle*, p. A1.

West, Rilla. (1995, May 10). *Guntersville Advertiser-Gleam*, p. 15.

Westergaard, J. (1977). Power, class and the media. In J. Curran, M. Gurevitch, & J. Woollacott (Eds.), *Mass communication and society* (pp. 95–115). London: Edward Arnold.

What they saw when they landed. (2004, May 31). *Time*, 51–61.

White, G. (2002, February 23). Last sacred rite. *Atlanta Journal-Constitution*, p. B1.

Whitman, D. (2001, September 24). Heroes, victims. *U.S. News & World Report*, 36–39.

Whoriskey, P. (2006, February 11). City to take custody of storm victims. *The Washington Post*, p. A4.

Wieberg, S. (1999a, May 6). Residents try to salvage scraps that are left behind. *USA Today*, p. A4.

Wieberg, S. (1999b, May 7). Amid chaos, toll is difficult to determine. *USA Today*, p. A4.

Williams, S. (2006, January 29). Remembering Layland details of 1915 mine disaster. *The Sunday Gazette-Mail* (Charleston, WV), p. 1B.

Willing, R., & Levin, A. (1999, May 14). Nothing left standing, except tough residents. *USA Today*, p. A17.

Willman, C. (2003, September 26). Johnny Cash, 1932–2003. *Entertainment Weekly*, 30–34.

Wills, G. (1987). *Reagan's America: Innocents at home*. Garden City, NY: Doubleday.

Wilson, K. (2002, February 28–March 6). Funeral directors don't see repeat of Georgia crematory disaster. *Cross Currents, 3.*

Wingert, P., & Campo-Flores, A. (2006, January 16). A dark place. *Newsweek,* 44–45.

Winter, J. (1995). *Sites of memory, sites of mourning.* Cambridge: Cambridge University Press.

Woestendiek, J. (2006, October 8). When worlds collide. *The Sun* (Baltimore, MD), pp. 1A, 6A.

*Wolf Blitzer reports.* (2004, May 28). CNN.

Words of wisdom. (2001, n.d. [fall]). *Newsweek: Commemorative issue,* 74–75.

*World news tonight.* (2004a, April 29). ABC.

*World news tonight.* (2004b, May 2). ABC.

*World news tonight.* (2004c, May 28). ABC.

*World news tonight.* (2004d, May 29). ABC.

*World news tonight.* (2004e, June 10). ABC.

*World news tonight.* (2006, March 30). ABC.

Wright, K. S. (2006, October 4). An Amish tragedy. *The Philadelphia Inquirer,* p. A19.

Wyo. Teen charged in 'car surfing' death. (2004, October 21). *The Denver Post,* p. B2.

Yaphet J. Aryee: Taxes and taxis. (2001, December 2). *The New York Times,* p. B8.

Yarbrough, S. K. (1965, August 29). *Guntersville Advertiser-Gleam,* p. 1.

Ysidro Hidalgo-Tejada: Seasoning with love. (2001, December 16). *The New York Times,* p. B8.

Zelinsky, W. (1988). *Nation into state: The shifting symbolic foundations of American nationalism.* Chapel Hill: University of North Carolina Press.

Zelizer, B. (1990). Achieving journalistic authority through narrative. *Critical Studies in Mass Communication, 7,* 366–376.

Zelizer, B. (1995). Reading the past against the grain: The shape of memory studies. *Critical Studies in Mass Communication, 12,* 214–239.

Zelizer, B. (1998). *Remembering to forget: Holocaust memory through the camera's eye.* Chicago: University of Chicago Press.

Zoglin, R. (2005, December 19). America's most beloved comic rebel. *Time,* 35.

Zweig, M. (2000). *The working class majority: America's best kept secret.* Ithaca, NY: ILR Press.

# INDEX